THE AUSTRALIAN SLANGUAGE

Mieliems Elonai ir Rimui,

su australiškais linkėjimais,

Teta Jadvyga.

28 liepos 1984

THE
AUSTRALIAN
SLANGUAGE

A look at what we say and how we say it

BILL HORNADGE

Cassell Australia

CASSELL AUSTRALIA LIMITED
44 Waterloo Road, North Ryde, NSW 2113
30 Curzon Street, North Melbourne, Victoria 3051
in association with Cassell Limited, Auckland

First published 1980
Reprinted 1981
Typography by Robin James
Jacket illustration by Jenny Coopes
Set in 10/11 Century by B&D Modgraphic Pty, Ltd., Adelaide
Printed and bound by Kyodo Shing Loong Printing Industries (Pte.)
Ltd., Singapore

National Library of Australia
Cataloguing in Publication Data
   Hornadge, Bill
      The Australian slanguage.

      Index.
      ISBN 0 7269 3733 9

      1. English language in Australia.
      2. English language – Slang. I. Title.
   427'.994

CONTENTS

PREFACE

This book had its genesis a few years ago when the thought suddenly came to me that I, who had lived all my life in Australia, sometimes had the greatest difficulty understanding what my fellow countrymen were saying. If this can happen to a native-born person, I thought, how much more difficult must be the art of oral communication for migrants and for visitors to these shores? From this thought arose the idea of putting together a book about some of the more unusual aspects of the Australian language, though I doubt whether I would have pursued the idea if I had then had any idea of the amount of research and effort such a volume would generate. However, once started I found myself becoming so interested in the subject matter that retreat from the project became impossible.

Research on the volume led me down many unexpected bypaths with a result that the work has considerably wider scope than originally planned. In many ways it has become a social history of Australia rather than a restricted study of the language of the continent. For this I make no apologies since I believe the additional material introduced in this way has fleshed out the bones of the original concept in a much more satisfactory manner than I could have envisaged when I first commenced the extremely laborious task of gathering the material and putting it all together.

With written communication there is only one basic problem —the interpretation of the meaning of the words set down on paper, i.e. *what we say*. With oral communication there is the additional hurdle of *how we say it*.

In this book the second hurdle has been dealt with first, chiefly because it is the shortest section, but also because it seemed logical to tackle at the beginning the many aspersions cast at Australians for their alleged sloppiness of speech, their tendency to speak through closed lips, and their peculiar accent. These things do not appear to worry the average native-born Australian because he has been surrounded by these speech patterns all his life and they have become part of the fabric of his existence. Unless he has travelled abroad he may not be aware that his speech differs considerably from that of other English-speaking peoples. However, judging by the trenchant criticisms voiced over the years, our speech patterns certainly do worry the visitor to these shores, so the issue cannot be swept under the carpet.

The main part of the book however, has been devoted to *what we say*, rather than to *how we say it*, and here I have attempted to trace the origins and development of what has come to be termed Australian-English. There are sound historical reasons why the inhabitants of this continent should have developed such a distinctive brand of English, but there is less evidence as to why our speech should be so peppered with slang as to leave us open to the charge of being the most slang-happy race on earth.

Because slang occupies such a large place in this book, I have chosen to title the work THE AUSTRALIAN SLANGUAGE, but this term is not my creation. Its origins are not known, but the Oxford Dictionary records that it was in use in England as far back as 1892. It was popularised by W T Goodge in his poem 'The Great Australian Slanguage' which originally appeared in the *Bulletin*, and gained even wider circulation when it was reprinted without authority in Davitt's *Life and Progress in Australia* in 1897.

Edmund Burke once wisely observed: *A very great part of the mischiefs that vex this world arises from words*. Words are indispensable to communication, but they tend to bring out the worst in people. Let a hapless writer of a letter to the editor or the author of a feature article or a book make a linguistic error and the whole world pounces on the unfortunate wretch. Perhaps for that reason, articles on various aspects of the Australian language and books on Australian-English have in the past aroused considerable controversy and debate on the continent. The appearance of such articles or volumes brings the critics out of the woodwork in droves to pounce on errors, real or imagined. Ah, they exclaim gleefully, this word or that word is not of Australian origin as the smart alec author claims —it was first used in England, or California, or Timbuktu, in the eighteenth century! And they may well be right, these self-righteous armchair critics, since philology is still a very inexact science, despite the many volumes devoted to it, and the origins of much of our language are lost in the mists of time. But we should not begrudge the critics their little bit of fun in mauling the hapless writers and authors who choose to venture into such dangerous fields. On the other hand, it might be wise to try and forestall some of the expected attacks of the knockers and critics by issuing a few disclaimers.

For a start this book is not put forward as a definitive study of Australian-English: it is simply a collection of material on the Australian language put forward to amuse and possibly to instruct readers. I have tried to avoid pontification of what is 'good English' or 'bad English' and make no positive pronouncements on pronunciation or enunciation. I do not even touch on such delicate matters as the ending of sentences with prepositions or expound on the terrible dangers to the community of the split infinitive. Such weighty matters I prefer to leave to the experts.

I would hope, however, that this volume would give my readers a better understanding and appreciation of Australian-English. It may even persuade some that a greater study of their language could prove extremely rewarding.

If they do pursue this course they will find that the field is dominated by two giants—both New Zealanders by birth. I refer, of course, to Sidney J Baker and Eric Partridge, both of whom have contributed very significantly to the understanding of English as it is spoken in Australia.

Baker's work *The Australian Language* (1945) still remains the definitive reference source for the origins of our language and is a goldmine of information on the origins of Australian slang. When reference is made to Baker, *The Australian Language* often is quoted as though it were his only achievement. Although this volume certainly stands at the top of the list, Baker made valuable contributions to our understanding of Australian-English in other volumes such as his early work *New Zealand Slang* (1935), *The Drum* (1959), *Australia Speaks* (1953), *Australian Pronunciation* and *The Pattern of Language*.

Eric Partridge's field has been a much wider one than Baker's, covering the English language in its entirety, rather than being restricted to the Antipodean scene. Nevertheless his studies of language frequently dealt in depth with the Australasian scene and his *Slang, Today and Yesterday* (1933) is an invaluable source document for the study of Australian-English, as is his *A Dictionary of Slang and Unconventional English*, and *Songs and Slang of the British Soldier 1914–1918*.

Another veritable goldmine of information on our language is that marvellous collection of quotations, *A Dictionary of Australian Colloquialisms* (1978) compiled by Professor G A Wilkes. I have also found the many books on Australian folklore assembled by Bill Wannan to be rich in source material on the language of the nineteenth century and would particularly recommend for study his *Australian Folklore* (1976). Another volume in similar style, and equally recommended, is Bill Scott's *Complete Book of Australian Folklore* (1976).

There are two other writers whose works I have not only enjoyed immensely but also have found to be invaluable source material on modern slang. They are John O'Grady, who has a keenly attuned ear for colloquialisms (particularly recommended for further study is his classic *They're a Weird Mob*) and Keith Dunstan, that indefatigable Melbourne researcher of unusual pieces of Australiana. I particularly recommend *Wowsers* (1968), *Knockers* (1972) and *Sports* (1973) for further study. For those seeking to study the language of the playground, barely touched upon in this volume, I would strongly recommend *Cinderella Dressed in Yella* (1969 and revised in 1978), a wonderful collection of school rhymes and sayings compiled by Ian Turner, June Factor and Wendy Lowenstein.

The classic nineteenth century reference work on the Australian language has long been considered Edward E Morris' *A Dictionary of Austral-English* (1898) but I must confess to some disappointment with this volume. It is certainly a comprehensive record of the newly developing language of the bush in the colonial period, particularly in the fields of flora and fauna, but Morris lived in a prudish era and he omitted, perhaps deliberately, a considerable amount of the more colourful language of the period, so his work is seriously marred by its selectivity.

I regret that the short list of further recommended reading mentioned above must serve as a substitute for a proper bibliography. It has not been possible to compile a bibliography because the notes used in the compilation of this work were assembled over a period of very many years, and in the case of most of the earlier notes details of original sources were not recorded. The volume contains many thousands of separate slang words and phrases drawn from a very wide variety of sources, and where known these have been listed in the text rather than in tedious footnotes.

My special thanks go to Mr C V Curnow, Marketing Manager of Kraft Foods Limited (Victoria) for interesting background information on the marketing history of Vegemite, and to the

Right Hon Sir Billy Snedden, Speaker of the House of Representatives (1978) for readily making available the quite extensive list of unparliamentary expressions of an earlier age which I have included in the volume. My grateful thanks also go to my daughter Lindy for sterling work in typing a very messy draft manuscript under considerable difficulties.

Bill Hornadge
March 1980

It may here be worthwhile to examine how it comes to pass that several readers who are all acquainted with the same language and know the meanings of words they read should nevertheless have a different relish of the same description.

Joseph Addison
(18th Century)

Chapter One

BLAME IT ON THE FLIES

Many Australians are mumblers . . . being a little deaf, I am frequently at a loss as to what they are talking about.

Lord Casey, 1970

For some years I regularly visited a barber shop where the chairs were tended by two barbers whom I shall call Fred and Ted—mainly because they are not their real names. Both Ted and Fred spoke through lips that parted only fractionally to emit sounds. As a result, neither could understand the other first time around and all their remarks had to be repeated. Their conversation ran something like this:

FRED: D'jahearabouolkellysbulllasni?
TED: Eh?
FRED: Did ya hear abou' ol' Kelly's bull las' ni'?
TED: Yairayetolmehhewenintathebrownceplacelikeabatter-tell.
FRED: Eh?
TED: They say he went inta the Brown's place lika bat outa hell.
FRED: Hairdidunnersaquidsadamagaysay.
TED: Eh?
FRED: He did 'undreds o' quids o' damage they say.

And so it went on. On the second time around Fred or Ted could pick up what the other had said, so long and close was their association, but even after years in those barber chairs I could never get more than twenty per cent of the conversation flow.

The accusation that Australians speak with lips half-closed has been directed at them from many sources. Hector Dinning in *The Australian Scene* (1939) noted:

The Australian often speaks without obviously opening his lips at all, through an immobile slit, and in extreme cases through closed teeth.

The belief is widely held that Australians speak through their teeth because of the prevalence of flies in the country. The fly problem certainly is one of long duration. As far back as 1629 the Dutch explorer Francois Pelsaert was obliged to record of his visit to the west coast of the continent:

. . . we also found such multitude of flies here, which perched on our mouths and crept into our eyes, that we could not keep them off our persons.

The fly problem hadn't gone away some seventy years later when William Dampier landed on the same coast (1699). He recorded his impressions in greater detail:

. . . their (aborigines) eye-lids are always half-closed, to keep the Flies out of their Eyes: they being so troublesome here, that no fanning will keep from coming to one's Face; and without the assistance of both hands to keep them off, they will creep into ones Nostrils; and Mouth too, if the Lips are not shut very close. So that from their Infancy being thus annoyed with these Insects, they never do open their Eyes as other People: and therefore they cannot see far; unless they hold up their Heads, as if they were looking at something over them.

From the time of the first settlement flies bothered the new settlers just as they had for centuries plagued the Aborigines, and early visitors to these shores were loud in their complaint about the nuisance. The early settlers took defensive action against the flies by developing a constant movement of the hands to brush the pests away. Since all things and all actions in Australia have to be assigned a nickname, the fly-swatting action quickly became known as THE AUSTRALIAN SALUTE. This persists to the present day in the outback but its days might be numbered if we are to believe the story in the *Australian* (3 March, 1976) which solemnly noted:

A sexually-mutated blowfly developed by CSIRO scientists in Canberra could lead to the demise of the great Australian salute.

It was not long before visitors to the country began to associate the prevalence of flies with the fact that most Australians (white) speak through their teeth. Certainly they don't seem to open their lips to express their sounds as do most other people of European descent.

In 1937 Judge Sheridan of Sydney voiced this opinion:

It seems an unfortunate habit of Australians to speak through their teeth as if they came from the 'fly country', afraid to open their mouths for fear of flies.

Or as the chant of the schoolyard has it:

Ask no questions,
Tell no lies,
Open your mouth
And catch the flies.

The belief was still being perpetuated as late as 1976, as was noted by Bill Peach in a magazine article:

There is a persistent theory, and I see that Professor Manning Clark is the latest to enunciate it in the Boyer lectures, that the Australian accent developed as it did because Australians spoke with their mouths half-shut to stop the blowies flying in.

An alternative theory was advanced by Dr Halliday Sutherland in 1940 when, in a letter to the Sydney *Daily Telegraph* he expressed the view that:

. . . I believe that the colonial accent in Australia is due to the effects of an inflammation of the nose, a complaint from which most Australians seem to suffer. The prevalent nose inflammation is probably due to pollen in the air. There are thousands of grasses in Australia which produce this pollen.

These theories are interesting but not entirely convincing. My own pet theory is that Australians developed as a nation of mumblers because of the climate.

The theory that Australian speech patterns are closely allied to the climate is not new. Hector Dinning in *The Australian Scene* (1939) expressed the view that:

. . . the slovenly speech of Australians is no doubt bound up also with the physical lassitude induced by their climate . . . their speech gives an impression of tiredness.

In a chapter in *Some Australians Take Stock* (1939), T S Dorsch examined this proposition but found himself unwilling to accept that slipshod Australian speech was due to the climate. He was more inclined to the view that . . . *it may in part be produced by a species of national sloth.*

In other words laziness. But this begs the question, because the laziness of which Australians are so frequently accused in itself may well be caused by the severe summer climate.

In his *Pronunciation of English in Australia* (1946) Professor

A G Mitchell addressed himself to the theory in more detail but he, too, was reluctant to accept it. He wrote:

If Australian speech were produced by climatic conditions, its comparative uniformity would be surprising in a country of such diversity in climate. If climate were the sole influence or even the chief influence some local variations in utterance would seem inevitable.

It cannot be shown that climate brings about differences in the physical structure of the organs of speech. There is a theory that a dry climate produces thinner mucous tissues in the nasal cavities and that this produces a harsher quality of voice, but this has nothing to do with the formation of sounds. Further, it cannot be shown that small changes in the physical structure of the vocal organs would necessarily produce a different speech. Individual differences in mouth-formation do not produce differences in speech unless there is gross abnormality.

Can the charge of national laziness in speech, allegedly brought about by climatic influence, be fully sustained? If we measure speech-energy in terms of muscular effort we shall find that consonants, on the whole, require more muscular movement than vowels or diphthongs. And the Australian's production of consonants does not differ in any way from that of the Englishman.

Professor Mitchell then went on to compare the speech patterns of Australians with those of educated southern Englishmen, Canadians and Americans. His conclusion was that it was not possible to show that the sounds in Australian speech had been evolved because of laziness of the speakers' habits or because of climatic influences, but he did admit that climate, among other things, might have something to do with the development of the so-called Australian character with its casual, free and easy leisurely mannerisms.

It seems to me that the above experts, Professor Mitchell included, have not fully taken into account the very harsh environment in which the early settlers of the continent found themselves, or the evolutionary pressures of nature in such circumstances. The long hot summers are extremely trying even for present-day native-born Australians aided by such benefits of civilisation as ice, refrigeration and air conditioning. For the majority of men and women who came here in the convict and colonial periods straight from the colder climates of the northern hemisphere, the Australian heat must have been like hell.

Sheer survival was at stake for most of the early settlers since they had to combat extraordinarily tough living conditions as well as the climate. In circumstances such as this the body tends to set up its own defence mechanisms to cope with a new environment. Given the extremes of temperature experienced in most Australian summers, the natural tendency for bodies unused to such conditions would be to use every trick to conserve energy since wasted energy in such an environment could easily make the difference between disaster and survival.

The charge of laziness has often been directed at Australians and it is true that they generally work at a more leisurely tempo, especially in outdoor conditions in summer, than the inhabitants of some other countries. The picture of the council labourer leaning on the handle of his shovel instead of wielding it, and of the Australian male leaning against the hotel verandah post is not entirely a caricature. It may be no coincidence that similar caricatures are painted of the siesta-prone stances of Latin Americans whose climate tends to parallel that of Australia. Far from this being natural laziness, such habits on the part of Australians and Latin Americans may well be perfectly justified bodily defence mechanisms to conserve energy and minimise dangers of bodily overheating and exhaustion in temperature extremes.

If this theory is valid, then it would be a perfectly logical bodily defence mechanism for the organs of speech to slow down their tempo in line with the natural slowing of other body rhythms. The opening of the mouth to enunciate clearly is wasteful of energy, whereas clipped and abbreviated speech uttered through lips that open fractionally reduces jaw action and conserves energy. If we are a nation of mumblers, there may be perfectly sound evolutionary reasons why this is so. I am well aware that such a theory is probably as incapable of scientific proof as the fly theory; but at least it is worth advancing as a possible explanation of our curious speech patterns and worth further study.

However, whether we blame it on the flies, the heat, pure bone laziness or some other factor, the fact remains that Australians, as a general rule, do tend to speak through clenched lips, and the physical restriction of tongue, lip and jaw which results does produce nasalised vowels, whilst vowels which tend naturally to be hard are also clipped.

In *New Zealand Slang* (1940) Sidney J Baker devoted a lot of space to the nasalisation of both Australian and New Zealand speech and commented:

A predominant feature of both New Zealand and Australian speech is the resistance against sounds in which the tongue is in a high raised position either at the back or the front of the mouth. This restricted movement of the tongue has an accompaniment in a restricted use of the jaw and lips. Vowels which therefore tend naturally to be hard are also clipped, and the general New Zealand inclination to speak rapidly results in delayed melodic phrasing—pleasing enough to the New

Zealand or Australian ear, but certainly not English.

The purely physical matter of restricted tongue, lip, and jaw movements also produces nasalized vowels. These are caused when the soft palate is lowered so that air escapes through both nose and mouth —a natural consequence when the mouth is not opened, in any case. The mistake should not be made of identifying New Zealand and Australian nasalization with that of the Cockney or American. Our nasalization comes mainly from attempting to pronounce acutely-sharpened frontal vowels with the mouth closed.

He then summarised as follows the concise form of the characteristics which follow from the restriction of tongue, lip and jaw noted above:

(a) A general sharpening of vowel values, though, by way of compensation final vowels tend to become long.

(b) A strong tendency to give the various vowels in a word the same value; an equalization of stress.

(c) Palatal speech, that is, retention of the tongue (tip and middle) well forward in the mouth in a flattened position.

(d) A restricted movement of the tongue, lips, and jaw.

(e) Rapidity of speech.

A book published in England in 1973, *Spoken English of People in Responsible Positions*, put it in a slightly different manner when it said that the nasalisation of the Australian speech was due to the velum at the back of the throat dropping down and allowing more air to escape through the nose. The book, which was published with an accompanying cassette, promised readers that they could train their velum to rise 'when appropriate'. Australians by the million ignored the temptation to train their velums and, by all reports, sales of the volume in the Antipodes were disappointing.

Chapter Two

THE AUSTRALIAN ACCENT

Twere better if thou never sang,
Than voiced it in Australian Twang.

From a poem in the **Bulletin,** 1894

When we are surrounded daily with the flat, nasal whine of the Australian voice we don't notice it; it is only after an absence abroad (even a short one) that it strikes the ear and jars the sensibilities. The trip into the city from the international terminal at Mascot (or Tullamarine) in the company of an Australian-born taxi driver can be a shattering experience for a returning traveller. The first half of the journey is spent wondering how on earth one has put up with such an assault on the ears for so many years. Then comes the moment of shattering self-revelation. 'My God, I must sound like that to people I met overseas!'

The nasalisation of the vowels of Australian speakers produces a sound which is of quite distinctive character. Various visitors have described it as a 'whine' or of a 'snuffling' nature and some of the comments are worth recording if only to illustrate how distressing the sounds are to the ears of visitors:

What puzzles me exceedingly to account for, a very large proportion of both male and female natives snuffle dreadfully; just the same nasal twang as many Americans have. This is an enigma which it passes my sagacity to solve.

Mrs Charles Meredith (1849)

The Australian Slanguage

The colonial twang was never at the beginning anything better than the twang of Cockney vulgarity. We imported it long before rabbits, sparrows, snails and other British nuisances were grafted upon our budding civilisation.

Chief Justice Madden (1892)

. . . their voices are almost unbelievably ugly, and one never quite gets over the shock of hearing some lovely girl speak for the first time. This is not merely a matter of the Australian accent, for many men have pleasant rough voices. Too many women talk with a strident, saw-like whine that is indescribable.

John Pringle in The Australian Accent

It is safe to say that however it came about no greater millstone was ever tied around the neck of any nation. The Australian accent at its worst brands every one of us, whether we speak it or not, as uncouth, ignorant and a race of second-class people.

A G Chambers (1974)

The fact remains that the common speech of the Commonwealth of Australia represents the most brutal maltreatment which has ever been inflicted upon the mother-tongue of the great English speaking nations.

William Churchill in Beach-la-mar (1911)

The Irish brogue is pretty in the mouth of a pretty Irish girl, and a Scots lassie can make the speech of that largely forsaken land sound heavenly. But the Australian twang, or whatever you like to call it, is never beautiful. It is hideous, and the thicker it gets the more hideous it becomes.

Sydney theatrical producer, George Highland (1923)

Quite a few visitors to these shores have commented that, to their ears, Australians appear to 'sing' their words rather than articulate them. Valerie Desmond in *The Awful Australian* (1911) even went so far as to claim that the practice had been copied from the many Chinese in the community! She wrote on the subject:

But it is not so much the vagaries of pronunciation that hurt the ear of the visitor. It is the extraordinary intonation that the Australian imparts to his phrases. There is no such thing as cultured, reposeful conversation in this land; everybody sings his remarks as if he were reciting blank verse after the manner of an imperfect elocutionist. It would be quite possible to take an ordinary Australian conversation and immortalise its cadences and diapasons by means of musical notation. Herein the Australian differs from the American. The accent of the American, educated and uneducated alike, is abhorrent to the cultured Englishman or Englishwoman, but it is, at any rate, harmonious. That of the Australian is full of discords and surprises. His voice rises and falls with unexpected syncopations, and, even among the few cultured persons this country possesses, seems to bear in every syllable the sign of the parvenu . . . The Australian's practice of singing his remarks I can only ascribe to the influence of the Chinese.

During my stay in Melbourne, I spent one evening at supper in a Chinese cookshop in Little Bourke Street, and I was instantly struck by the resemblance between the intonation of the phrases passing between the Chinese attendants and that of the conversation of the cultivated Australians who accompanied me.

Valerie Desmond seemed obsessed with the daily assault on her ears and in another part of her book returned to the attack on the Australian accent as follows:

One of the strongest prejudices that one has to overcome when one visits Australia is that created by the weird jargon that passes for English in this country. Created is too mild a term to apply to the process. It comes as a positive shock, and I recall with actual pain the morning I awoke as the mailboat lay at Fremantle breakwater, and I heard this horrible patois filter through my porthole to offend my ear for the first time. Strangely enough, English people who have lived in the colonies for any length of time grow accustomed to the pronunciation of the Australian, and, worst of all, it insinuates itself into their own language until it is really difficult to find a resident of more than ten years' standing in Australia who does not sing-song like a native . . . In conclusion, it is only necessary to point out that so objectionable is the Australian accent that theatrical managers resolutely refuse to employ Australian-born actors or actresses. Though a few of these are possessed of talent—or what passes for talent in Australia—the managers prefer to import English artists of inferior merit, solely because they possess the essential qualifications that Australians lack—the ability to speak the English language.

The effect that the Australian accent and intonation can have on American ears is perhaps best reflected in the comment made in 1979 by Robert Easton, US actor and expert on speech patterns:

I've heard John Newcombe describe a tennis match, and if I came close to imitating that I believe I could impersonate a wild duck singing Annie Laurie under water.

Many first-class Australian films have perished on the rock of accent when attempts have been made to market them abroad— particularly in the United States where our vowels are a special problem.

In 1978 the award-winning film *Newsfront* was widely acclaimed in the US, but even so the accent caused problems and one New York critic felt compelled to make the unkind comment that there was a case to be made for English subtitles to the film, thus placing Australian speech very firmly in the category of French, German and Spanish where American audiences were concerned.

Over the years the editorial writers of the nation's newspapers have returned, again and again, to the subject of the Australian accent. One of their problems in tackling the issue always has been in trying to define objectives towards which Australians should strive in their aim for better speech patterns. One editorial writer who tried to come to grips with the issue penned the following words in an editorial in the *Sydney Morning Herald* on 28 December 1933:

We would define Australian-English as that pleasant oral communication which is audible and instantly apprehended by reason of its clear enunciation and rate of articulation; which is expressed in correct grammatical form and is free from solecisms; it has the vowel quality and absence of nasality associated with a person of respectable attainments and the inflections are such as do not provoke a sense of antagonism or resentment in the auditor by virtue of such speech.

In 1924, an editorial writer in the Melbourne *Age* penned these words on the subject:

Whether we deserve it or not we are being very widely branded as 'orful orstryllyins'. The youngsters are the greatest sinners. They are growing up inured to the nasal discords of Australian colloquial speech, and it is common knowledge that in each successive decade the evil is not being eliminated but accentuated. If the process continues the Australian speech will become unrecognisable as the English language . . . only in homes where there is some form of culture can Australian children hope to escape the blight.

On 22 August 1923 the *Daily Telegraph* expressed a somewhat different viewpoint on the subject:

It is true that for a long time signs have not been wanting of peculiarities of intonation developing in our outback settlements. We know what happened to English in its passage across the Atlantic. The twang of Americans is a fearsome thing, though it has contributed not a little to that gaiety of nations . . . As a whole, Australians, without a doubt, speak better English than the English themselves, for outside of London, England is a maze of dialects from Land's End to the Tweed. Australians have no desire to contribute a 'third kind' of English for the amusement of foreigners.

However, an editorial in the Sydney *Daily Telegraph* of 22 December 1926 took a different stand when it advocated the development of a distinct Australian accent as a patriotic necessity. The editorial expressed it this way:

An Australian accent is as essential to Australian patriotism as an Australian flag. It matters little whether it be a twang or a brogue or a bleat, so long as it is real. And to be real it must be a spontaneous production of the Australian's environment. Anything else is shoddy.

Another writer who saw the development of a (pleasant) Australian accent as a matter of patriotism was Ruby Board who, in an Australian English Association pamphlet of 1926, expressed these views:

Granted that inevitably each country will develop its own distinctive variation of speech, is it necessary to be proud of the fact that our own is ugly, and appears to other English speaking peoples as uncultivated and crude, and are we going to allow these unpleasing qualities to become each year more intensified, because, forsooth, they are Australian? Surely a true patriotism will try to guide that development so that the national speech may be euphonious and worthy of pride.

In 1978 the *Australian* columnist Buzz Kennedy wrote a light-hearted piece on the speaking habits of his fellow Australians, in which he observed:

The broad Australian accent is not a lovesome thing, I grant you. At its worst, it is reminiscent of a dehydrated crow uttering its last statement on life from the bough of a dead tree in the middle of a claypan at the peak of a seven-year drought . . . Proper Australian is spoken while moving the lips as little as possible—making life hell for deaf lipreaders, but keeping the flies out of the mouth. Indeed, it has been said, quite seriously, that our flies are the cause of our mode of speech.

The noise which comes out should be gratingly flinty and half should be through the nose. Inflection should be minimal, as should facial expression. No hand gestures, of course—hands should be in the pockets.

Although Kennedy was voicing a tongue-in-cheek point of view, he succeeded in encapsulating the essence of the criticism hurled at Australians for a century or more by visitors with sensitive ears. The only difference is that Kennedy was defending his fellow Australians where others have condemned them out of hand.

Chapter Three

A STRINE
ON THE EARS

A second language had evolved, an Australian gaelic called
strine but conversation could still be conducted
undemandingly by affirming alternatively, 'I'd give it a go';
and 'I'd shoot the bastards'.

Dr Richard Gordon, British author, 1967

In 1964 the English authoress Monica Dickens was autograph-
ing copies of her latest book in a Sydney bookshop. A woman
handed her a copy of the book and said 'Emma Chisit'. Assuming
that this was the woman's name, the authoress wrote on the
flyleaf above her signature 'To Emma Chisit' and handed the
book back. In a more positive voice the customer said, 'No,
Emma Chisit?'

After some further (confused) exchanges the visiting authoress became aware that what the woman was saying was
'How much is it?'

When this incident was reported in the *Sydney Morning
Herald* the heavens opened and the newspaper was flooded with
examples of similar verbal mishaps, which were given the name
of Strine.

The correspondence columns soon began to overflow, and to
help them out the newspaper enlisted the aid of one Alastair
Morrison of Sydney University who, under the strine *nom de
plume* of Professor Afferbeck Lauder (alphabetical order), for
some time ran occasional articles on his findings into the
mysteries of Strine. Eventually the good Professor brought his
findings together in two slim volumes published by Ure Smith
Let Stalk Strine (1965) and *Nose Tone Unturned* (1966).

Some typical examples of Strine as dredged up by Professor Afferbeck Lauder and his legion of researchers were:

AIR FRIDGE (average)
AIRPSLY FAIR BILLIS (absolutely fabulous)
AIRP'S TREKS (abstracts—the art galleries are full of them these days)
AORTA (they ought to . . .)
BAKED NECKS (bacon and eggs)
BANDRY (boundary)
BARE JET (bed yet, as in 'Did ya make yer bed yet, Shirl?')
CHEQUE ETCHER (Where did yer get yer . . .?)
DIMENSION (Don't mention [it])
DINGO (Didn't go)
EGG NISHING (air conditioning)
EBB TIDE (appetite, i.e. 'I dunno Norma, I've got no ebb tide f' anythin' these days')
EGG JELLY (actually)
EMENY? (How many?)
GARBLER MINCE (couple of minutes, i.e. 'I'll be with yer in a garbler mince, luv')
GESS VONNER (guest of honour)
GISSA (Give me, as in 'Gissa lookat them photos Norm')
IKE NARDLY BLEEVIT (I can hardly believe it)
JEGGODA (Did you go ter . . .)
TERM NIGHT SEAR (terminates here)
X (axe)
YEGGOWAN? (Are you going?)
ZARF TRAWL (after all)
WEZZME (Where is my . . .?)
WEZZME HEMBAIRG? (Where is my handbag?)
TRINE (train, i.e. something that runs on a rhy why line)
TO GORF (Took off, i.e. 'He to gorf like batter to hell')
SKETTIN TWOLD (He—or she—is getting too old)
IBEY SEA (Australian Broadcasting Commission—the ABC)
GLORIA SOAME (glorious home)
SLY DROOL (slide rule)
SINNEY YOONEY (Sydney University)
MARE CHECK (magic)
LONDGER RAY (lingerie)
TERROR SOUSE (terrace house)
SAG RAPES (sour grapes)
SANDER'S LAPE (sound asleep)
GLORIA STY (a glorious day)
CHEAT WAS SCOLD (Gee, it was cold)

WINE CHEVVER COLE SHARE? (Why don't you have a cold shower?)
SEMMITCH (sandwich)
SCUMMIN GLERSER (coming closer)
SCONA (It is going to)
SCETTIN LAIRDER (It is getting louder)
DINT NOTE WAS (I did not know it was . . .)
TAN CANCEL (town council)
STEWNCE (students)
STAR GINTER (stuck into as in 'get star ginter 'im mate')
SOUP-MARKED (supermarket)
SPARGLY GUYS (sparkling eyes)
TEA NATURE (teenager)
DENT-SHOE WORRY (Don't you worry)
ILER CALF TRIM (I'll look after him)
WATSY EFFRIS TEA? (What does he have in his tea?)

Long exposure to a flow of Strine along the lines of the examples quoted above is taken in their stride by most Australians. But imagine what it does to the self-confidence of migrants or visitors to Australia who (before their arrival) are reasonably sure they possess a good command of the English language! This point was summed up neatly by Professor Richard Blandy of Flinders University Institute of Labour Studies when he was commenting (in 1977) on the language problems of migrants:

In a society as monolingual as Australia, where you're a linguist if you speak both Strine and English, this is an appalling disability for a worker.

An attempt (apparently unsuccessful) was made to solve this problem in 1970 when the Student Counselling Unit and the multi-racial Asian Club of the University of New South Wales jointly sponsored a six-weeks course in Strine and Australian Slang. The course was the brainchild of Commonwealth court reporter Ron Bates, a Licentiate in Speech and Drama from the NSW Conservatorium, who felt that the course might help Asian students bridge the wide gap between Osfud and Sinney. Some twenty students from Indonesia, Malaysia, China, Hong Kong and Thailand enrolled in the original course, but subsequent reports on the progress of these cultural guinea pigs were mixed. It was clearly felt by many members of the community that such courses might widen the cultural gap between Australia and south-east Asia rather than perform any bridging work.

When the news of the course ultimately seeped through to

London it was greeted with some incredulity. Writing in *Punch*, John Taylor no doubt summed up the feelings of every Britisher when he commented:

Australia is the one country in the world where coarseness is proudly regarded as a national heritage. Only last year news was leaked that evening classes had been established there to coach newly enlisted citizens in the nasal esoterics of Strine, as opposed to the pure and proper delivery of our lovely English tongue. Culturally, such an exercise might justly be regarded as the equivalent of tutelage on how to eat with your fingers, or a concentrated course in hawking and spitting. Such resolutely chauvinistic manifestations reflect the incorruptible pride of a Visigoth who would rather burn down a Roman villa than accept the effete civilising influence of living in it.

A Melbourne *Herald* report of 14 April 1967 indicates how the insidious Strine cult can infiltrate the bureaucracy. This is the *Herald* report of this momentous event:

Colac's new free kindergarten was officially named 'Wydinia' by Cr Derek Mathews at the opening ceremony last night.
Why 'Wydinia'?
The kindergarten committee retiring president, Dr Alexander Reid explained that when the committee was considering a name it thought of all the advice it received while the weatherboard building was going up . . .
'Why dinya build it of brick?', 'Why dinya build it in the east?', 'Why dinya do this?', 'Why dinya do that?'.
'It's up to date, and there'll never be another kindergarten called this,' said Dr Reid.

An amusing example of how Strine can cause official upsets on an international level came to light during the Queen's Silver Jubilee Celebrations in 1977.

The Chairman of the Australian Silver Jubilee Committee, Mr Harry M Miller, was in London at the time telling the press about the wonderful things being planned in Australia for the event. The celebrations, he said, would commence with a chain of 3 000 bonfires lit simultaneously across the nation by some 200 000 boy scouts. Only one council in Australia had refused permission for a bonfire, he said. Asked to name the offending town involved, Mr Miller spoke a name which a British reporter (unused to Strine) transcribed as Quirindi (in the north-west of New South Wales). When this appeared in print the residents of Quirindi were most upset at having their loyalty challenged in this way and the Town Clerk said that he would be demanding an apology from Mr Miller. A hasty phone call to London elicited the fact that the guilty council which Mr Miller had named had in fact not been Quirindi at all but the Sydney suburban council of Ku-ring-gai.

Finally, to test your skills in Strine, how about translating this poem from *Nose Tone Unturned*:

> *With air chew, with air chew,*
> *Iker nardly liver there chew,*
> *An I dream a badger kisser snite and die*
> *Phoney wicked beer loan,*
> *Jar-chewer mere non-nair roan,*
> *An weed dreamer batter mooner pinner sky . . .*

Chapter Four

THE WHINE OF STRINE FALLS MINELY ON THE PLINE

Even tolerably well-educated Australians in pronouncing words containing the long A vowel fall into a branch of Cockney twang, as for instance, pronouncing lady as though it were spelt lydy.

A writer in the **Bulletin,** 1892

If there is one letter of the alphabet that can be singled out as setting the average Australian apart from his English-speaking brothers in other parts of the world it is the vowel 'a'. The rest of the world *insists* that we pronounce this as 'i'. Susan Kaldor in *Asian Students and Australian English* (1970) spoke for many when she quoted the complaint of an Asian student: *One has sometimes to pronounce 'male' as 'mile' before one can be understood.*

I have found that the 'a' problem is not so acute in England, where the English take it in their stride, but it can be a source of constant misunderstandings in the United States of America where our accent causes the locals considerable bafflement. If a visiting Australian should need to secure a manual phone connection to a number in MAINE, the prelude will probably go something like this:

OPERATOR: 'Operator, may I be of service?'
DINKUM AUSSIE: 'I want to call MAINE 560-590-666.'
OPERATOR: 'I'm sorry Sir, there is no such exchange as MINE.'

DINKUM AUSSIE: 'I want MAINE, not MINE.'

OPERATOR: 'I'm sorry sir there is no such exchange as MINE.'

DINKUM AUSSIE: 'I want MAINE. MAINE. Get it. M for Maude, A for Arthur, I for Indian, N for Nelly and E for Ernie. MAINE, not MINE.'

OPERATOR: 'Oh, you want MAINE. I'll connect you now, Sir.'

DINKUM AUSSIE: 'And not before its flamin' time.'

OPERATOR: 'Thank you, Sir, have a nice day.'

After a visit to the United States in 1941 Australian art critic Richard Hughes related (in the *Sunday Telegraph* of 12 October 1941) the following tale:

> I inquired at the *New York Times* office for the editorial file of clippings on aliens.
>
> I asked, very clearly, 'May I have your "Race" file?' They handed me very efficiently, a voluminous and informative dietetic file labelled "Rice".
>
> Learning from experience, I tried to spell the name 'Bailey' on the telephone.
>
> '"B" for "bread", "A" for "Adam"' I began.
>
> '"Eye" for "Adam",' the girl repeated in surprise. 'You mean "Eye" for "Izzy", don't you?'

The problem with the vowel 'a' in the United States should not be underestimated. It is very real in the field of communications and can even cause serious problems in the commercial field. In support of this, I would like to relate a true incident.

Back in the 1960s when I owned Seven Seas Stamps, the firm did a considerable business in packaging low-cost packets of postage stamps which it supplied to various commercial firms as giveaways or 'premiums', as they are known in the United States. Because Australian labour costs were then much lower than those in the US the firm developed an extensive trade in premium packets of stamps to North America. Amongst our customers was a chain of restaurants in Kentucky which, over a period of several years, bought extremely large quantities of premium packets which they gave away to customers visiting the outlets.

In 1965 I appointed a new American sales representative for our premium packets. While on a trip to New York I was briefing him on the costings and potential and existing markets for the line. During the course of the briefing I mentioned the success we had had in supplying many repeat orders to this chain of restaurants in Kentucky.

I noticed a puzzled look came over the face of the New Yorker at this reference. Americans are a very polite people and usually will do anything to avoid giving offence, but he felt that he had to clear up what was rapidly building up into a monumental misunderstanding.

Finally, he said: 'Excuse me, but I want to get something clear. How could a China restaurant in Kentucky possibly use the quantities of premiums you mention?'

CHINA RESTAURANT . . . CHAIN OF RESTAURANTS . . .

The penny dropped, and explanations were forthcoming which cleared up the mystery.

As early as 1892, G L James in *Shall I Try Australia* made this comment on the troublesome vowel 'a':

> As to the English spoken in Australia, I believe it has already been remarked how correct, as a rule, it is, and I think it is free from any distinguishing accent or provincialism to a marvellous extent, while the tone of voice is pleasing and well modulated. In Sydney, however, more particularly the young girls, especially of the lower classes, are apt to affect a twang in pronouncing the letter 'a' as if it were 'i', or rather an 'ai' diphthong.

Whilst it is perhaps understandable that Americans should become confused when they hear 'a' sound as 'i', the extraordinary thing is that even WITHIN AUSTRALIA confusion sometimes arises because of the habit. Writing in the *Bulletin* on 11 July 1934 a solicitor related the following experience:

> I have two typists, part of whose duty is to read over and check engrossments of documents when typed. If I happen to catch the context it is all right, but otherwise I find myself wondering how I used such words as 'light' and 'bight' in the draft of a document which couldn't possibly require them. Then I realise that I wrote 'late' and 'bait', and when the document comes in find both words correctly spelt. I noticed a case in the law reports only last week where counsel had to apply for leave to substitute the name 'Ada' for 'Ida' in a document. I have had exactly the same trouble. I couldn't make out which name the lady bore, even after she had spelled it aloud, and when I asked her to write it down I nearly lost a client.

Another example of the confusion that can arise from Australian speech patterns was reported from Melbourne in March 1979. A group of women planned a protest against the proclamation of the Ayatollah Khomeini's ruling that women in Iran should return to traditional Moslem dress. A spokesperson for the group rang Telecom enquiries to find out where the IRANIAN Consular Office was located but didn't make herself clear and was given the address of the URANIUM Information Centre in South Melbourne. The Uranium Centre is used to demonstrators turning up on its doorstep but officers there were somewhat bemused to be confronted with twenty-four women dressed in veils and Moslem clothes chanting slogans about the Ayatollah Khomeini and events in Iran. The demonstrators eventually departed when they realised that there had been a breakdown in communications somewhere along the line.

Because Australians tend to pronounce 'a' as 'i' in the same manner of the English Cockney, the belief has long persisted that Australian language is an Antipodean form of Cockney. To this day many Americans, for instance, baffled by our 'i'-oriented accent, insist that we speak pure Cockney.

Of course there was a considerable Cockney element in early colonial speech since Londoners comprised a fair percentage of our compulsive emigrants—the convicts—but by the end of the last century the mix of population was so broad that the Cockney element was a very small one indeed.

This did not prevent the Cockney theory gaining considerable credence from the 1890s when the talk of Federation for the first time sparked a lot of interest in aspects of Australian life and culture that had previously been largely ignored.

The *Bulletin* was one of the chief offenders in this respect, stoutly maintaining the Cockney origin of basic Australian speech without adducing any concrete evidence to support the claim. In one stirring editorial of 6 January 1893 the *Bulletin* was to proclaim that:

... early Australian parents were too busy, and generally too uneducated, to notice that their offspring had caught the (Cockney) complaint, and said 'kike' for 'cake' and 'gripes' for 'grapes' ... but whether the 'colonial twang' dies out of Australian mouths or grows and strengthens and is improved on the American system, the fact will remain that it was never at the beginning anything better than the twang of Cockney vulgarity. We imported it, long before rabbits, sparrows, snails and other British nuisances were grafted on our budding civilisation.

Students of language have been attempting, apparently without too much success, to counter this view since the turn of the century. In *Australia, the Making of a Nation* (1910) J Foster Fraser wrote:

To charge a person with talking like a Cockney has behind it an intention to be supercilious and rude ... To say that all Australians talk Cockney is just one of those exaggerations which the mass of people have a right to repudiate ... Yet that Cockney is spoken is undoubted ... To say that it is an inheritance from London settlers is absurd. My own belief is that it is an independent growth, partly due to climate, but mainly due to carelessness in speech.

An even stronger stand was taken in 1934 by Thomas Wood when he wrote in *Cobbers*:

Australians don't (talk Cockney). People who say they do know nothing of accents and nothing of voices. They judge by vowels and inexpertly then. They disregard intonation, inflexion and quality. Are the Cockney and the Australian voice alike in these? They are not. The first is husky and the second is thin. The first flicks up and down; the second stays level. The first slides its words into groups; the second drawls them, one at a time. You do not find the Cockney stresses in Australia, nor, incidentally, the wit ... Australian vowels ... reminded me of vowels I heard in the South Midlands rather than those I had heard in East London; they are the malformations you can make for yourself if you keep your tongue flat and tighten your lips. Ugly? That is a question of taste. But ugly or not, these vowels, like the characteristic intonation that goes with them, show how our tongue has developed in a particular country, and a condemnation based simply on prejudice is not justified.

A J Marshall in *Australia Limited* (1942) also took up the cudgels on behalf of the anti-Cockney theory when he wrote:

The only product besides wool that Australia has anything like a corner in is her inimitable accent and nobody is likely to want to take that off our hands ... A lot has been written about the Australian accent, but one thing only has been agreed upon. That is, that of all the accents evolved by British-speaking man, it is along with that of the Cockney, by far the most unpleasant ... Americans and Englishmen say briefly that 'Australians talk like Cockneys.' A sensitive ear will tell you that there are noteworthy differences ... There is nothing unnatural about the Australian accent. It is a legitimate, local variation of speech. The trouble is that it is so damnably unpleasant.

All these efforts to put distance between Australians and the Cockneys on the score of accent seem to have fallen on deaf ears because on numerous occasions I have heard non-Australians— mainly Americans—assert their very firm belief that we talk 'Cockney' and it is all because of that 'i' instead of 'a' in our speech.

I fear the wretched thing will haunt us all to our collective graves.

In a letter to the Editor of the *Sydney Morning Herald* in 1978 Michael Boylan suggested that the 'o' syllable was also heading for trouble. He claimed that there was increasing tendency, particularly on the part of young women, to produce 'o' in words such as 'throw', 'blow' and 'go' not with the familiar long 'o' sound but with a short 'o' as in 'hot'. He said he could think of only three possible explanations for this:

(1) It was a further corruption of our dialect by the New Zealanders;

    (2) Possible changes in the jaw structure of a large segment of the population;

    (3) An affectation.

This letter brought a response from Mrs R M Edelsten, Licentiate of the Trinity College of London for Speech and Drama, who gave a long technical explanation on sound production, and wound up with this comment:

> . . . however, I agree with him that these sounds are very often very badly pronounced by Australians, and that is because they do not shape their lips, but just allow the sound to escape from their mouths.

Chapter Five

SHORTEN IT

One word's as good as ten. Wire in. Amen.

Shearers' Grace before meals. Author unknown

A feature of Australian speech is the excessive use of diminutives. Australians have been accused of pure laziness in shortening words, but whatever the reason for this verbal shorthand, the use of diminutives certainly is widespread. Some examples:

ABO for Aborigine.
ARVO for afternoon.
BARBIE for barbecue.
CARBY for carburettor.
COMP for (workers) compensation.
CUPPA for cup of tea.
CURRY for Cloncurry.
DARLO for Darlinghurst (a Sydney suburb).
DELI for delicatessen.
EV for have ('Ev a frosty, Mate').
GABBA for Wollongabba (a cricket ground in Brisbane).
JOURNO for journalist.
KERO for kerosene.
LOO for Woolloomooloo (a Sydney suburb).
MOONY for Moonee Ponds (a Melbourne suburb—its residents are
    known as 'Moonies').
MOSSIE for mosquito.
NEWK for (John) Newcombe.
OZ for Australia.
PADDO for Paddington (a Sydney suburb).
PREGO (or PREGGERS) for pregnant.
REGO for car registration (use of this diminutive is widespread in
    advertisements for used cars).

ROO for kangaroo.
SCHOOLIE for schoolteacher.
TATTS for Tattersalls (a lottery).
TELLY for television and also for Sydney *Daily Telegraph*.
UEY for U-turn.
UTE for utility truck.
UNI for university.
UPTER for up to no good.
VAG for Vagrancy Act (i.e. 'On the vag').

A visiting English heart surgeon was said to be very surprised when informed that the word in most common usage in Australia was AORTA. He thought this indicated an extremely high interest in his own field of heart surgery but was said to have been quite disillusioned when examples of the usage of the word were pointed out to him such as 'AORTA do sumpin' about those drains', 'AORTA lower taxes and raise wages', 'AORTA be shot fer such a silly bloody action'. And so on. The list is endless.

AORTA is simply an Australian abbreviation for 'They ought to' and is just one of the examples of Australian laziness in shortening words to reduce effort and save wear and tear on the vocal chords.

Writing in the *Sun-Herald* in 1978, Penelope Rowe reported on a conversation she had overheard on a Sydney bus:

'What are you having for dinner tonight?'
'Ard.'
'Ard? What's Ard?'
'Ardunno.'

Although Australian laziness usually expresses itself by dropping letters from the end (or beginning) of established words, sometimes an entire word is eliminated in the pursuit of vocal economy. There is, for example, an increasing tendency by readers of television and radio commercials to drop the 'and' from prices such as 'a hundred and ninety-nine dollars'. The abrupt 'a hundred ninety-nine dollars' jars on the ear but does save a word, and since TV and radio advertising rates are based on the number of words used, this form of desecration of the English language may well be inspired by economics rather than laziness.

However, it is pure laziness, not economics, that prompts me to adopt the Australian habit of shortening it, by abruptly ending this chapter at this point!

Chapter Six

PRONUNCIATION

Little care is apparently taken to correct vicious
pronunciation . . . this inattention has a tendency to foster
an Australian dialect which bids fair to surpass the
American in disagreeableness.

NSW School Commission Report of 1854-5

In the field of language probably nothing causes more debate—
at times at quite heated levels—than pronunciation. The
popular American song neatly sums up a problem that is world-
wide: 'You say ba-NAN-as, I say ba-NARN-as; you say tom-
ATE-oes, I say to-MART-oes'.

Australia does not have regional dialects which are such a
cause of confusion on the pronunciation front in other parts of
the world, and this in itself can be a problem for visitors long
used to being able to place the origin of a speaker by his or her
pronunciation of certain words.

In *The Pronunciation of English in Australia* (1946) Professor
A G Mitchell makes the point that there is no such thing as
standard English pronunciation determined by any authorised
body. There are, he points out, many different forms of English
pronunciation: national, dialectal and social, and amongst the
many forms of English pronunciation, that spoken in Australia
takes its place. Professor Mitchell then goes on to make this
interesting observation:

. . . Some critics, it would seem, imply that Australians had set out in
cold earnest to evolve a distinctive dialect of English, and that in doing
so they had selected all the most unpleasing characteristics of some
English dialects. Australian pronunciation has its own history, though
we may not be able to trace that history satisfactorily. It has developed
through a combination of social, psychological, acoustic, physiological

and other influences. Such divergent linguistic development in an isolated community is inevitable. It is still going on in Australia . . . The Australian is at some disadvantage in understanding the characteristics of his own pronunciation because there is little diversity of speech in Australia, and the Australian has little opportunity of hearing other forms of English speech, less opportunity still of hearing foreign languages . . . The Australian is probably too complacent in the belief (universal, after all) that his is the normal, plain, unmannered way of speaking and that all other ways are a little queer. He too seldom has the salutory experience of discovering that his own speech may sound a little queer to other speakers. Many Australians, unable to hear anything characteristic or individual in Australian speech, affirm that talk about the Australian accent is argument about what does not really exist.

Professor Mitchell's viewpoint still holds good though the three great post-war forces of television, large-scale influx of non-English speaking migrants and the event of cheaper air fares encouraging mass travel overseas have all tended to reduce Australia's isolation and in time may invalidate some of the arguments he puts forward.

In *World Words*, published in New York in 1945, Professor W Cabell Greet put forward an interesting theory, which I have not seen, challenged or tested, that some Australian pronunciations are based on income! To illustrate his point he took the word CANBERRA and noted:

There is a story that Government employees who receive more than £500 yearly pronounce the name of the capital with the accent on the first syllable, and those who receive less put the accent on the second.

Although Australia lacks regional dialects, there are two other factors which tend to cause a lot of confusion on the pronunciation front. These are the very extensive use of slang terms, which in themselves often have differing pronunciations, and the widespread use of Aboriginal place names. The pronunciation of these differ very widely from place to place since there was wide variation in the interpretation placed by the early settlers on the words they had learned from Aborigines. When written records of Aboriginal place names were attempted, the differences became even more pronounced with widely varying spelling of words of the same pro-nunciation, as well as differing pronunciation of words spelled the same way.

For example, EUNGELLA, located near Murwillumbah on the north coast of New South Wales, is called YOON-GELLA by the locals; but in the mountains behind Mackay, in Queensland, there is another EUNGELLA which is pronounced EE-YUN-GLA.

Variations usually arise from differing traditional usage in widely separated communities. If someone in authority decided a hundred years ago that their place was pronounced a certain way, the locals went along with that, oblivious of the fact that in another part of the country a name with identical spelling was being pronounced quite differently.

In *Australia Speaks* Sidney Baker gives some interesting examples of place names with similar—or in some cases identical—spelling but with vastly different local pronunciation. These include:

BYABARRA is pronounced By-a BARra but BYABURRA is pronounced By-AB-ra

GOONDIWINDI is Gun-da-WINdy but GOONDOOBLUIE is Goon-da-blu-EE

MUNDARLO is Mun-DAH-lo but MUNDAROO is MUN-da-roo

YOUNGAREEN is Yun-gar-REEN but YOUNGERRINA is Young-ERRina

GEURIE is GEAR-ee but GWABEGAR is woBBy-gah

ECHUCA is Ee-CHOO-ka but SOBROAN is Sa-BRON

CONGI is Cong-I but MOONBI is MOON-bee

Baker noted that pronunciation peculiarities abounded in Australian place names and he records some which are worth noting:

DUMARESQ pronounced Da-MERrick

ROUCHEL pronounced ROO-kal

SCHEYVILLE pronounced SKY-vill

FAVEAUX pronounced Fa-VO

LAHEYS CREEK pronounced LAZE Creek

BOONOO BOONOO pronounced Bunna-baNOO

MUNGIE BUNDIE pronounced Mucker-BUN-dye

GHINNI GHINNI pronounced GHINnee-ghin-NEE

COBRABALD pronounced KAW-bra-ball

PINDARI pronounced Pin-da-ROY

BENANDARAH pronounced Ba-NAN-dra

CANOWINDRA pronounced Ca-NOWN-dra

BOOROORBAN pronounced Ba-ROO-a-ban

BOURBAH pronounced BOO-a-bah

And if you really want to get tied up in knots you can always visit WAGINGOBERAMBI which is pronounced Wa-GHING-go-ba-RAMbee, or go to YATTEYATAH which is pronounced YATtee-ya-TAH.

The usual arbiter on such matters is a standing committee of the Australian Broadcasting Commission which meets regularly to decide the pronunciations of words and place names which its announcers must use when on air. The committee fights a valiant battle to maintain national standards on pronunciation, but one suspects that it may in time be overwhelmed by the sheer weight of the problem of slang, local differences and the well-known Australian inertia on all matters relating to reform—linguistic or otherwise.

Chapter Seven

THE EVOLUTION OF LANGUAGE

Words strain,
Crack and sometimes break, under the burden,
Under the tension, slip, slide, perish,
Decay with impression, will not stay in place,
Will not stay still.

T S Eliot

Many people speak of 'good', 'bad' or 'correct' English as though language were a static thing, capable of standing still and being precisely formalised. Nothing could be further from the truth, of course, as language is as just as much a living thing as any organism, ever growing and changing so that it cannot be frozen in any single frame of time or space.

The evolution of Australian-English has been carried through at a much faster pace than most languages because of the circumstances of its birth and development. To understand the Australian language, therefore, one must have some understanding of the circumstances of its origin, some of which have no parallel with other countries.

A key factor—though by no means the only one—was the convict origins of the colony. For more than half a century the country was used as the dumping ground for tens of thousands of convicts of the worst type—the refuse of the English prisons and hulks. Drawn from the lowest orders of English society, and bringing with them a variety of dialects and the FLASH language—the slang of the eighteenth-century criminal class—the pattern was set early for the development of a language quite different from *proper* English of the middle and upper classes of the homeland. In the early and vital years of development, these classes were represented only in very small numbers in the Antipodes.

The new white inhabitants of Australia found themselves in a completely foreign environment with a harshness of climate and landscape beyond their comprehension. It was a land where everything seemed upside down and totally alien. As Brian Penton expressed it through one of his characters in *Landtakers* (1934):

> It's a long way from your merry old England out here, and it's a funny sort of place, where nothing happens like it should. Christmas comes in the middle of summer. The north wind's hot and the south wind's cold. Trees drop their bark and keep their leaves. The flowers don't smell and the birds don't sing. The swans are black and the eagles white. You burn cedar to boil your hominy and build your fences out of mahogony. Aye, it's not the same as the Old Country at all.

The new inhabitants were faced with a completely different type of flora and fauna, all of which had to be identified and named. They found the land inhabited by Aborigines who themselves were divided into hundreds of (often warring) tribes without a common language. When the early settlers started to move about the continent they frequently attempted to apply native names to the new flora and fauna or geographical features they encountered, but immediately ran into the problem that the name ascribed to an object by one tribe was completely different from the name for the same thing by another tribe.

Being some 12000 miles from their homeland also meant that the new settlers—whether convicts or freemen—had to improvise heavily to survive in such a harsh environment. This improvisation meant completely new ways of daily living and new words had to be coined to cover experiences which had no counterpart in the Old Country.

Given the circumstances of the origin of the colony, the environment and the influence of the many Aboriginal dialects, it is little wonder that there quickly developed in Australia a language distinctly different from that of the Mother Country when the new settlers came.

George P Marsh, in *Lectures on the English Language* (1859) summed the changes up very well when he wrote:

> Whenever a people, by emigration into a different soil and climate, by a large influx of foreigners into its territory, by political or religious revolutions, or other great and comprehensive changes, is brought into contact with new objects, new circumstances, new cares, labours and duties, it is obviously under the necessity of framing or borrowing new words, or of modifying the received meaning of old ones, in such a way

as to express the new conditions of material existence, the new aims and appetencies, to which the change in question gives birth.

The evolution of language follows the same basic evolutionary laws as apply to flora and fauna. The most important of these laws—as in the animal kingdom—is natural selection. New words are pushed up by new circumstances, and either thrive, if the environment for them is favourable, or die if it is not. Imposed on the pattern of natural creation are small groups of words or sayings brought into being not as a response to any community need but by clever individuals playing with words. Barry Humphries (see chapter 31 entitled BAZZA McKENZIE) is a typical example of such a word creator. Perhaps his methods of foisting new words on an unsuspecting populace through his writings, comic strips or stage presentations could best be described as 'creation by linguistic artificial insemination'. Such creations can only survive if they gain wide currency or quickly capture the public imagination with their cleverness or aptness. But for every such artificial word that survives to become part of the language, perhaps a hundred others wither on the vine in their infancy. For instance one would not expect that the invented words in the following advertisement which appeared in a 1978 issue of *Nation Review* would be given a high survival rating:

MELBOURNE. Sizar, 20, proud of his blossoming viraginity, yet fearful of his insalubrious posteriority, needs pusillanimous votaries or similar pedants for relief of his occupational disease rather than leave everything to chancre. Ring Steve 386.5043.

The rapidity with which a language evolves is perhaps best illustrated by the well-known poem *The Great Australian Slanguage*, by W T Goodge, first published in 1897. In this poem, Goodge took a large number of then typical Australian slang expressions and wove them cleverly into his verse. At the turn of the century these words all had extremely wide currency. Today they have almost all vanished from the language, having been replaced by different slang terms for the same objects. Goodge's poem is worth reprinting in full, if only to illustrate how fleeting is the life of most slang terms:

> *Tis the everyday Australian*
> *Has a language of his own,*
> *Has a language, or a slanguage,*
> *Which can simply stand alone.*
> *And a 'dickin pitch to kid us'*
> *Is a synonym for 'lie',*
> *And to 'nark it' means to stop it,*

And to 'nit it' means to fly!
And a bosom friend's a 'cobber',
  And a horse a 'prad' or 'moke',
While a casual acquaintance
  Is a 'joker' or a 'bloke',
And his ladylove's his 'donah',
  Or his 'clinah' or his 'tart',
Or his 'little bit o' muslin',
  As it used to be his 'bart',
And his naming of the coinage
  Is a mystery to some,
With his 'quid' and 'half-a-caser',
  And his 'deener' and his 'scrum',
And a 'tin-back' is a party
  Who's remarkable for luck,
And his food is called his 'tucker',
  Or his 'panem' or his 'chuck'.
A policeman is a 'johnny'
  Or a 'copman' or a 'trap',
And a thing obtained on credit
  Is invariably 'strap'.
A conviction's known as 'trouble',
  And a gaol is called a 'jug',
And a sharper is a 'spieler'
  And a simpleton's a 'tug'.
If he hits a man in fighting
  That is what he calls a 'plug',
If he borrows money from you
  He will say he 'bit your lug'.
And to 'shake it' is to steal it,
  And to 'strike it' is to beg;
And a jest is 'poking borak',
  And a jester 'pulls your leg'.
Things are 'cronk' when they go wrongly
  In the language of the 'push',
But when things go as he wants 'em
  He declares it is 'all cush'.
When he's bright he's got a 'napper',
  And he's 'ratty' when he's daft,
And when looking for employment
  He is 'out o' blooming graft'.
And his clothes he calles his 'clobber'
  Or his 'togs', but what of that
When a 'castor' or a 'kady'
  Is the name he give his hat!

And our undiluted English
Is a fad to which we cling,
But the great Australian slanguage
Is a truly awful thing!

In the evolutionary process, words pop up, have a short or long life span and then disappear. Except for the purely artificial creations, it is seldom that the origin of slang words can be traced back to a specific time and place or originator.

The Furphy family of Shepparton, in Victoria, had the distinction of contributing two distinct and widely different expressions to the English language, and both are interesting examples of the evolutionary process of words.

John Furphy was the owner of a foundry established at Shepparton in 1874. During World War I the foundry supplied metal carts to the army for water carrying and sanitary purposes, and each cart had embossed on it the firm's name and the slogan.

GOOD, BETTER, BEST: NEVER LET IT REST,
TILL YOUR GOOD IS BETTER, AND YOUR BETTER, BEST.

Camp rumours and idle latrine gossip came to be known as FURPHIES, a military term which spread into general usage in peacetime. The term is still occasionally used.

John's brother Joseph Furphy was the well-known author of *Such is Life*, written under the *nom de plume* of Tom Collins. By coincidence, 'Tom Collins' was a much earlier synonym for gossip. Bill Wannan in *The Australian* (1954) explains Tom Collins as follows:

Tom Collins was a synonym for idle rumour. This Tom was a mendacious fellow at whose door was laid the leg-pulling that flourished in hotel bars and wherever men gathered to gossip. A newcomer, breasting the bar of a hotel in Little Collins Street or Little Bourke Street, Melbourne, would be greeted with the latest scandal uttered against him. The victim, trying to run it to earth, would be told that Tom Collins said it, and Tom always had just gone to do the block in the pub line.

Bill Wannan also quotes a verse which appeared in the *Bulletin* in 1893 which indicates that Tom Collins was a bit of a wowser who did not drink or gamble or play around with wild women.

When Joseph Furphy chose this name as a pseudonym he must have been aware of 'Tom Collins'' reputation—no doubt it was the reason for the choice. It was therefore distinctly ironic that his brother John's iron carts some years later would give rise to the term FURPHY with almost exactly the same meaning as the original mythical character of Tom Collins.

Tom Collins proved to be the most enduring of the two expressions, however, as this later became the name for a popular cocktail whose name spread around the world. Nowadays bartenders from Rio de Janeiro to Timbuctoo will quickly respond to a drinker's call for a TOM COLLINS without having the faintest idea of the nineteenth century Australian origin of the term.

Some words disappear or develop new meanings through over-use or a change in community attitudes. The expletive SHIT is a good example. Long used as a scatalogical term for faeces, it joined the ranks of the expletives in the 1960s when it became the fashion to air four-letter words at every opportunity. Probably the most widely used four-letter expletive on a world-wide basis in the 1970s was SHIT. Its usage was so common that it popped up regularly in American-made movies from the mid-1970s.

And this was the start of its downfall as an expletive. It was used so extensively, by both men and women, that it lost its aura of 'naughtiness'. When that happens it is almost inevitable that a word either disappears from common usage or there is a change in direction of its meaning or use.

In 1978 a friend informed me that the 'in word' in Sydney was GUANO which is the excrement of sea fowl. Someone, looking around for a substitute for the expletive SHIT, had obviously hit upon this perfectly innocuous foreign-sounding word, with the same basic meaning as SHIT when it was an 'underground' term, and decided to launch it on the unsuspecting Australian community—with some success if my informant is correct in its Sydney usage. Only time will tell whether GUANO will make it as another Australian expletive used nationally. Perhaps it will do so if some TV personality adopts it and starts to use it on air!

Incidentally, SHIT still survives as an Australian prison term for tobacco, and in more recent years has become the most common international underground term for hashish.

Language evolves at such a fast rate that this constitutes a trap for those who do not keep a close ear to the linguistic ground.

Take the common English word GEAR, a product of the Industrial Revolution having reference to machinery. In Australia it had a fair run in pre-war years as a slang word referring to one's luggage, or to sporting equipment (i.e. cricket gear, fishing gear).

It was no doubt in this sense that in 1978 the conductor on

board the FISH (a train running between Sydney Central and the Blue Mountains) was recorded as announcing over the train's public address system:

We are now arriving at Springwood, and will those passengers intending to alight, don't forget to get off. Also, don't forget to get your gear off.

This brought guffaws from the passengers who were aware, as the conductor apparently was not, that GEAR had long been obsolete as a term for luggage and was then the current 'in word' for CLOTHING. To 'get one's gear off' is to do a strip which would hardly be appreciated by the law if attempted in daylight on a railway platform.

But by then (1978) the meaning of the word GEAR was already in the process of changing again as amongst the young it was rapidly becoming a slang term for heroin and hard drugs generally. This caused some red faces in Qantas when the fact was pointed out that as late as in 1978 their youth travel brochure *Detours* carried a line stating they could advise young travellers 'where to sack down, how not to get ripped off, where to get gear'.

The writer of the brochure made extensive use of slang to reach his particular audience, but fell into the trap of using the word GEAR in an obsolete form so far as the target audience was concerned.

The way that a slang word can acquire new meaning in the evolutionary process is interesting. For instance the word HOOT (from the Maori UTU) was transported across the Tasman in the last century and for a long period was the slang expression for money. It was still around, though not in frequent currency, in the post-war years. I thought it had disappeared from the scene but noted its use in the *Sun-Herald* (Sydney) as late as 1977:

... It's about a Q.C. and his wife, who live in Point Piper and obviously have lots of hoot.

In more recent times the word was used in a different way such as 'I don't give a hoot.' ('I don't give a damn.') It seems there is another version floating around according to the following quotation by Norma Hayman from *Nation Review* of 17–23 November 1977:

On the face of it the Women of the Year Luncheon in aid of the National Heart Foundation promised to be a hoot.

A HOOT here obviously doesn't refer to money or 'giving a

damn', but rather as something being 'a bit of a laugh'. Jim Ramsay's *Cop It Sweet* provides the clue as it gives the alternative slang definitions of HOOT as MONEY and STINK.

Here the going gets heavy as STINK by itself is a slang word with several meanings. The commonest usage is as a vulgar term for a bad smell or unpleasant odour, but it is also a fairly common term for an uproar and its use in that form in Australia goes back to the convict era as it is listed by Vaux as an underworld expression. Grose's *Classical Dictionary of the Vulgar Tongue* (1823) gives an interesting definition:

STINK: When any robbery of moment has been committed which causes much alarm, or of which much is said in the daily papers, the FAMILY PEOPLE will say, there is a great STINK about it. See WANTED.

WANTED: When any of the TRAPS or runners have private information against a FAMILY PERSON, and are using means to apprehend the party. they say, such a one is WANTED; and it becomes the latter, on receiving such intimation, to keep out of the way, until the STINK is over, or until he or she can find means to STASH THE BUSINESS through the medium of Mr Palmer, or by some other means.

In World War II a STINK became a popular term amongst Australian troops to describe an official uproar over some misdeeds, real or imagined, on the part of the troops. In such cases the culprits lay low until the STINK or FLAP (an alternative word) was over.

The word is also used in the extended form of STINKER, a term for an excessively hot and oppressive day. A man who has objectionable characteristics is also referred to as a STINKER, while a man can also get STINKING drunk. The nickname STINKER is also applied to the Australian bird the Blue-winged Shoveller. Another variation on the word is STINKIES, the term used by Australian schoolboys everywhere for certain types of marbles, whilst schoolboys also have long referred to a certain type of fireworks as STINKPOTS.

The variations of the term seem endless; but what emerges from all this is that Ms Norma Hayman was probably trying to convey the message that the National Heart Foundation luncheon would be a fairly lively occasion. Why didn't she say just that and save all the chasing off to our dictionaries in search of definitions of the seldom used word HOOT?

Chapter Eight

GUTENBERG AND THE GLOBAL VILLAGE

Today we're beginning to realise that the new media aren't just mechanical gimmicks for creating worlds of illusion, but new languages with new and unique powers of expression.

Marshall McLuhan

The previous chapter dealt with the evolutionary processes of a language such as Australian-English, but paid no heed to the communication systems by which these changes came about.

The development of speech was the greatest single step that man took in his long evolutionary march from the past, and it was a step that set him apart, in a quite remarkable way, from every other living creature.

For the many millions of years when early man was developing crude speech patterns, the sole method of communicating them was the human voice. Gestures and signs could be used and understood to convey general messages and attitudes, but speech was the *only* medium for transmitting, understanding and recording word patterns—the very foundation of language.

The invention of writing was another enormous breakthrough in the development of language. It meant that word patterns could be preserved in some concrete form for future unborn generations instead of being dependent on the unreliable oral traditions of the past. And the invention of moveable type by Gutenberg was yet another giant step forward in the development of language since the magic of the written (or printed) word could at last be taken from the conservative hands of the few, the traditional guardian scholars of know-ledge, and put into the hands of the masses in the form of pamphlets, newspapers, magazines and books.

It is difficult to assert, with any degree of accuracy, which communication methods played the major roles in the develop-ment of Australian-English. My own guess, and it is only a guess, is that the oral tradition was the predominant influence until near the end of the nineteenth century, when it was superseded by the influence of the print media in their many forms.

From the middle of the last century newspapers were published at regular intervals, daily in all the larger centres of population, and were widely read. There seems little doubt that they were extremely successful in keeping the populace adequately informed of what was going on, both on the local scene and in the world at large. And their influence on the commercial and political life of the country was very considerable—at times decisive. Yet, I have a doubt as to whether they played any major role in the development of the decidedly raffish, larrikin-oriented language that we under-stand today as Australian-English.

Critics of newspapers often accuse them of leading the populace down the path to a new linguistic Sodom and Gomorrah by printing all the indecencies and obscenities voiced in the community, which all right-thinking persons would prefer to be swept under the carpet along with all the other nasty things lurking there.

This is unfair. In my long experience of the press, as both a working journalist and a keen observer, I know the reverse to be the case. With a few notable exceptions, the Australian press is very prudish in its approach to social issues and to language, and even the most brazen scandal sheets display a remarkable conservatism in the actual words they use to describe the sensational events reported in their columns. By and large, the press lags well behind in the use of slang words that have long become accepted by the general populace. All newspapers have their guidelines of dos and don'ts on language usage, and sometimes they display a sensitivity to public reaction that is positively hilarious. In support of this I will cite an incident to which I was a witness.

In 1949 Lord and Lady Mountbatten announced that they would be paying their first visit to Australia. The sub-editor who handled the story on the *Sydney Morning Herald* came up with a fairly unexciting but seemingly innocuous heading which (from memory) ran something like this:

MOUNTBATTENS
TO COME
HERE IN JUNE

After the first (country) edition has been printed around 10 pm it is common practice in most sub-editors' rooms of morning newspapers to hold a brief post mortem on stories. Headings are changed where it is thought necessary. The late morning edition often bears little resemblance to the first edition of a paper and many a potential libel has been picked up and eliminated in the period between editions.

On this particular occasion one of the sub-editors queried whether or not the word COME in the heading on the Mountbatten story might have sexual connotations. The matter was debated (quite seriously) for some minutes but opinion seemed inconclusive. Then the late Sidney J Baker, who at that time was a special writer on the *Herald*, happened to walk into the sub-editors' room. As the author of *The Australian Language* and several other works on slang, he was immediately asked his opinion on the debate then taking place. Baker considered the matter for a moment and then delivered judgement: Yes, he said, the phrase 'to come' did mean to ejaculate during intercourse, though the term wasn't in general usage.

Baker's words were the kiss of death for the offending heading which was changed for all subsequent editions.

Another example of editorial nervousness when faced with words of dubious character was cited by former journalist Randolph Bedford in *Naught to Thirty-three* (1944) when he told the following story:

> In my passion for realism, I once put in a report of a burglar's arrest that I had witnessed:
>
> 'The prisoner's wife, who opened the door, was dressed in a chemise.'
>
> It passed the sub-editor; but the leader of the staff, who was, for that day at least, a man easily shocked, altered it to 'her sleeping robe'. By accident the Editor, a very direct man, saw the proof.
>
> '"Sleeping robe",' he said. 'Sleeping robe! That boy is too direct to write "sleeping robe". Where's the copy! What did he write? ... "Chemise"! He was nearly right. Why not use English?'
>
> And he altered it to read: 'The prisoner's wife, in her shirt, opened the door.'

Because of their conservative policies, most daily newspapers are extremely reluctant to allow new words—especially those classified as slang or vulgar—into their columns, but the editorial front against colloquial speech is not united and can be breached in many ways. Columnists and distinguished contributors are allowed far more latitude than reporters and often take advantage of this to introduce into their writings words and phrases that would be considered taboo in the news columns. Sub-editors also are faced with problems in handling copy containing verbatim speeches or comments by famous men and women. Again, they may hesitate to wield a blue pencil to strike out some colloquialism by a prime minister or the prominent community leader, whereas they would not hesitate if it were uttered by a lesser mortal.

By and large however, the daily press does not give general support to evolutionary trends in the development of Australian-English, though once a word or phrase *has* gained general community acceptance, and is recognised as such by the newspapers, it is accepted as suitable for print and quickly gains very wide circulation—thus further bolstering community usage.

If the newspapers are slow to accept new words into their hallowed columns, the same does not apply to other print media such as magazines and books.

In the latter part of the nineteenth century and the early years of this century the *Bulletin* magazine (often referred to as the *Bushman's Bible*) was a tremendous force in introducing to readers in the cities the new language of the bush through the endless stream of stories and pithy paragraphs which graced its pages.

Sidney J Baker in *The Australian Language* paid this tribute to the *Bulletin* as a repository of the new Australian-English which developed in the nineteenth century:

> . . . The simple facts are that the material on bush lore, slang and idiom collected by thousands of writers in the *Bulletin* pages is absolutely irreplaceable. Perhaps never in the history of world journalism has a paper stood nearer to the heart of a country than the *Bulletin*; probably never again will so much of the true nature of a country be caught up in the pages of a single journal.

Other literary, political and general journals also played a more significant role in the evolution of language than the daily newspapers, though their influence collectively probably was not as great as the *Bulletin* which specialised to such a degree in stories of the bush and its characters.

The nineteenth century novelists and poets such as Henry Lawson, Banjo Paterson, Rolf Boldrewood, Tom Collins and Marcus Clarke, and the later generation of writers which included Louis Stone and C J Dennis, were also prolific in their use of the new language of the bush. In fact some of them were accused of excessive over-use of slang terms, whilst others undoubtedly misused colloquial terms in artificial settings. The end result however, was that the writings of such men as Dennis (in particular), and of the bush balladists of the last century, comprise a vast repository in print of the Australian colloquial language of the latter colonial period.

Another twentieth-century writer who tapped the vein of basic Australian speech with enormous success was Lennie Lower, probably the most prolific humorous writer any English speaking country has ever produced. His output in the form of newspaper and magazine columns from the late 1920s to his death in 1947 was prodigious and he had an enormous following throughout Australia. Lower was not a great user of slang, but his columns were always written in a simple colloquial form, understandable at the lowest levels.

I once discussed with his mother the methods he used in writing his only novel *Here's Luck*, that great epic of Australian humour. At the time he was a columnist on the Sydney *Daily Guardian* and much of his work on the novel was done at the office in between his columns. Each night he would bring home the bits and pieces of chapters that he had put together and would read them out to his mother and sister for reaction, comment and suggestions. His mother, a rather formal, elegant lady who would have been described by a former generation as being 'well brought up', told me that she strongly disapproved of what she termed 'vulgarisms' in the book, such as 'pub' and 'grog', and she strongly urged her son to make the book more 'respectable' (her term). Lower resisted and in this showed much better judgement than his mother as it was the colloquial down-to-earth style that gave it such force—and saleability. The fact that *Here's Luck* has only been out of print on rare occasions since it was first published in 1930 is a fair indication of its enduring qualities and how seriously Australians are wedded to their peculiar form of colloquial speech. Lower's mother was well advanced in age when I spoke with her and was still torn between great pride in her only son's great literary achievement and the secret wish that his fame could have rested on a work more in line with her own elitist upbringing. And this seems the eternal dilemma facing the educated Australian who has a constant love-hate relationship with an Australian-English language which he or she feels is a caricature of the real thing, yet which he or she feels compelled to use as one of the key factors in the assertion of national aspirations.

I thought this dilemma was summed up very well by

Greenough and Kittredge in *Words and Their Ways in English Speech* (1902):

> Slang . . . is a peculiar kind of vagabond language, always hanging on the outskirts of legitimate speech, but continually straying or forcing its ways into the most respectable company.

In more recent times the influence of Gutenberg has waned considerably under the assault of the new electronic communication systems of radio and television. These have taken us forward into what Marshall McLuhan calls the 'Global Village' of instant world-wide communication. But in one sense it may have meant a step back in time with language evolving mainly by word of mouth transmission as it did before print became a form of mass communication, though the process has been speeded up enormously as new words or phrases gain instant exposure electronically to millions of ears.

The electronic media have not only a far greater impact on listeners and viewers than the old print media had on readers, but their immediacy makes censorship more difficult. Whereas a sub-editor on a newspaper can ponder for minutes, blue pencil poised, on the wisdom of allowing a certain word or phrase to creep into print, the radio and television controllers frequently have no such latitude since so much of their material goes over the air waves 'live'. Even where there is a time-delay button to exercise control, it is rarely used except when it is considered necessary to bleep out some four-letter word. By its very nature an electronic medium is 'instant action' and therefore must present a 'warts and all' picture of the world quite different from more selective print media. Professor R Downing, Chairman of the Australian Broadcasting Commission in 1975, recognised this when he readily confessed:

> When we invite Bob Hawke to appear on a programme we expect him to use some colourful language. Otherwise we wouldn't invite him.

Sometimes an obsolete word or expression can gain a new lease of life and be recycled back into the linguistic mainstream as a result of unexpected exposure in the electronic media of its use by a prominent personality. For instance, before the December 1977 Federal elections, a well publicised golf match between leading women political figures attracted a lot of media coverage. During the match Mrs Tamie Fraser, wife of the Prime Minister, made a faulty stroke and her cry of exasperation, 'Wouldn't it rot your socks' was heard by TV viewers around the nation.

It was perhaps thirty years since I had heard the expression, which obviously had survived in such outposts of civilisation as western Victoria, but no doubt the term gained a new lease of life, at least in the school playgrounds of the nation, as a result of its unexpected TV airing. The expression was, of course, an offshoot of the many 'Wouldn't it . . .' terms of exasperation so popular during World War II, i.e.:

'Wouldn't it haunt you?'

'Wouldn't it make you sick?'

'Wouldn't it rip you?'

'Wouldn't it make you mad?'

'Wouldn't it rot your guts?'

'Wouldn't it rotate you?'

and of course the good old genuine army version:

'Wouldn't it root you?'

In a sense the wheel has come full turn with the evolution of Australian-English becoming again dependent on an oral tradition, but with the process speeded up to a degree that would have been unthinkable even a generation ago. There is no knowing where this headlong electronic rush will lead us, but of one thing we can be positive: Australian-English will not stand still but will go down the years of destiny ahead, dancing this way and that, nimbly but at great speed, as future generations continue their pursuit of their ultimate destiny in the great Land of the South, and change their language and their speech patterns to meet the needs of their quest.

Chapter Nine

AUSTRALIAN-ENGLISH

Among the male Australians there is a taciturnity
proceeding from natural diffidence and reserve, not from
any want of mental resources; this led one of their more
lively countrymen to observe 'that they could do everything
but speak'.

G Bennett in
Wanderings in New South Wales, 1834

From the earliest years, visitors to the Australian colony were
loud in their condemnation of the type of English spoken by
native-born residents of the Antipodes. These early commentators on the Australian scene, however, saw the matter of
speech in plain terms of black and white. The language of the
educated gentlefolk of southern England was to them 'correct
English'. Any departure from this was 'bad English' and they
despaired when their ears were assailed with nasalised
Australian speech with its curious mixture of the vulgar
tongue, and peculiar local idiom, slang and colloquialisms.
They blamed it all on our convict origins, of course, and Edward
Gibbon Wakefield's well known observation of 1829 perhaps
best sums up the views of all 'right-thinking' persons of the time:

Bearing in mind that our lowest class brought with it a peculiar
language, and is constantly supplied with fresh corruption, you will
understand why pure English is not, and is not likely to become, the
language of the colony.

But Wakefield's view was far too simplistic. It failed entirely
to take into account the fact that the mass of humanity dumped
into Sydney town in the first half-century of the colony brought
with them a great diversity of regional and social dialects so

that the adoption of any one dialect of the Mother Country became unlikely—if not an impossibility. Given the nature of the convict and emigrant mix, and the challenges of a new land with vastly differing landscapes, climate and social life the emergence of a distinct 'colonial parlance' was inevitable.

Noah Webster in the preface to his *American Dictionary of English Language* (1828) summed this up very well, and in a far more perceptive manner than Edward Gibbon Wakefield did when he wrote:

Language is the expression of ideas; and if the people of one country cannot preserve an identity of ideas (with the people of another country), they cannot preserve an identity of language. Now, an identity of ideas depends materially upon a sameness of things or objects with which the people of the two countries are conversant. But in no two portions of the earth, remote from each other, can such identity be found. Even physical objects must be different.

Commenting on the environmental factors which helped shape the Australian language, Sidney J Baker in *The Drum* (1959) made these points:

The material differences marking Australia as distinct from England are so varied that only the misinformed or the wilfully blind can ignore them. Generations of Australians have contributed towards the development of linguistic habits that reflect many of these differences. Moreover, these habits are not localised, but are spread with great evenness over the whole of Australia. There is little immediate distinction, for instance, between the expressions used and the pronunciation of Western Australia, the Eastern States, Northern Australia and Tasmania. Minor differences exist, it is true, but for a country of Australia's size they are extremely few. So here is preliminary evidence of an egalitarian levelling.

When a person in Albury speaks of BLUDGING, COBBER, FURPHY, POMMY, LARRIKIN, RATBAG, ROPEABLE, RORT, SHEILA, WOWSER, ZACK and ZIFF, the gold fossicker on Cape York and the cow cocky in the Mallee know what is meant. And when the Sydneysider refers to SP BETTING, DRINKING WITH THE FLIES, WHINGEING, SWY, NO-HOPER, BUCKLEY'S CHANCE, HARD CASE, OFFSIDER, GAME AS NED KELLY, FULL AS A GOOG, DRUNK AS CHLOE, WHIPPING THE CAT, PUTTING THE ACID ON, DROPPING ONE'S BUNDLE and CRACKING HARDY, there is probably not a single Australian who does not understand immediately. The most important thing to note about these terms is that they are Australian; they do not belong to the language of either Britain or the United States.

In the last century those who fought to uphold traditional English language forms fought a game but losing battle. One such was Sir Redmond Barry, and his efforts were such that *The Australian Sketcher* of 4 December 1880 took the unusual step of commenting on this aspect of his life in an obituary it published of him:

The very stateliness of his manner was a standing protest against the free and easy demeanour of a generation which, in its reaction against the stiffness, formality and restraint of former times, has gone to the opposite extreme, and is discarding all the amenities of good society, while his language . . . was greatly preferable in its measured precision and studied balance to the slipshod English and the slang which are so popular in many circles.

One person who quite early in the piece, and unlike Sir Redmond Barry, saw some hope in the way the Australian speech was developing, was James Dixon who, in his *Narrative of a Voyage* (1820), expressed a view that would certainly not have been endorsed by most of his compatriots of that period:

The children born in these colonies, and now grown up, speak a better language, purer, and more harmonious, than is generally the case in most parts of England. The amalgamation of such various dialects assembled together, seems to improve the mode of articulating the words.

For a long time everyone tried to maintain the myth that what was spoken in Australia was basic English with some local variations. That belief can no longer be sustained and it is now generally recognised that what is developing in Australia is an entirely new form of English.

Back in 1945, the newly appointed Minister for Immigration, the late Arthur A Calwell, commented: *All newcomers, of course, will have to learn to speak Australian.*

Since Calwell was noted for his oddball remarks, no one took him up on the matter, but by 1974 the chickens were starting to come home to roost on the linguistic front, as was clear from the following report in the *Bulletin*:

Radio Interviewer: 'What did Princess Anne say to you when she presented the medal?'
Mark Tonelli (after winning the 'gold' at Christchurch in the 100 metres backstroke): 'I could not understand her. She speaks English and I speak Australian.'

In 1973 Singapore's Prime Minister Lee Kuan Yew commented on the matter as follows:

The Australians speak perfect Australian-English and they are understood, albeit with a little effort, by those who hear them for the first time.

In 1978, Robert Burnfield, the chief editor of the *Oxford*

English Dictionary, set the cat among the linguistic pigeons when he predicted that the term 'English speaking peoples' eventually would become obsolete and that in 200 years time Americans and Britons would speak such utterly different English that they would not be able to understand each other. Burchfield did not extend his speculation on this theme to the Antipodes but, had he done so, he probably would have come up with a similar prediction. Already the rift between 'British-English' and 'Australian-English' is widening rapidly and a few more generations may see chaos in the field of communications between the two hemispheres.

It is interesting to note that while many people railed against the development of 'Australian-English' and saw the widening gap between it and 'British-English' as a tragedy to be avoided, some authorities (a minority perhaps) took a contrary view. For instance Sir Keith Hancock, Emeritus Professor at the Australian National University, in 1973 deplored what he felt to be internationalisation of 'Australian-English' and a drying up of the old colonial inventiveness. He expressed his views as follows:

There was a time, not so long ago, when the English language was enriched by the steady inflow of words that bore the stamp of life in Dorset, Kerry, the Mississippi Valley, the Riverina and many other distinctive regions. From pastoral Australia came words like buckjumper, billy, cooee, damper, dillybag, gullyrake, humpy, jackeroo, jumbuck, rouseabout, sliprail, sundowner. From the goldfields came words like digger, dolly, fossick, John Chinaman, nugget, pan out. From the weird mobs in Sydney and Melbourne came words like barrack, clobber, cobber, dinkum, larrikin, stonker, wowser. These springs of Austral-English are now drying up. 'OK' is ousting 'My Bloody Oath' and 'Too Right'.

In an earlier book *Australia* (1930) Professor Hancock noted the development of an Australian intonation which, though thin and narrow in its range of tone, he found expressive and pleasant to the ear. He went on to make this comment:

Those teachers who struggle against the common curse of debased English would do better to develop the resources of this legitimate accent rather than attempt the impossible task of impressing upon scoffing pupils Oxford English thrice removed.

A similar view was expressed early in 1940 by Mr B H Molesworth, Federal Talks Controller of the Australian Broadcasting Commission:

Clear Australian speech is nothing to be ashamed of. We don't want imported Americanisms any more than assumed Oxfordisms.

Chapter Ten

SLANG

All slang is vulgar. It lowers the tone of society and the standard of thought. It is a great mistake to suppose that slang is in any manner witty. Only the very young or the uncultivated so consider it . . . The woman who exclaims, The Dickens! or Mercy! or Goodness! when she is annoyed or astonished is as vulgar in spirit, though perhaps not quite so regarded by society, as though she had used expressions which it would require but little stretch of the imagination to be regarded as profane.

Author of **Australian Etiquette,** 1885

In dealing with SLANG I wish to make it clear from the outset that I do not intend to stray into the morass of controversy over definitions of the term. The experts from Fowler to Partridge, and others, have been arguing for decades, without much success so far as I can see, on what constitutes SLANG. They haven't even been able to come up with a definition of the word, acceptable to all parties. About the only consensus on the matter seems to be the rather generalised view that SLANG is the very foundation of colloquial speech. A language without a good smattering of slang words and expressions would be a very sterile thing indeed.

In an article on Slang in an early edition of the Encyclopaedia Britannica, Professor Krapp touched on the influence of the 'melting pot' of races in developing colloquial styles of speech. Whilst his remarks referred to the United States of America, they apply with equal force to Australia and are worth quoting:

The mixture of races and the general breaking of old associations which accompanied the first great western migrations were peculiarly favourable to the development of a highly flavoured colloquial style. And in general it may be said that the frontier in America, after the colonial period, has always been a border line of romance between reality and unreality in which slang expressions have made a vigorous growth.

The critics of slang have been many, and extremely vocal, in their quite unsuccessful attempts to drive it from the English language. In the 1850s Oliver Wendell Holmes thundered:

The use of slang is at once a sign and a cause of mental atrophy.

Around the turn of this century Ambrose Bierce joined in the chorus condemning it when he wrote:

Slang is the speech of him who robs the literary garbage cans on their way to the dumps.

However, it is interesting to note that SLANG has not been without its distinguished supporters. Carl Sandburg wrote very approvingly of it when he commented:

Slang is language that rolls up its sleeves, spits on its hands and goes to work.

This is a sentiment with which most Australians would probably agree as they have taken SLANG to their collective hearts in a fairly massive way in the development of their quite unique brand of Australian-English.

Perhaps the one thing that distinguishes the use of slang in Australia from its usage in other countries is that it is not confined to the lower classes—where vulgar speech can be expected—but has been used by the highest in the land. The use of slang by men and women of education in Australia has always been a source of some amazement (and concern) to visitors from England. Valerie Desmond in *The Awful Australian* (1911) commented on this aspect of life in the Antipodes as follows:

... But, in addition to this lack of good breeding and the gross mispronunciation of common English words, the Australian interlards his conversation with large quantities of slang, which make him frequently unintelligible to the visitor. This use of slang is so common that the public memory forgets that it is slang, and it finds its way into most unexpected places. Chief Justices on their benches, leading newspapers in their editorials, statesmen—such as Australia boasts— all disfigure their utterances by jarring slang terms and phrases, so commonly used as to pass unnoticed by either their hearers or themselves.

English slang has a foundation of humor. There is a note of whimsical comedy about the Oxford undergraduates' practice of calling a bag a bagger, and nobody can repress a smile the first time he hears a coster call eyes 'meat pies' or trousers 'round-the-houses'. But there is no humor in Australian slang. It is drawn from the lowliest sources—the racecourse, the football match, and the prize-ring. Like most of the imagery of primitive people, it is largely metaphorical, so involved as to require an interpreter.

Whilst I would concede that Valerie Desmond had a good point in noting that slang is used to a far greater extent by all classes in Australia than it is in other parts of the English speaking world, I would strongly contest her claim that Australian slang lacks humour or inventiveness. The examples given on these pages belie that statement and show that when it comes to inventiveness on the linguistic level the Australian is without peer.

Commenting on the development of the Australian language, Sidney J Baker in *The Drum* (1959) observed that Australians seemed to have a notable capacity for linguistic invention. He speculated that this told us quite a lot about the Australian character, and indicated a sharp-witted innovativeness and adaptability tied to a restless discontent with the orthodoxies of the English language and a clear indication of rebellion against established authority. Baker made the point that innovation is justified (and inevitable) when the environment of one linguistic community differs from another, but in Australia there is linguistic novelty for novelty's sake. What he termed word-making exuberance extends to many corners of the Australian speech, and examples he cited in support of this include:

STOCKWHIP, STOCK ROUTE, TUCKER, PIG-JUMP, BUSHRANGER, DUFFING, SOUTHERLY BUSTER, DINKUM, BRUMBY, BOWYANGS, BARRACKING, GOGGLY, GUYVER, NITKEEPER, SHANGHAI, SMOODGE, BOMBO, SLY GROG, SKERRICK, WALTZING MATILDA, RAFFERTY RULES and JOHNHOP. And such phrases as to POKE BORAK, BALD AS A BANDICOOT, NO GOOD TO GUNDY, PUT THE HARD WORD ON, HOME ON THE PIG'S BACK, TO GO HOSTILE, DO A PERISH, ROUGH AS BAGS and SEND HER DOWN, HUGHIE!

Perhaps the strongest objection that can be directed at slang is that it causes acute problems of communication between English-speaking people of different countries. The visiting Englishman or American has the greatest difficulty understanding what passes for English in this country, whilst Australians who venture abroad have also been known to become greatly confused with the colloquial speech of the English-speaking countries they visit.

A couple of examples will suffice to indicate the nature of this problem in communications. The first is culled from Sidney J

Baker's *The Drum* and is an example of modern Australian idiom compiled by Baker, who also provided the translation:

THE ORIGINAL
Shove this spin down south and mote along to the rubbity for a fiddley's worth of bombo. My sort's ratbag cobbers are turning on a shivoo sarvo. Dice your yacker and get your chop of the plonk, why don't you? With all the galahs and dills that'll drag on this yike, it'd be ridge to have someone who's a wake-up to yabber with.

THE TRANSLATION
Take this £5 and hurry down to the hotel and buy £1 worth of wine. My girlfriend's eccentric acquaintances are having a party this afternoon. Why don't you leave your work and take a share of the liquor? Anyway, with all the unimportant people who will be there, I would like to have someone who is intelligent to talk to.

Another very interesting example was provided by ABC personality Bill Peach in 1976 when he launched *The Australian Pocket Oxford Dictionary*. Peach made the point that the words that Australians use are mostly standard English words, but here they have different meanings. When added to the smattering of purely local slang that peppers the everyday speech of the average Ocker, the result can be very confusing indeed. To illustrate his point, Peach related a story in straightforward English, and then provided an alternative couched in Australian terms selected only from the 'B' section of the Dictionary he was launching. The two stories are printed below and are quite instructive:

STORY IN STANDARD ENGLISH
Let's suppose that a station cook from out west is getting sick of the constant criticism of his cooking, and the nagging of his wife has brought him out in a rash, so he decides to drive his old car down to the city for a holiday. When he arrives, he naturally parks outside the first hotel he sees and goes in for a drink. The hotel is a bit of a shambles, because there's been a stag party there the night before, but he finally gets the publican to give him a drink, and he looks out the window and sees a parking inspector slapping a ticket on his car.

The cook is naturally upset, not being used to parking restrictions. He rushes outside and gets into an altercation with the inspector, who tells him that he's an ignorant country oaf. The cook is so upset by this remark that he jumps straight into his car and heads back to the country forthwith.

SAME STORY IN AUSTRALIAN-ENGLISH
Well, this babbler from Back of Bourke is feeling pretty butchers. The bull-artists and bludgers are all bagging his bacon and beans, and the barracking from his old battleaxe is giving him the Barcoo rot. So he

does his block, drops his bundle, bungs himself into his old bomb and battles down to the big smoke.

Naturally he makes a beeline for the nearest boozer. There's beer all over the floor and blowies all over the bar. 'Bit of a brothel in here,' he tells the boss cocky. 'Yeah,' the boss cocky says. 'Had a big buck show in here last night. Have a beer. And just take a bo-peep out the window, because there's a brown bomber booking your bomb.' 'Well that's bloody beautiful,' the babbler cries.

He races outside and bungs on a blue with the brown bomber, whose name by the way is Blue because he's got red hair. 'What brand of bastardry is this, you bludger?' the babbler cries. 'Break it down. Don't get off your bike,' says Blue the Brown Bomber as he calmly writes out a bluey.

But the babbler's not taking any of that bulldust, and he buckets the brown bomber boots and all for trying to make him the bunny. But the Brown Bomber buckets him back. 'Blind Freddy can see you're a blow-in from the Black Stump. What do you think it is—Bush Week?'

And then the babbler jumps into his old bomb, and tears up the bluey and blows through back to the bush, bellowing as he goes. 'I can see I've got Buckley's here. You're a bunch of bushrangers, and the bloody big smoke's not worth a bumper.'

The difficulty that outsiders have of 'tuning in' on the Australian wave length was also extremely well illustrated by Bill Scott in an article in *The Australian Author* in April 1975. I would like to quote his comments verbatim:

. . . Communication is indeed the problem. The following statement was heard in the public bar at Chardon's Corner Hotel in Brisbane, Christmas Eve, 1974:   'You should've been here last night. Two wogs bunged on a blue. One of them got into holts with some young lair from Inala, but his china wouldn't back him, so he did his block and went the knuckle on his mate.' End of quote. This communicated all right. The hearer said, 'Go on!' The first speaker then said, 'Yeah, we nearly pissed ourselves.'

I submit that the above, and I vouch for its veracity, would convey the sort of fellows they were to another Australian who knew the language, but would be meaningless to someone who only spoke English . . .

An example of how Australian slang words can cause international problems when addressed to people who cannot comprehend them was given by the Melbourne *Herald* in December 1955. It concerned the extensively used word WHACKO, an enthusiastic exclamation to proclaim delight in a situation, for example:

'Whacko, you beauty' or 'Whacko the Diddelo'.

The term has wide currency in Australia but apparently is unknown in Holland, and this fact almost caused the break-up of a romance, which had started when Dutch-born George Schmidt met Joan van Oort at a party in Indonesia in 1952. George came on to Australia whilst Joan went home to Holland. They maintained contact by correspondence and then in August 1955 George cabled a proposal of marriage to Joan. She cabled back the single word 'Ja' (Yes). George decided to be equally economically minded in his reply. His cable was a single word: 'Whacko'.

The cable would have been understood instantly by anyone in Australia, but in Holland there was consternation. No one knew what it meant and Joan, fearing the worst, wept for days, believing that George had broken off the brief engagement. Finally the Dutch Post Office took a hand and cabled back to the Sydney Post Office asking what the word meant. The Australian Post Office used some initiative in the matter and cabled back to their Dutch counterparts that the word was Australian slang for 'wonderful' or 'very good'.

Joan's tears dried up immediately and in December that year there was a happy ending to the story when she flew to Australia to marry her slang-happy fiance.

One of the confusing things (for a visitor) is the way an Australian slang word can be used with so many variations. For instance in Australia an ARTIST is not necessarily someone who can paint a good portrait or landscape. When the term is used it is far more likely to be one of admiration for someone very accomplished in a certain field, even if the field itself lacks social approbrium.

A very heavy drinker in general is a BOOZE ARTIST whilst an old derelict who consumes vast quantities of methylated spirits will attract the more specialised term METHO ARTIST. Someone who is renowned for his constant boasting will invariably attract the title of BULL ARTIST, which is also a term of contempt applied to someone who is suspected of currying favour with the boss. In World War II prisoners of war sometimes applied the term BASH ARTIST to particularly brutal Japanese camp guards.

Although Australian language at times seems top-heavy with slang, there are some areas where its use is barred. The veteran actor Bill Lyle found this out the hard way in 1976 when he persuaded the Catholic Communications Centre in Sydney to try a series of 'ocker' television advertisements about Christianity and religious values. Mr Lyle had the best of intentions and saw the advertisements as reaching a new audience—the Australian working man—by using his accents and mannerisms. Mr Lyle explained that the advertisements were composed to maintain maximum impact and he defended their use by remarking:

> . . . Christ lived with the common people, had roughened hands from carpentry, helped fishermen with their nets and probably smelt of fish scales when leaving the Sea of Galilee.

The advertisements were unusual, to say the least. One of them had this line of text:

> G'day, 'ave you 'eard about the day Jesus says to Peter: 'Let's push off in the boat and go for a row.' Peter says, 'Bewdy, me and the boys can toss a line over the side and get some fish for tea.'

Another, dealing with the Miracle of the Loaves and Fishes, told the story this way:

> G'day. 'Ave you 'eard about the day Jesus and His mother had been working flat out with this big mob, curing warts and leprosy and all that?
>
> After a while the Apostles said, 'It's time to tie on the feed bag—but there's not enough tucker for this mob.'
>
> Andrew said, 'Here's a kid with five loaves of bread and two fishes.' So Jesus said, 'Righto, bring me the bread and the bream.' He blesses it —breaks it into bits and the Apostles take it around.
>
> Jesus said, 'Collect what's left over, or we'll be in strife for littering.'
>
> They found there was twelve baskets of food left over. Jesus had fed 5 000 blokes—that's not counting all the sheilas and kids.

The advertisements got to air, but only just. They caused such a furore in church circles that the Catholic Communications Centre beat a hasty retreat and decided that the ockers of the nation weren't quite ready to hear the Christian message in their own peculiar language.

The issue was raised again in 1979 when an Anglican clergyman, the Reverend Bruce Wilson, suggested that Christianity needed to adopt an OCKER image to recapture the interest of the Australian masses. As he put it:

> We don't know how to express the Gospel, and to maintain our integrity, in Ocker.

For his pains he was jumped on very firmly by other clergymen of his own and other denominations. Mr Philip Oliver, Director of Information of the Anglican Church in Sydney, rather frostily commented:

> Not all Australians would want religion identified with T-shirts and tinnies.

The Reverend G W Hardy of St Stephen's United Church in Sydney was even more outspoken when he commented:

The mind boggles at the possibilities the Reverend Bruce Wilson opens up for 'ocker Christianity'—barechested, beer-bellied parsons knocking it back with the best, scraggy legs beneath 'shortie' cassocks, and shocked old ladies walking out of swinging services while the menfolk reassemble for a singalong to the TAB.

Perhaps the kiss of death was given to the controversy when the *Sydney Morning Herald* published a cartoon by Molnar showing a singlet-clad Ocker clergyman addressing his congregation from the pulpit, on which rested a can of beer, with the words 'Dearly beloved mates and sheilas . . .'

Chapter Eleven

DESCRIPTIVE SAYINGS

Clerks must work more Sundays than the Pope, more Saturdays than Roy Higgins, more midnights than your friendly neighborhood rapist and more holidays than a call-girl on a cruise.

Member of the Federated Clerks' Union, 1977.

Australians display a great deal of inventiveness in creating new slang words, some of which have done a great deal to enrich the language spoken 'Down Under'. And they haven't stopped at mere words: the everyday speech of the man in the street literally abounds with unusual, and sometimes extremely witty, phrases and expressions of Australian origin.

When Sidney J Baker, author of many books on the Australian language, died in 1976, a Sydney newspaper printed the following tribute drawn entirely from sayings extracted from Baker's best known work *The Australian Language*:

Your blood's worth bottling, you're as clumsy as a duck in a ploughed paddock, you're as aggressive as a bull ant, but there's no need to do your block, or to get as drunk as Chloe, so fair crack of the whip, or we'll be as dead as mutton chops, which would make us as miserable as a chromo at a Christening, then roar the tripe out of everyone in sight and run around like a decapitated chook, go through like a Bondi tram and end up so poor you'd be licking the paint off the fence.

Some well known expressions are simply exclamations, for example: 'Stone the crows and starve the lizards', usually prefacing some other remark, whilst others are merely disconcerting throwaways designed to halt a flow of rhetoric such as:

'What's *that* got to do with the price of fish?' Yet others are delivered in the form of verbal insults: 'May all your chooks turn into emus and kick your dunny over.'

Some of the best examples pop up in the most unexpected places. On the edge of the Simpson Desert in 1978, Sydney journalist Ron Saw met an outback character who expressed the firm opinion that diesel motors were 'gutless wonders that wouldn't pull a greasy stick out of a dog's arse'.

Quite a few slang expressions start off as purely local allusions but through regular usage gain wide currency far beyond the place of origin.

UP KING STREET is an expression fairly widely used for at least the first half of this century to describe any one who was bankrupt or insolvent. The term originated in Sydney where the Bankruptcy Court was located at the top end of King Street. This expression seems to have inspired a number of other expressions: UP SHIT CREEK (in trouble); UP THE SHUTE or UP A POLE (worthless); UP THE DUFF or UP THE STICK (pregnant) right down to the contemptuous expression UP YOU or the alternate UP YOU FOR THE RENT, SPORT.

Another term of Sydney origin is TO SHOOT THROUGH LIKE A BONDI TRAM, meaning to make a speedy departure (when Sydney had trams those running to the seaside suburb of Bondi were noted for their speed records). Thus John Morrison in *Twenty Three* (1962):

He shot through like a Bondi tram the minute the telegram arrived.

In national usage the term has been shortened simply to SHOOT THROUGH, for example, Randolph Stow in *The Bystander* (1957):

Just shoot through, son, and leave us to settle this.

One amusing expression of Australian origin is 'To get the rough end of the pineapple'—meaning to get a raw deal or unfair treatment.

Cartoonist Larry Pickering used this slang expression in a very clever way in 1976 when he produced a cartoon for the *Australian* as a sequel to the constitutional crisis of November 1975, when the Governor General Sir John Kerr dismissed the Whitlam (Labor) Government.

The following year Gough Whitlam, the aggrieved former Prime Minister, visited London and had an audience with the Queen. Although the subject of this talk was not publicly disclosed, it was widely assumed that Mr Whitlam had taken the opportunity to press the point strongly that Sir John Kerr's action had been wrong and unfair. In dealing with the meeting, Larry Pickering drew a sketch of a scene at Buckingham Palace with Gough Whitlam sitting down in a room in the distance. The Queen was shown at the door, anxiously beckoning to an equerry and whispering: 'Psst, what's the rough end of the pineapple mean?'

One expression in fairly common usage is HE'S HAD THE ROGER, meaning that 'He has had it', 'He is finished' or 'He has had the skids put under him'. Even top people in the land find on occasion that they have HAD THE ROGER and sometimes they are given to complaining about it publicly.

In 1975 the long-time Labor Premier of Tasmania Eric Reece was manoeuvred out of office when his party introduced a new rule requiring parliamentarians to retire at the age of sixty-five. He complained to the press about the manoeuvre this way:

> One of them should have come to me and said, 'Eric, you've had the Roger, son. It's just about time you gave it away.' That would have been a kindness.

To impose on someone in Australia is to COME THE RAW PRAWN—an expression which originated in the front lines of World War II. Whilst Rohan Rivett in *Behind Bamboo* (1946) used the term RAW PRAWN as being something far-fetched, absurd or difficult to swallow, its general usage is as an alternative for 'putting one over' someone else. For example, Sumner Locke Elliott in *Rusty Bugles* (1948):

> The filthy rotten Crab, he'd better not come the raw prawn on us.

Another interesting saying is HE DOESN'T KNOW WHETHER HE'S ARTHUR OR MARTHA or sometimes I DIDN'T KNOW WHETHER I WAS ARTHUR OR MARTHA meaning that the person referred to was in a state of some confusion. It has never been established whether there ever was a real Arthur or Martha, nor are there any clues on its origin but it is a term in wide use. The following example by D'Arcy Niland in *Call Me When the Cross Turns Over* (1957) provides a fairly typical example of its usage:

> Don't try the Barcoo spews. A cow of a thing. Get a feed into you, and then you want to chuck it up again. You chuck it up and you're right as pie till you eat again. And so it goes on. You don't know whether you're Arthur or Martha.

When the Prime Minister Malcolm Fraser in 1976 revived an old saying, 'Life wasn't meant to be easy', he set in train a whole spate of allied pieces of folk wisdom, which didn't stop at the borders. In 1978 it was reported that a Port Moresby Oyster Bar had doggie bags imprinted with the message, 'Life wasn't meant to be greasy'. One character (also in 1978), took the message a bit too far when he scratched on the shiny paintwork of a brand new Mercedes in a Sydney street: 'Life wasn't meant to be *this* easy'.

If there is one Australian expression capable of driving resident American efficiency-conscious executives into a frenzy it is SHE'LL BE RIGHT, MATE (sometimes extended to SHE'LL BE RIGHT, MATE, SHE'LL BE APPLES).

At its best it is merely a term of general reassurance that all is well with the world, that the job will be finished on time, or that some deadline will be met. In practice it has come to express the lackadaisical attitudes of Australians towards work and personal achievements. Australians have frequently been accused of shoddy workmanship and it must be said that they do seem to lack the dedication to a task (unless it takes their fancy) that other nationals sometimes have. This often means that they will take an assignment only to the minimum (rather than maximum) degree of efficiency, and hand it over with the hopeful injunction, SHE'LL BE RIGHT, MATE, SHE'LL BE APPLES. Unfortunately on many occasions it *isn't* right and it *isn't* apples and the unfortunate *mate* who has been handed the slipshod workmanship has to bear the brunt of this national happy-go-lucky characteristic. The trait is most evident in planning events or functions. The Australian is a willing enough worker when he sees something has to be done, but he is a very poor planner and leaves all sorts of things to chance in a manner that gives ulcers to those who have to come along and pick up the bits and pieces. Henry Williams in *Australia—What Is It?* (1971) put it this way:

If the madmen triumph and the button is pressed and this earth is reduced to a smouldering radio-active cinder, maybe, out on the old Barcoo or somewhere out west, there will be a survivor, a lone battler to emerge from his timber-and-corrugated shack, look out across the ruined planet, roll himself a smoke, and say, 'She'll be right, mate'.

The way this phrase irks Americans was perhaps best summed up by Richard R Ronald when he wrote (1966):

The biggest drawback as overseas visitors see this country is your oft-quoted remark, 'It'll do mate'. This horrible sentiment is truly holding back this country from ever becoming a first-class nation. But then who cares? The gorgeous sunshine is still available, the blue harbour still shimmers, the beautiful beaches still beckon, and life for so many is easy in the main, so effortless compared with the daily struggle for bread, shelter and sustenance in so many lands. Could this

71

be the reason behind your famous slogan which sits astride this lovely land like a deadly plague, 'It'll do mate'?

A closely allied expression is NO PROBLEM (meaning 'it can be done' or 'it will be done'). The only problem with this particular comment is that in many cases actions don't follow words and it (whatever *it* happens to be) isn't done. NO PROBLEM therefore tends to be an expression which irritates visitors almost as much as SHE'LL BE RIGHT, MATE or SHE'LL BE APPLES.

There are a number of expressive sayings used when someone has landed in trouble in Australia including: 'up to the armpits in shit', 'up shit creek without a paddle' and 'caught by the short and curlies'. When his Computicket operation failed in 1979, Harry M Miller was on record as saying:

Now I know what they mean by the saying 'being up to your arse in alligators'.

Perhaps a majority of sayings in general are similes as the average Australian seems to delight in comparing a person, an object or action to a familiar subject. Henry Lawson, away back in 1896, set the standard when he observed of a certain character that:

... he was meaner than a goldfield Chinaman, and sharper than a sewer rat.

Other well known Australian similes include:

The harvest was so poor the sparrows had to kneel down to get at the wheat.

The crop was so poor you couldn't find a straw to clean your pipe in the whole paddock.

That farm was so run down you could flog a flea across the paddocks, go home to dinner, and come back and *still* find him.

He's got more corrugations on his belly than a thousand gallon tank.

Dry as a kookaburra's khyber in the Simpson Desert.

She was as skinny as a sapling with the wood scraped off.

She was a whopper . . . fully three axe-handles across the hips.

It was cold enough to freeze the balls off a brass monkey.

He was as happy as larry (or 'as a possum up a gumtree').

It spread like a bushfire.

It was as rough as a pig's breakfast.

It was as dead as mutton.

He had more kid in him than a pregnant goat.

He was as drunk as Chloe (or 'an owl', or 'as a bastard').

He was as fat as a poddy calf.

More hide than Jessie (an elephant at Taronga Zoo).

Sore as a snouted sheila.

All behind like Barney's Bull.

It was as cold and dark as a bushman's grave.

Me mouth is as dry as the bottom of a birdcage.

He shot through like a Bondi tram.

He went through like a packet of salts.

He (usually a racehorse) ran like a hairy goat.

He's got Buckley's chance (or 'He's got two chances, his own and Buckley's').

He's as silly as a two bob watch (or 'Mad (or silly) as a cut snake').

Lousy as a bandicoot.

Weak as a gin's piss.

Mad as a meat-axe.

He was too mean to hang himself.

He's so mean that when a fly lands in the sugar he shakes its feet before he kills it.

Clumsy as a duck in a ploughed paddock.

He's lower than a snake's belly.

She'd talk ten feet under water with a snorkel in her mouth.

Awkward as a Chow on a bike.

Flash as a rat with a gold tooth.

The scrub was so thick a dog couldn't bark in it.

He was as miserable as an orphan bandicoot on a burnt ridge.

They sat on the stage like a bank of faded geraniums.

Miserable as a bastard on Father's Day.

He's got more degrees than a thermometer (description of an academic).

Flat out like a lizard drinking.

He was running round like a headless chook.

Dressed up like a pox doctor's clerk.

Busy as a one-armed taxi driver with crabs.

He's got a chip on his shoulder like a telegraph pole.

He was flyblowed as usual in regard o' cash.

So windy it 'ud blow a dog off its chain.

It's as scarce as hen's teeth.

Miserable as a shag on a rock.

He's got more problems than there are beef steaks at a butchers' picnic.

He lay there like a stunned mullet.

He was sitting up like Jacky.
He was as bald as a bandicoot.
He was as game as Ned Kelly.

Other general expressions which appear to be of Australian origin include:

More than you could poke a stick at.
Know yer! I'd know yer skin if I saw it hangin' on a bush.
His blood's worth bottling.
Wouldn't know him if he fell out of a packet of cornflakes.
He hasn't got a pot to piss in.
He's so unlucky, if he bought a kangaroo it wouldn't hop.
If it was rainin' pea soup, he'd only have a fork.
Gawd we're unlucky. If it were raining virgins we'd be washed away with a poofter.
If it was raining palaces, he'd be hit on the head by a dunny door.
He did his lolly (i.e. lost his temper).
It was on for young and old (referring to the start of a brawl or disturbance).
He has some palings off the fence (he is mentally disturbed).
I didn't come down in the last shower (sometimes 'He didn't . . .').
He couldn't knock the skin off a rice pudding.
He's not the full quid (meaning he is slightly unbalanced).
He has straw coming out of his ears (derogatory term usually used by a city man about a countryman).
He couldn't give away cheese at a rat's picnic.
He gave it the herbs (i.e. accelerated the car).
He kicked the tin (i.e. made a contribution).
It was upta putty (i.e. no good).
Aw, give it a go, or 'Give it a burl' (to have a try).
He came a GUTZER (He had a big fall).
It was a great run up for the books (A long chance came home).
To kick the arse off an emu (to be in high spirits).
To come the raw prawn or 'Don't come the raw prawn with me, Mate' (to try to put something over).
Who's robbing this coach? (A warning; hands off).
To treat with ignore (to disregard).
It'll put lead in yer pencil (usually pertaining to the eating of

oysters, widely but probably wrongly believed to be an aphrodisiac).

There's no flies on him (He is smart).

Put in the boot (Drive home the advantage).

Take a screw at this, Get a load of this, will ya or Take a dekko at this (Invitation to have a look at something).

Chapter Twelve

THE CONVICT STRAIN

Bearing in mind that our lowest class (the convicts)
brought with it a peculiar language, and is constantly
supplied with fresh corruption, you will understand why
pure English is not, and is not likely to become, the
language of the colony . . . Terms of slang and flash are
used, as a matter of course from the gaols to the Viceroy's
palace, not excepting the Bar and the Bench. No doubt they
will be reckoned quite parliamentary, as soon as we obtain
a parliament.

Edward Gibbon Wakefield
in **A Letter from Sydney,** 1829

Much as we might like to sweep under the carpet the convict
origins of the white settlement of Australia, the legacies of that
grim period are still far too evident to allow us this luxury. And
the legacy is powerfully present in everyday Australian
language.

Professor Eric Partridge clearly set out the way our language
has been shaped by our convict ancestry when he wrote:

The rise of American closely resembles that of Australian. The first
settlers in both countries were adventurers and exiles. Men and women
of a brave and independent spirit, no great respecters of rank,
authority, or custom. Then came the convicts, who ceased to be sent to
America when the War of Independence broke out and who, a
generation later, began to be transported to Australia. Convicts were

'marinated' over a much longer period to America than to Australia, but in larger numbers, in proportion to the ordinary population, to Australia than to America. When convicts were no longer sent to these two countries, those in servitude either, and mostly, died out or became settlers, and the latter were soon absorbed and their pasts forgotten. To both countries, too, have gone many ex-convicts or other ex-prisoners, as also those criminals who found Britain 'getting too hot' for them: and of these, far more have gone to the United States than, because of the very much greater distance and consequent expense of the journey, have emigrated to Australia. Therefore, though I can offer no statistics, I should say that the actually and the potentially criminal elements, taken together, were roughly equal in the two countries until Prohibition was introduced into the States, from which date the criminal and near-criminal proportion of the population has been very much larger in the States than in Australia. But there are further analogies between America and Australia: the settling of both countries was a difficult and dangerous task, calling for bravery, endurance, and a sense of humour, and if the colonists in America ran a greater risk from the Red Indians than did those in the island continent from the Aborigines, the latter, once they left the coast lands, had a far less fertile and well-watered country to conquer; moreover, the Australian settlers did not proceed in such large groups as, for safety and in mere good sense, the American settlers. In both lands, however, immense distances had to be contended with, and hardihood and physical hardness were equally necessary in America and Australia. What wonder, then, if—quite apart from the American influence so marked on the Australian vocabulary—the everyday, as well as the underworld, speech of the two countries has so many features in common!

However, we should not assume that the 'slanguage' that developed in Australia in the formative period of the nineteenth century was solely of convict origin. Sidney Baker in *The Drum* pointed out that there was very little difference in education and speech patterns between the convicts and the immigrants. His observations on this point are worth noting because they are very pertinent to any study of Australian language in the early years of settlement:

On a general basis, there was not a great deal of difference in social status between our earliest (involuntary) immigrants and the bulk of those who came later from Britain. If contemporary reports are any guide, the free migrants to Australia last century came mainly from the lower classes. The upper class and upper middle class of Britain were too well-lined to have anything but a patronising interest in the 'blawsted colonies'. They had no reluctance in using a dividend or two from Australian investments, but they were not the stuff (fortunately, perhaps) of which immigrant pioneers are made. No; the thousands of people who came to us from Great Britain were socially and educationally dispossessed—or a great many of them, anyway. So, unquestionably, were our convicts. They were burdened with discontents and unhappiness.

Watkin Tench, Captain of the Marines, in his *Complete Account of the Settlement at Port Jackson* (1793) made the following interesting observation on the early use of 'flash' language in the colony, and the problems that it posed in the reformation of convicts:

A leading distinction, which marked the convicts on their outset in the colony, was an use of what is called the 'flash', or 'kiddy' language. In some of our early courts of justice, an interpreter was frequently necessary to translate the deposition of the witness, and the defence of the prisoner. This language has many dialects. The sly dexterity of the pickpocket; the brutal ferocity of the footpad; and the deadly purpose of the midnight ruffian, is each strictly appropriate in the terms which distinguish and characterize it. I have ever been of opinion, that an abolition of this unnatural jargon would open the path to reformation. And my observations on these people have constantly instructed me that indulgence in this infatuating cant, is more deeply associated with depravity, and continuance in vice, than is generally supposed. I recollect hardly one instance of a return to honest pursuits, and habits of industry, where this miserable perversion of our noblest and peculiar faculty was not previously conquered.

The first attempt at documenting the language that was starting to develop in the colony was made by that extraordinary convict James Hardy Vaux, who in his career of crime was three times sentenced to transportation to Australia. In 1812, while serving a sentence at Newcastle, NSW, he compiled his *Vocabulary of the Flash Language* and this was included in his *Memoirs*, published in 1819. His vocabulary, of course, was more of a guide to the current argot used at that time by the lower classes of England, but this argot was transported almost intact to Australian soil where it thrived and produced many offshoots, some of which still linger on in current speech.

The basic convict origin of the colony in itself led to the coining of new words to sort the 'sheep from the goats' as it were.

In *Felonry of New South Wales* (1837), James Mudie laid claim to have invented the word FELONRY to describe the convicts of the colony and he justified this linguistic invention as follows:

The author has ventured to coin the word FELONRY, as the appellative of an order or class of persons in New South Wales—an order which happily exists in no other country in the world. A legitimate member of the tribe of appellatives ... as peasantry, tenantry, yeomanry, gentry.

One of the earliest nicknames for convicts was CANARIES, a term derived from the yellow prison garb. Its usage was noted as early as 1827 by P Cunningham in *Two Years in New South Wales*:

Convicts of but recent migration are facetiously known by the name of CANARIES, by reason of the yellow plumage in which they are fledged at the period of landing.

Rolf Boldrewood also used the term in *Colonial Reformer* (1890) as follows:

Can't you get your canaries off the track here for about a quarter of an hour, and let my mob of cattle pass?

Perhaps the slang expression most commonly used in the nineteenth century for convicts was LAG—a term of English origin which received an Australian appendage in the form of the prefix OLD. In Australian terms an OLD LAG was an ex-convict. From the name was derived the term LAGGED, referring to the apprehension and conviction of the prisoner, i.e. 'What was he lagged for?'

When a convict had served his sentence he was free to return to England (if he could raise the fare for the journey) or stay on in Australia as a free man. If he chose the latter course, which most ex-convicts did, he may have been free in the eyes of the law, but he certainly was not equal in the eyes of those residents of the colonies who had arrived as emigrants or 'free settlers'. The latter class considered themselves far superior in status and character to the ex-convict and were determined that the convict stigma should remain attached to the man and his descendants. Murray in *An Unfinished Autobiography* attributed to a Mr Dalhunty words that expressed the sentiments of the gentry of the time:

When a man's carriage splashes me with mud, I always stop and try to recollect what his father was lagged for.

To set the ex-convict apart from the rest of the community it was necessary to coin a word for him and that word was EMANCIPIST (an alternate but less used expression was EMANCIPATIST).

The term was in use from the early part of the nineteenth century. P Cunningham in *Two Years in New South Wales* (1827) defined it as follows:

Emigrants who have come out free from England, and emancipists, who have arrived here as convicts, and have either been pardoned or completed their term of servitude.

The term was not without its critics who objected to such a perfectly good English word being wasted on ex-felons. James Mudie in *Felonry of New South Wales* expressed his displeasure with the term as follows:

> The author begs leave to record his protest against the abuse of language in the misapplication of the terms EMANCIPISTS and ABSENTEES to two portions of the colonial felonry. An emancipist could not be understood to mean the emancipated but the emancipator. Mr Wilberforce may be honoured with the title of emancipist; but it is as absurd to give the same appellation to the emancipated felons of New South Wales as it would be to bestow it upon the emancipated negroes of the West Indies.

The local sensitivity on the issue of names for convicts, ex-convicts and free settlers was perhaps best summed up by Charles Rowcroft in *Tales of the Colonies* (1843) when he wrote:

> I must warn you, that we never speak of the convicts in this country by that term; we always call them 'government men', or on some occasions, prisoners; but we never use the word 'convict', which is considered by them as an insulting term.

The gaols of every country breed a special idiom derived partly from outside society and partly from the circumstances of life within closed walls. Australian prison argot is a riot of sounds quite incomprehensible to ordinary citizens or, in the words of a former criminal, Neil James:

> ... a unique and esoteric language understood only by thieves, prisoners, schizophrenics and acid heads.

James, who has spent thirty years of his life behind prison bars, in 1975 wrote an interesting article on prison language for the *Bulletin*. Appropriately it was headed: Nodding the Nut for a Swy and One and this set the tone for an instructive tour through linguistic bypaths which (fortunately) are never explored by the vast majority of citizens.

·In his very instructive article on prison language, James constructed a number of imaginary conversations between inmates to illustrate their total divorce from the ordinary world. Just one brief quote from one of these conversations will illustrate that the spoken word inside an Australian prison bears no resemblance to English as we know it:

> 'Went down. Two with a one for duddin'—unheard of! Dead set the best bake in history they gave me and I got the book for a shit pod dud. When I got buckled they asked for a two spot for the no-bake, but I put 'em on the arse bit for being big askers . . .'
> 'What about flyin' the flag, mate?'
> 'No way in the world I won't.'

The prisoner is telling his cell mate that he has been found guilty and sentenced to a two year term, with parole period set at one year, on the charge of falsely representing the value of goods he was selling. The detectives in court had given him a maliciously bad character reference (A BAKE) to put him in a bad light and the magistrate had given him the maximum sentence (THE BOOK) for what the prisoner conceived as a very minor crime (selling a dud watch). His cell mate asks him will he appeal against the severity of the sentence to a higher court (TO FLY THE FLAG) and the aggrieved one says that he will.

The mysteries of prison jargon are outside the scope of this work, but a few examples will give an idea of its complexity and perhaps may spur some student to explore this much neglected linguistic field.

Some forms of crime have their own prison terms and it might be illuminating (for the victims) to know some of them:

SNOWDROPPING: Stealing garments from clothes lines.

ROCK-SPIDERING: Stealing the clothes and wallets of amorous couples in parks.

SCRANNY-THROWING: Throwing a fake fit to distract attention while an accomplice carries out a theft (usually in a supermarket or department store).

TEA-LEAFING: Stealing.

HAWKING THE DOT: The act of soliciting for prostitution on a street.

DUDDING: Selling stolen or worthless merchandise and representing it as being of good quality.

HOISTING: Shoplifting.

The *Australasian Post* in 1960 published the following list of then current gaol slang sent to it by a former Long Bay prisoner:

BOB HOPE: soap.
BO-PEEP: sleep.
DAD AND DAVE: shave.
BARGO: someone who will eat anything.
BIFFING: bashing.
FRED ASTAIRE: lair.
JOHN DORY: crim's story.
JUKEBOX: radio.
LAGGING: sentence.
SCREWS: wardens.
ST. LOUIS BLUES: shoes.
TEDDY BEAR: lair.
TUB: shower.

VERBALER: conman.
BRACES: horse or dog races.
BOB POWELL: towel.
CIGGERS: tailor-made cigarettes.
FAIRY BOWER: shower.
FRONTED: went to court.
LAGGER: pimp.
MICKEY MOUSE: grouse (good).
SLOT OR PETER: cell.
SWY OR TWO OXS: two of something.
TOM THUMB: the drum (a useful tip; sound advice, vital information).
YOGI BEAR: boob lair.
WEED: tobacco.

Newspaper reports of the 1970s indicated that a new craze of BOOB TATTOOS was prevalent amongst Australian teenage girls. The BOOB TATTOOS were not, as might be surmised, anything to do with breast tattoos, but comprised the initials of boyfriends tattooed on to shoulder blades. The tattoos were not professionally done but were applied by the girls themselves using needle, ink and cotton. The name BOOB TATTOOS came from the slang BOOB for gaol where the practice of self-tattooing originated.

FLOG is a good old Anglo-Saxon word that has had its ups and downs in this country. The lash scarred so many Australian backbones in the convict era that one would think the word FLOGGING would forever be barred from the vocabulary of the country.

However in World War II the word FLOG was revived by the armed forces as meaning 'to steal' or 'to sell that which doesn't belong to you' (i.e. Army stores on the black market).

The term passed over into general civilian use and the word is still used ambivalently as meaning 'to steal' or 'to sell', though in the latter usage no illicit act is implied. For instance in 1977 Charles Wright, the *Australian* columnist used the term thus:

This Silver Jubilee has certainly fired and inspired the British, as ever a nation of shopkeepers. Having failed to sell Concorde, they are now flogging the Queen for all she is worth.

The term was used in an entirely different way however, in 1975 when a Perth mechanic, Wayne Letts, won $500 000 in a lottery. His reaction to the news of his win was rather unusual: *It flogged up a good party* he told a reporter.

Another prison slang word with grim overtones is TRAC the

name given to so-called intractable prisoners. Some gaols, such as Grafton in New South Wales, were specially designed to receive and hold such prisoners and over a period of time it became prison policy to administer to each new batch of TRACS what became known as a reception BIFF. John Pettit, a former NSW prisoner officer described the BIFF reception at Grafton gaol in NSW in the 1962–4 period as follows:

He (the prisoner) was received by four or five officers selected as a reception committee. He was checked out by his warrant, identified, and then double-marched into the A wing—which is the intractable wing—stripped, searched everywhere. He was then set upon by officers with batons and flogged until he was so unconscious that he urinated and his nervous system was dead. He was then thrown into a cell and left there to recuperate. When he became conscious, he was then marched down and showered. He was then taken back to his cell and, depending on what he was there for, given the same treatment again. That went on all that day. He was left in his cell for a few days before being put into the routine of Grafton Gaol itself.

TRAC should not be confused with TRAK, which is pronounced the same way but is a slang word of vastly different meaning. TRAK is short for TOORAK, a very exclusive Melbourne suburb (its residents probably would claim it as Australia's most fashionable residential address). Residents are referred to—often in a derogatory way—as TRAKS or TRAKKERS, or, in the words of Bette Midler (1978):

. . . you know, the TRAK pack. Vogue on the outside . . . vague on the inside.

Chapter Thirteen

ANTI-AUTHORITARIANISM

Hostility towards authority in all its forms is a living, if latent, Australian tradition, liable to spring into rampant action if the temperature and alcohol mix is right.

British Journalist Paul Johnson, 1976

The convict heritage seems to have left a legacy of hostility to all forms of authority to a degree not found in any other western society. For instance, when a Wollongong solicitor, Mr P Grainger, appeared in a local court in 1970 to defend a client he remarked in the man's defence:

As an ordinary Australian, he was naturally suspicious of authority.

The anti-authority sentiment of the convict period is perhaps best summed up in the widely recited ballad:

>And some dark night when everything
>Is silent in the town,
>I'll kill the tyrants one and all
>And shoot the floggers down.
>I'll give the law a little shock—
>Remember what I say,
>They'll yet regret they sent Jim Jones
>In chains to Botany Bay.

Possibly because they were so visible, and more directly responsible for actions against civilians, particular hostility has, from the earliest period of settlement, always been directed at uniformed police. British author George Mikes in 1968 commented on this phenomenon as follows:

One surviving trait from convict days is the Australian's open detestation of the police. There is no other civilised country in the world where people are so indifferent, nay hostile, to the police.

A ditty which had wide circulation in the middle of the last century summed up the general attitude of the populace towards the police of the day:

> *Oh, the traps, the dirty traps;*
> *Kick the traps when e'er you're able;*
> *At the traps, the nasty traps;*
> *Kick the traps right under the table.*

In some areas of Australia the anti-authoritarian attitude of adults finds expression at an early age in school-yard ditties. The compilers of *Cinderella Dressed in Yella* (second edition, 1978) report this school-yard rhyme in use in the Melbourne area in 1973:

> *We hate you coppers*
> *Oh yes we do,*
> *We hate you coppers*
> *And that is true,*
> *When you're near us*
> *We spew,*
> *Oh coppers, we hate you.*

In the forefront of the anti-police name callers was Ned Kelly and two of his quotes of 1879 (the year before he was captured and hanged) are typical of the man and of the period. They are worth quoting for the record:

... A parcel of big ugly fat-necked, wombat-headed, big-bellied, magpie-legged, narrow-hipped, splay-footed sons of Irish bailiffs or English landlords which is better known as Officers of Justice or Victorian Police.

I would like to know who put that article that reminds me of a poodle dog half clipped in the lion fashion, called Brook E Smith, Superintendent of Police, he knows as much about commanding Police as Captain Standish (the Victorian Police Commissioner) does about mustering mosquitoes and boiling them down for their fat on the back blocks of the Lachlan.

Slang terms used for policemen in Australia over the years have included TRAPS, JOHNNIES, JOES, COPPERS, NARKS, TROOPERS, DEMONS, WALLOPERS, ROZZERS (or ROSSERS), PIGS and BOMBERS (or Brown Bombers—a term for once brown-uniformed traffic police).

The majority of these terms were not of Australian origin but direct imports from the lower-class slang of the convict period. Even the most widely used term for a policeman COPPER, an expression still current, was an import derived from COP (to catch). The word itself has many offshoots such as COPPER'S NARK (a police spy), SILENT COP (small traffic island), COPMAN (long obsolete) and COP SHOP (a police station), whilst COPPER is also the slang expression for low-value coins made of bronze.

Perhaps the only true Australian slang terms for police are JOES, TROOPERS, WALLOPERS and BOMBERS.

On the Victorian goldfields police were widely known as JOES, a derisive name coined after the appointment of the unpopular Joseph Latrobe as Governor of Victoria in 1851. Latrobe sent the police to the goldfields to enforce the gold licence laws, and cries of 'Look out, the Joes' were soon ringing around the diggings as miners took evasive action against the laws. The nickname JOES did not have wide currency outside Victoria and is long obsolete.

WALLOPER (and occasionally THUMPER) came into use much later and reflected the widespread suspicion in the Australian community that police take a delight in WALLOPING or THUMPING everyone in sight. Whilst the term COPPER is not always used in a derogatory sense, this certainly doesn't apply to WALLOPER. Nor is the term PIGS, imported from America by demonstrators in the Vietnam war protest era, used in any friendly way. Australian police have been particularly sensitive about this word and have hailed before the court and convicted more than one person who has merely imitated the 'oink oink' of a pig in the presence of a uniform.

In the period of the gold rushes, labour was in such short supply that police forces of the colonies were forced to take whatever recruits they could get—even ex-convicts. As they were said to have come with the Exodus (of prisoners) from England, this led to a curious nickname being applied to such recruits—'Israelites'. Frank Fowler in *Southern Lights and Shadows* (1859) explains the long-forgotten slang term as follows:

The Australian boy is a slim, dark-eyed, olive-complexioned young rascal, fond of Cavendish, cricket, and chuckpenny, and systematically insolent to all servant girls, policemen, and new chums. His hair is shiny with grease, as are the knees of his breeches and the elbows of his jacket. He wears a cabbage-tree hat, with a dissipated wisp of black ribbon dangling behind . . . he calls policemen 'Israelites', because the majority of them came out with the Exodus.

In 1965 the Sydney satirical publication *Oz* magazine claimed that the Sydney Police Force had recruited an undercover group known as *The Dogs* who lived like tramps and hoodlums to trap would-be lawbreakers. 'Only trained detectives, sergeants and the more intelligent constables from outer Sydney are recruited', the article went on to say.

Since it was never possible to tell with any degree of certainty whether *Oz* magazine was speaking the truth or with tongue firmly planted in cheek, I have no way of knowing whether a force such as *The Dogs* existed in the 1960s, but the matter is noted here for the record.

Not unnaturally the police have long resented these attacks and at times have responded with a bit of name-calling directed at their tormentors. For example Detective Sergeant Ronald Edington, President of the Queensland Police Union, was in 1971 goaded into this comment:

You see a child born a mongol, and you have to give it respect—well, it's the same with demonstrators.

At the same time Senior Detective Donald Lane, the newly-elected Queensland Member of the Legislative Assembly rather mildly commented:

We don't really like being called ning-nongs.

Constable (Miss) Nerida Keeley expressed herself a little more forcefully in the same year when she commented:

The mug cops line might have been valid once but it is not valid any longer.

Of course, the police are not the only targets of Australian anti-authoritarian attitudes. The bureaucrats of the nation have long been sniped at and abused, often with justification, by the man-in-the-street. The bureaucrats have, perhaps as a defence mechanism, bred like imported rabbits to such an extent that they now comprise about thirty per cent of the workforce and therefore are themselves rapidly becoming the man-in-the-street. Maybe this will lead to the bureaucrats developing a new vocabulary of insults to hurl at non-government workers.

The ultimate target of any anti-authoritarian outburst must, of course, always be the government—any government, Local, State or Federal. The good Australian, like the good Irishman, is always AGIN THE GUVMINT. Back in 1900 Henry Lawson summed it all up very neatly when he wrote:

Curse the Government, and say the country's done. It doesn't matter what Government it is, for he's always against it. I never knew a real Australian that wasn't.

Chapter Fourteen

THE
CLASSLESS
SOCIETY

The Master Class
Can kiss my arse,
I've got a Guv'mint
Job at last.
              Nineteenth century doggerel

Given the nature of Australia's origins, and the class of men and women who settled here—some voluntarily, some without choice—it is not surprising that they should have aimed at the creation of a society without the class distinctions of 'Mother England'.

Many of them considered they had succeeded in this aim and even quite perceptive visitors have for long been under this delusion. For instance, Francis Adams exclaimed:

This is a true republic, the truest, as I take it, in the world. In England, the average man feels that he is inferior, in America that he is superior: in Australia he feels that he is equal.

And in the 1870s the visiting Anthony Trollope made note of this in similar vein when he wrote:

The humbleness, the hat-touching, the servility which is still incidental to such work (labouring) as theirs in this old country, and which is hardly compatible with exalted manhood, has found no footing there (Australia).

Adams and Trollope and the many others who have expressed similar sentiments, of course, have been well astray of the mark.

Australian society is not a classless one by any means, though the class forms that have developed are somewhat different from those of the older democracies. Visitors who have looked in vain in Australia for some of the worst examples of class division as it operates in Mother England, for example, have been unaware that other, sometimes quite subtle, class distinctions of an entirely different kind have developed in the Antipodes.

Although Australia is by no means a classless society, in some areas the distinctions have been broken down to a remarkable degree. For instance, nowhere in the world is there found the easy-going social mixing of the classes, and clubs abound where employees meet with and drink with their employers without much thought being given on either side to the unusual nature of this system. Visiting Englishmen are given to apoplexy when they encounter the situation for the first time.

It should be recognised however, that such practices are all part of a quite conscious effort by Australians to eliminate the type of class distinctions that exist in the 'Old World' of Europe. Such efforts take many unusual forms, some of which are quite disconcerting for visitors. One of these is the common practice of Australians of sitting in the front seat of taxi cabs to demonstrate to the drivers that they do not consider them to be inferior. A male passenger who clambers into the backseat of a cab may be regarded by the driver as 'putting on airs' or, as English comedian Harry Secombe put it in 1974:

> The first time I was there I hopped into the back seat of a Sydney taxi and the driver asked me if I had leprosy.

Nicknames have long been used in Australia to make social distinctions. The term THE BLUE RINSE SET (or BRIGADE) is used to describe (derisively) the social matrons of Vaucluse (in Sydney) and Toorak or North Balwyn (in Melbourne). Thus in 1973 when Bill Hayden MHR, as Social Security Minister in the Whitlam Government, was encountering strong opposition to his Medibank proposals, he lashed out:

> I'll give you an assurance here and now that the North Balwyn blue rinse brigade and their ilk are not going to stop the health care financing system.

In Australia anyone who wields power is regarded as a TALL POPPY to be cut down to size. Although not an original Australian term, it gained widespread acceptance in the depression years of the early 1930s when the Labor Premier of New South Wales, Jack Lang, campaigned vigorously on a policy of high taxation of the wealthy classes, whom he repeatedly referred to as the TALL POPPIES.

The *Sydney Morning Herald* of 6 August 1931 reported:

'I'll put it on the shoulders of those able to bear it', he (Mr Lang) shouted when it was pointed out to him by the Opposition that '"lopping the tall poppies" meant in some cases 80 or 90 per cent'.

In his book *The Turbulent Years* (1970) Jack Lang explained as follows what he had meant by his 1930s term TALL POPPIES:

The next (step) was the introduction of the bill to reduce all government salaries to a maximum of £10 a week. I referred to those being paid more than that amount (in 1931) as the 'tall poppies'.

Taxing the TALL POPPIES seems to have developed into a bit of an obsession with Labor politicians. In 1973, Mr Clyde Cameron, the Minister for Labour and National Service in the Whitlam Government, complained that the Public Service Board had developed a compulsive urge to lavish funds on the 'tall poppies' of the Public Service. Mr Cameron varied his choice of epithets a little when later on he referred to the higher paid Public Servants as FAT CATS—a term that immediately gained even wider currency and usage than TALL POPPIES.

Not all Australians, of course, agree that TALL POPPIES or FAT CATS should be cut down to size. In 1975 a former Liberal Prime Minister, John Grey Gorton, expressed a contrary view:

Labour is obsessed with the 'tall poppies', and seems determined to pull them down. But tall poppies, more and more tall poppies, are what this country needs. The chance to grow to a height is the chance for many to express themselves.

It is not always easy to determine class demarcations in Australia. Wealth by itself is certainly not one of the determining factors, possibly because there is before every Australian the constant dream of 'striking it rich', of even the most humble BATTLER making his fortune through a mineral strike, a lucky run at the races or a big win in the lottery. However, when wealth is used to exercise power over others, considerable hostility is generated in the breasts of the not-so-rich in the community.

If there is one single thing that seems to act as a RED RAG TO A BULL to the ordinary Australian, and to bring out his worst instincts, it is a title bestowed by the Monarchy; although by some paradox a majority of Australians believe in the institution of the Monarchy itself. It is only the system of titles that the average Australian objects to and as a result knights and baronets have been the object of considerable antipathy in the Antipodes.

When in the 1850s the emancipist W C Wentworth sought to introduce a plan for colonial peerages such a wave of derision swept around the country that the idea was stillborn. Daniel Deniehy described it derisively as a BUNYIP ARISTOCRACY —a phrase that lingered on in the language long after Wentworth's plan was forgotten. In 1853 the *Sydney Morning Herald* reported a speech by Deniehy as follows:

... here they all knew the common water mole was transformed into the duck-billed platypus, and in some distant emulation of this degeneration, he supposed they were to be favoured with a bunyip aristocracy.

More than a century later the same newspaper was able to use similar words when (in 1960) it reported that:

... the ALP in NSW is building up a bunyip peerage of its own, even if the bunyips aren't titled and sit in the Lower, not Upper House.

Even the Whitlam Government's scheme for a system of Australian awards was greeted very suspiciously by its own Labor followers when introduced in 1975, and the venom and abuse heaped on the head of the Queensland Trade Union figure Jack Egerton when he accepted a knighthood in 1976 reverberated up and down the land. Even Liberal politicians in Australia have been known to decline offers of knighthoods on the ground that such titles are considered an electoral liability. In some cases, where titles have been accepted, they have amounted to the 'kiss of death' to political ambitions.

At the other end of the scale, and distanced from the affluent and titled classes, has always been the BATTLER, the almost indestructible 'little man', always trying hard, but seldom making the grade. Frank Hardy in *The Four-Legged Lottery* (1958) summed up the species very well when he wrote:

Sparks was a typical Australian battler, tall and angular, a sardonic wit, a kindly cynic who favoured the under-dog ... Tom Sparks had tried every way known to man of making a 'more or less honest quid', from gold prospecting to inventing gadgets. Now he eked out a living punting horses and, during a bad trot, 'turned over a quid' as a salesman.

The term is still in general use and in 1975 the *Australian* newspaper noted that:

... there are not signs that the forthcoming Federal Budget will give any help to the small Aussie battler.

The extension of the quite deliberate policy to create a classless society means that anyone differing from the 'norm' is regarded with suspicion, if not downright hostility. This national tendency to mock and ridicule anyone not of the common mould was clearly recognised in the following advice tendered by Edward Kinglake in his 'Useful Hints to those Intending to Settle in Australia' incorporated in his book *The Australian at Home* (1891):

Let me whisper it softly. You will be far more popular if you leave the fact of your being English to take care of itself, and do not put on what the Americans call 'frill'. Do not try to impress 'the Colonials' or they may succeed in snubbing you.

Australians dislike anyone who they feel is a phoney or who acts in a way they consider as PUTTING ON SIDE. When this happens the person concerned is said to be BUNGING IT ON. The term can be used for men or women and in fact the fair sex are probably criticised most for this type of behaviour. Alan Seymour in *The One Day of the Year* (1963) directs this broadside:

Well, she bungs it on a bit, don't she? . . . that young lady's too lah-dee-dah for us.

And William Dick in *Naked Prodigal* (1969) refers to the male who BUNGS IT ON as follows:

These flash bastards . . . give you the shits bunging on side like they do.

Whilst to BUNG IT ON is a term of approbation, to GO BUNG has a different meaning entirely. It means to be bankrupt or insolvent or to have lost your money in a business venture. Thus Dymphna Cusack and Florence James in *Come in Spinner* (1951):

What's wrong with 'er? The bank gone bung?

The term is also used for something such as a car, radio or television set that has ceased to operate. It has, in Australian terms, just GONE BUNG.

Anyone who adopts an affected speech or manner in Australia is said to be PUTTING ON THE JAM, a saying which probably had its origin back in the nineteenth century when jam was a luxury. In those days what was spread on bread was more likely to be dripping or Golden Syrup (also known as COCKY'S JOY), the 'poor man's jam'.

The Sydney Slang Dictionary (1882) defined PUTTING ON

JAM as 'assuming false airs of importance', and E Finn in *Chronicles of Early Melbourne* (1888) noted:

Putting on Jam, a phrase of modern slang, and increasing in importance.

In 1911 Alfred Searcy in *By Flood and Field* wrote:

A new chum fellow with notions of city decorum, and not a little 'jammy', ran over from the store.

The phrase is not now in general use, though it crops up occasionally, possibly because these days people are more likely to put peanut butter or Vegemite on their bread. Somehow PUTTING ON THE PEANUT BUTTER does not have the same derisive ring to it as PUTTING ON THE JAM.

In an article in the *Australian* in 1978, columnist Max Harris disclosed the interesting fact that ever since he had started writing his various newspaper columns he had been baffled by the venomous anger that was fermented by his occasional use of unusual words. He said he received more insulting correspondence and angry radio talk-back because of vocabulary than anything else.

After noting that there might be some argument that the writer has a responsibility to 'temper his verbiage according to the shornness of the lambs', Harris made these comments on the Australian gut-reaction to words outside the normal vocabulary of the man-in-the-street:

When Australians are baffled by a word it triggers off the defensive aggressions of an easily precipitated inferiority complex. The old chip-on-the-shoulder. The inverted snobbery. The mateship egalitarian dogmas. We Australians aren't good at words. Words are for smoothies, foreigners, arty-farties and pretentious poofs. The language I've got is good enough for me. I do all right. It should be good enough for bloody Harris or anyone else. Logophobia is an atavistic survival from a crude and insulated period of Australia's culture. It has survived almost unperceived at a time when the last traces of frontier bigotry, prejudice, and defensiveness have just about bred out of the national psyche. It is a dangerous survival. It is a pity that it expresses itself with such a virulent knee-jerk reflex.

Being well-educated can at times be a hazard in Australia. In 1970 David Francis Fraser, a process server, stated in an affadavit tended to the Sydney Equity Court that he had attempted to serve a summons on two men hiding out in a house in Glebe. When told that he (Fraser) had an Equity Court Summons to be served on the occupants, a young man in the house said: *We do not want to get involved in any bourgeois court.*

The affadavit went on to say that he (Fraser) did not know what the word 'bourgeois' meant and told the young man to 'speak Australian', whereupon the young man made an obscene reply!

Another example of the perils of a good education was related by the *Bulletin* in 1978. The story told how a Judge of the New South Wales Supreme Court while holidaying on the North Coast had strolled down a jetty and had attempted to elicit some information from a local fisherman with these words: *And how are they biting, my piscatorial friend?'* The local turned bright red and shocked the judicial gentleman when he replied: *'None of your bloody business, shitface.'*

Chapter Fifteen

CLASS AND SPEECH

Dr H V Evatt . . . spoke with an Australian accent that made
it difficult for me to understand despite my having been
familiar, forty years before, with the colloquial speech of
uneducated inhabitants of Australia.

Admiral Leahy, of US World War II Fleet

Although Australians haven't succeeded in creating the true
classless society, they have gone such a long way along the road
that it is not always possible to determine a man's class (or
status) by his speech. Whether this is due to the egalitarian
nature of the society, or of a desire by the educated classes to
avoid criticism, is not clear, but the fact remains that Australia
is one of the few countries in the world where there are
remarkably few differences between the speech of a labourer
and the self-made millionaire.

It has always been a shock to visitors to Australia to find that
the use of what they consider to be bad speech is not confined to
the 'lower classes' (as in England) but often is the norm for the
so-called educated classes. Valerie Desmond brought this point
out in *The Awful Australian* (1911) when she complained:

Neither the coster of today, nor the old-time Cockney of the days of
Dickens, would be guilty of uttering the uncouth vowel sounds I have
heard habitually used by all classes in Australia. For the dialect of this
country differs from those of other lands in being as strongly developed
among the educated people as among the peasantry. Were its use
restricted to the bullock-driver and the larrikin one could make
excuses; but this is not so. Judges, scientists, university graduates, and
bottle-gatherers use the same universal Australian esperanto. The
doctor, who has attained eminence in Australia, and who, in point of
merit, is probably quite up to the standard of the average provincial
practitioner at Home, will give such words as 'light' and 'bright' (the

same exaggerated vowel sound as the cabman and the bootblack. The barrister will not say, 'May your Honor please,' but 'May-ee yer Honor please.' The scientist will refer to 'Me researches.' There is no such word as 'my' in the Australian language. 'Me husband, me yacht, me motor,' one hears everywhere. But the most striking instance of vowel mispronunciation occurs in respect of the diphthong 'ow', a cow is invariably a 'keeow', brown is 'breeown', town is 'teeown'.

There is a nouveau riche in culture as well as in material things, and the accent of the cultivated Australian proclaims to the world that his acquisition of learning belongs to his generation alone. At Home, we are occasionally forced to encounter individuals whose sudden access to money is revealed by their tongues, but we are spared from such unpleasant revelations when we meet the intellectuals. These are products of generations. In Australia, they are turned out while you wait, with all the uncouthness of their fathers. Australia alone of all the countries in the world has lingual hobnails on its culture.

In the counties of Great Britain and the provinces of continental Europe the possession of a marked dialect denotes lowly origin. The educated gentleman of Yorkshire or Sligo is differentiated only by a very slight and not displeasing accent. In fact, in Great Britain, the dialect is of some benefit in indicating the origin of the man who uses it. I have frequently found it of value in engaging servants and in dealing with the lower classes generally. But in Australia, this abominable pronunciation pervades the entire continent. The native of Perth and the native of Townsville use precisely the same phrases pronounced precisely the same way, gentleman and laborer alike. Possibly this is one of the results of the extraordinary democracy of this country—a democracy which makes Jack as good as his master. Perhaps it is a cause rather than an effect. When Jack finds his master speaking in the same manner as he does himself, and, making no effort to maintain his position as a gentleman, he is not so much to be blamed for thinking that he is as good as his master—and in Australia he probably is.

More than half a century on, the speech of Australia's ruling classes was still a matter of concern to visitors. When the British journalist Peregrine Worsthorne visited Australia in January 1979 he stayed with a large landholder in the Western District of Victoria on a property which had been in the hands of the same family for more than a century. Of his host's family Worsthorne was later to write:

> . . . yet his son speaks with the very worst kind of Australian accent, which would unquestionably preclude him from membership of the exclusive Melbourne Club.

Worsthorne later stopped off at a country hotel on the way to Adelaide where the three bars were crowded with clientele *indistinguishable, with no visible graduations of rank or style.* He went on to comment:

Perhaps this is as it should be. But it does not make for good social theatre, so to speak, since everyone seems to be cast in the same minor role. The British class system at least forces people into different moulds, which produces a far more interesting social landscape than Australia's shapeless uniformity. And because everybody here is equal, and superficially at ease with each other, there is no need for manners or politeness, which are the gears required only in societies whose wheels do not all revolve at the same speed. So there is good will galore, unrestricted affability, but a total lack of grace and courtesy; without the tensions and frictions of a class hierarchy there is no call for social lubricants.

The extent to which 'British English' has been mangled by the ruling classes in Australia has been the subject of many comments. Alan Marshall in *Australia Unlimited* made this point:

It is a very sobering experience to hear a Lord Mayor of the second city of the British Empire (i.e. Sydney) drop his aitches and mangle his vowels at a public reception to a notable visitor. It is odd to talk with a Minister of Education who obviously has never been educated beyond sixth grade. It is a weird experience to come back to a country and find cabinet ministers, school headmasters, clergymen, bank managers, medical officers, with accents like wharfingers.

Those who have been unfortunate enough to have been contaminated by prolonged contact with the Australian accent, sometimes feel it necessary to apologise for the fact. In 1974 the Australian Associated Press reported from London that the former Conservative MP. Mr Enoch Powell, campaigning in Ulster in the British elections, had apologised for having an 'ugly' accent. He had picked it up partly in Australia where he was professor of ancient Greek at Sydney University from 1937 to 1939!

In 1970 the then Premier of NSW Sir Robert Askin put forward the interesting proposition that Australians were inclined to take more heed of the way a speech was delivered than its linguistic content. He expressed his view as follows:

In Parliament you can have people speaking with the most brilliant vocabulary, but they don't draw people in. But some cove will get up and start to speak with deep sincerity, and he may be butchering the Queen's English but he will fill the House.

In 1973 Max Harris made the point that there are two kinds of Australian speech which he said were 'educated Australian' and 'degenerate Australian'. He wrote:

What the present generation don't apprehend, because of an enfeebled and stupefyingly undisciplined educational system, is that there are two kinds of Australian speech—educated Australian and degenerate Australian. At the same time the Australian accent has degenerated until it is on a par with the working class slum speech of the north of England.

Harris is supported in this viewpoint by Professor A G Mitchell who in *The Pronunciation of English in Australia* (1946) claimed that there were two well-defined types of speech in Australia: an educated, cultivated, professional speech and an uncultivated, popular speech. He described these loosely as Educated Speech and Broad Speech and maintained that annual surveys of the speech of students enrolled in English I at Sydney University indicated that at least seventy per cent of the population were reckoned to be speakers of Broad Australian.

Professor Mitchell's views aroused little comment when the book appeared, but when he repeated the claim in a letter to the *Sydney Morning Herald* in 1952 a spirited controversy quickly developed, with a number of readers challenging his assertions.

The *Herald* finally closed the correspondence but allowed the Professor a last word on the subject. Professor Mitchell was at some pains to point out that the definitions he had given were not perfect but were the best he could think of to describe Australian ways of speech without desirable implications. He went on:

One possible undesirable implication left, even so, is that those who use broad speech are uneducated. In all the opinions that I have ventured on the subject I have been at pains to point out that this is not and cannot be implied. The expectations—highly educated men who use the broad speech—are too clear and too numerous.

The characteristics of uneducated speech are much the same wherever English is spoken—mainly the dropping, substitution and assimilation of sounds. When I refer to uneducated Australian I mean this quite specifically.

If you want to classify the types of speech that are heard in Australia a principle of division is hard to find. There are no class divisions as in England; there are no local divisions as in England and America.

In 1958 Professor Mitchell and Arthur Delbridge, Senior Lecturer in English at Sydney University, carried out an Australia-wide survey involving some 7000 students in the 16–18 age group in more than 300 high schools—both state and independent, to try and determine the extent of speech patterns and differences in Australia. The tests included individual taped interviews of students, backed up by questionnaires. The results were examined in various ways measuring the patterns of speech of boys against girls, patterns in state and independent schools (both Catholic and non-Catholic) on a basis of the occupation of the student's father, the birthplaces of the students and their parents, and on regional locations of the schools involved.

The results of the findings were published in 1965 in a book *The Speech of Australian Adolescents*, by the authors of the survey. Although differences of speech patterns did emerge in the survey, they were by no means clear-cut in their delineation. A reading of the survey results indicates that there is a remarkable uniformity in speech patterns throughout Australia and that such factors as class and geographical location play a significantly lower role in determining speech and voice patterns than they do in many other countries, such as Great Britain.

Although all the concrete evidence is to the contrary, there still persists the myth that residence in some of the 'better class' suburbs of Australian cities affects accents. An unusual example of this was reported in November 1978 by the *Sydney Morning Herald* columnist. The report noted that when Mrs Sheila Cohen of Neutral Bay (a fashionable Sydney suburb on the north shore) rang a Federal Government department to ask about a cheque she was expecting, the clerk who answered the phone asked her to wait while he fetched her file. On returning to the phone the clerk said:

I hope you won't be offended if I tell you this, Mrs Cohen, but when I answered the phone I thought you sounded like an upper class twit. Now that I see your address on file I know I was right.

Chapter Sixteen

OUTBACK

Australian poetical writers invariably get the coastal scenery mixed up with that of 'Out Back' . . . We wish to Heaven that Australian writers would leave off trying to make a paradise out of the Out Back Hell.

Henry Lawson, 1893

Although eighty per cent of Australians live—and have always done so—in the cities and towns on the coastal fringe of the continent, the remaining twenty per cent living in relatively isolated inland areas have always exerted an influence on the life and mores of the country far greater than their numbers seem to warrant.

This paradox is reflected in many ways, from the political to the economics of the land. Australia's economy for long rode 'on the sheep's back'. If the phrase no longer strictly applies, it is still fair comment to say that many a city dweller catches cold when the outback sneezes as it is prone to do in this land of fierce extremes of floods, bushfires and drought. A whole succession of astute Country Party leaders have been able to exploit this fact to wield influence far greater than their meagre numbers would normally justify.

It has been the case of the tail wagging the dog down through the years, and nowhere has this paradox been more evident than in the shaping of the Australian language. Whilst the timid city dwellers clung to the safety of the coastal belt, the pioneers went forth into the wilderness and not only produced primary goods to set the young nation on its economic feet, but also developed a language rich in slang and idiom of the harsh environment they sought to conquer.

Many visitors to these shores have commented on the vast

emptiness of the interior of the continent, and how this has shaped the thinking of the inhabitants.

The best outside view on this point that I have seen was expressed by Senator Eugene McCarthy, the former United States Presidential candidate, after he made a brief visit to Australia in 1978.

McCarthy saw Australia as a kind of no-security prison with its people confined by distance from other places rather than by walls or prison bars. He then went on to make these pertinent comments:

Actually the problem with Australia is not so much one of time as it is one of space. Australians, as a rule, do not say that it will take too long to get somewhere—they say it is too far. They are more concerned with the size of the football field than they are with the length of the game. Their common, non-reflective language is the language of distance. Australians refer to their interior as 'the outback'. In other countries, like the United States, if one lives in the interior it is common to refer to the east as 'out east' and to the west as 'out west'. This is not so in Australia. Whether an Australian is from the north, south, east or west, the interior is out! What the people of Australia say of the periphery of the country I do not know. One can only wonder who is 'in' in Australia.

From the earlist days of settlement the interior of Australia has been referred to as the OUTBACK, but it is very difficult to define just where this starts (or finishes). Some place it beyond the equally mythical BLACK STUMP, whilst other so-called experts are convinced that the OUTBACK doesn't really start until you go beyond Bourke in western New South Wales (hence another popular expression BACK O'BOURKE). Bill Wannan quoted a bushman's description of OUTBACK which seems to sum up in a nutshell the general confusion on the actual location of this piece of Australia:

Outback is away out west, out in the never-never where the crows fly backwards; it's away out west o' sunset and right out back o' beyond; it's away out back o' Bourke in the great open spaces, where men are men and women are few and far between; it's right away out—well, it's away out back, yer can't miss it.

The OUTBACK has an identical geographical twin in the NEVER NEVER, and to reinforce the myth of the actual existence of such places the old timers invented equally mythical place names such as BULLABAKANKA (there are several alternate spellings), SNAKE GULLY and WOOP WOOP.

In the OUTBACK there is only one certainty: that 'things are pretty crook'. If it's not a drought, it's a flood or a bushfire conspiring to wipe out the settler. It is all encapsulated in G H Gibson's poem on the perils of life OUTBACK:

> Sing a song of saltbush,
> Sandy Blight an' drought.
> Forty thousand weaners
> Slowly pegging out.

From OUTBACK is derived the untidy word OUTBACKERY, meaning the conscious cultivation of pioneering rural values. Tom Ronan in *Once there was a Bagman* (1966) described the term very well when he wrote:

The phase of life, now sneered at by our pharisaical, suburban, scholarship-nurtured intelligentsia—'Outbackery' they call it—has its intervals of excellence.

A book review in the *Bulletin* in 1971 also made reference to the term:

No violence, no sex, no self-conscious outbackery; the only complaint, the book is too short.

Just as the early Australian settlers decided on the word BUSH to describe the wooded areas of the country instead of the more traditional WOODS or FORESTS of England (see chapter 17 entitled SYDNEY OR THE BUSH), so they adopted new names for other features of the landscape. It was as if they had decided that the only way they could conquer this harsh, brown environment in which they found themselves was to turn their backs on all the familiar names of their homeland.

Professor W K Hancock, in *Australia*, summed it up very well when he wrote:

The Australian . . . has rejected almost at a blow the beautiful names of an intimate countryside—fields and meadows, woods, copse, spinney and thicket, dale and glen, vale and coomb, brook, stream and rivulet, inn and village. But in their place is a new vocabulary of the Bush—billabong, dingo, damper, bushwhacker, billy, cooee, swag, swaggie, humpy, stockman, jackaroo, squatter, bushranger, sundowner, brumby, drover, never-never, outback, backblocks . . . Many of the words have come from the Aborigines, some have worked upward from 'St Giles Greek', others derive from the gold rushes, and still others are originals coined offhand out of experience and matter-of-fact humour.

Some of the local substitutions for names in the new landscape are quite interesting. Whilst Australians retained the English word RIVER for their larger waterways, they rejected the traditional English STREAM for their tributaries in favour of CREEK. Although this is a term of English (not Australian) origin, it has a different meaning here as explained by Cassell's *Picturesque Australasia* (1887):

Generally where the English language is spoken a creek means a small inlet of the sea, but in Australia a creek is literally what it is etymologically, a crack in the ground. In dry weather there is very little water; perhaps in the height of summer the stream altogether ceases to run, and the creek becomes a string of waterholes; but when the heavens are opened, and the rain falls, it reappears a river.

It should be added that most Australian farmers I know pronounce CREEK as CRICK.

In Australia, rough, untamed country with trees of stunted growth is referred to as the SCRUB or SCRUB-LAND or even SCRUBBY. This is a term used as early as 1802 by James Fleming in *Journal of the Exploration of C. Grimes*:

The land appeared barren, a scrubby bush . . . The trees low and scrubby.

Cattle that have taken to the SCRUB and run wild are referred to as SCRUBBERS. The Melbourne *Argus* of 29 April 1893 referred as follows to these animals:

The scrubbers, unseen of men, would stay in these fastnesses all day chewing the cud they had laid up the night before, and when the sun went down and the strident laugh of the giant kingfisher had given place to the insidious air-piercing note of the large-mouthed podargus, the scrub would give up its inhabitants.

It should be noted that the term SCRUBBER survives in present day language as a slang word for an unattractive or promiscuous woman!

As language is the chief—although not the sole—means of communication of humans, there is one Australian word which has special meaning as in itself it refers to a form of outback communication. The word, of course, is COOEE, an Aboriginal word for a call The cooee itself is a penetrating cry made to attract attention, so that 'within cooee' means 'within hearing distance' (i.e. 'he wasn't within cooee of the right spot').

The cooee has been credited with saving many a life in bush country and has been used since the earliest colonial days. J D Land in his *Phillipsland* (1847) spelled the word 'cooey' but nevertheless had an interesting story to tell about its usage, even outside its country of origin:

Cooey is the Aboriginal mode of calling out to any person at a distance, whether visible or not, in the forest. The sound is made by dwelling on the first syllable, and pronouncing the second with a short, sharp, rising inflexion. It is much easier made, and is heard to a much greater distance than the English Holla! and is consequently in universal use among the colonists . . . There is a story current in the colony of a party of native-born colonists being in London, one of whom, a young lady, if I recollect aright, was accidentally separated from the rest, in the endless stream of pedestrians and vehicles of all descriptions, at the intersection of Fleet Street with the broad avenue leading to Blackfriars Bridge. When they were all in great consternation and perplexity at the circumstance, it occurred to one of the party to COOEY, and the well-known sound, with its ten thousand Australian associations, being at once recognised and responded to, a reunion of the party took place immediately, doubtless to the great wonderment of the surrounding Londoners, who would probably suppose they were all fit for Bedlam.

Chapter Seventeen

SYDNEY OR THE BUSH

Don't you fancy that the poets better give the bush a rest,
Ere they raise a just rebellion in the over-written west?

Henry Lawson

If I were asked to name one word which sums up the ethos of Australia I would unhesitatingly plump for BUSH, a word which has emotive overtones stretching far beyond its original use as a substitute for the English terms WOODS and FOREST.

BUSH is not exclusive to Australia as it was a term (now obsolete) in use in the United States in the nineteenth century and still has some usage in Canada and Africa, but only in Australia has it gained meanings far beyond the original use as a noun.

BUSH is derived from the Dutch word BOSCH and arrived here at the turn of the nineteenth century from the Cape of Good Hope. It was first recorded in an adjectival form of BUSH NATIVE in 1801 in a letter by George Caley (recorded in Bladen's *Historical Records of Australia*) whilst its first appearance in print in its more common form of a noun was in the *Sydney Gazette* of 17 April 1803. Within a few years it had completely superseded the English terms WOODS and FOREST as a description of timbered areas. In this sense it is still in use, but by the 1830s it was spreading its wings and taking flight in many directions.

It soon became—and continues to be—a general term to describe all countryside away from the cities and towns—irrespective of whether there are any trees in evidence. It must be quite disconcerting for a visitor to these shores, to stand on a treeless plain and hear a local man of the soil speak with affection of THE BUSH.

Anthony Trollope commented on this contradiction in *Australia and New Zealand* (1873) when he noted:

... folk who follow a country life are invariably said to live in the bush. Squatters who look after their runs always live in the bush, even though their sheep are pastured on plains ... nearly every place beyond the influence of the big towns is called 'bush', even though there should not be a tree to be seen around.

At times the word BUSH is used with such wide meaning that it can refer to almost anything away from a capital city. When Mr John Mason MLA was appointed Leader of the Liberal Opposition in NSW State Parliament in 1978 several Sydney newspapers referred to him as the BOY FROM THE BUSH. In fact Mr Mason's place of residence is Dubbo—a provincial city in its own right. Dubbo residents certainly would not see themselves as being bushmen but that is how some city newspapers evidently pictured them.

Given the reverence which the average Australian attaches to the BUSH, it is perhaps not surprising to find that the word has developed a remarkable crop of variants, most of which are still in everyday use though coined in the last century. Some examples: The first rural dwellings were BUSH SHANTIES; the early outlaws were BUSHRANGERS; a person who lacks social graces or acumen is a BUSHWACKER; one who hikes in hill country is a BUSHWALKER; a man who talks in legal terms is a BUSH LAWYER; a rough and ready tradesman is a BUSH CARPENTER; a person of doubtful religious persuasion is a BUSH BAPTIST; to take to the hills or to disappear is to GO BUSH whilst rumours and news spread on the BUSH WIRELESS.

There are also quite a number of other slang words involving BUSH which are now obsolete. They include BUSH BELLOWS for hat (used to fan a campfire alight); BUSH OYSTERS for bull's testicles; BUSH LIAR for a spinner of tall tales; BUSHMAN'S CLOCK a kookaburra whose raucous laugh is heard at daybreak; the BUSHMAN'S BIBLE the long-used name for the *Bulletin* because of its influence in the outback; BUSH PICKLES a gruesome concoction of plum jam laced with Worcester sauce and BUSH TRIFLE an equally repellent mixture of johnny cakes, jam and condensed milk.

The term even extended to items of furniture. Canon Goodman's *Church in Victoria During the Episcopate of Bishop Perry* (1848) quotes a letter from a Mrs Perry which contained the sentence: ... *a hard bush sofa, without back or ends.*

BUSHFIRES create such havoc throughout the land that the word still strikes a chord of terror in the heart of any Australian living within sight of trees. So great is the apprehension of fire in rural areas that almost every country community has its extremely well organised and equipped BUSHFIRE BRIGADE, most of whose work comprises the extinguishing of GRASS fires rather than BUSHFIRES.

Not unnaturally the term BUSHFIRE has bred some off-shoots, the most interesting of which is the phrase TO GET ON LIKE A BUSHFIRE, meaning to develop a project at a fast pace. The term is also used to describe a rapidly developing friendship between two newly-met Australians. Sarah Campion in *Bonanza* (1942) expressed it this way: *They got on like the proverbial bushfire.*

Another offshoot (now obsolete) was the term BUSHFIRE BLONDE to describe a red-headed girl.

To be lost, whether in the outback or in a city, is to be BUSHED and this can even be achieved at sea if we are to take heed of Charles Barrett who in *Coast of Adventure* (1941) wrote of a small ship and commented:

Had we gone wide of the light; become bushed in the great Van Diemen Gulf where a small craft could easily be wrecked in half a gale?

Nor is the term confined to those who are physically lost. On occasion even Parliament can get BUSHED if we are to judge by a report in the Melbourne *Argus* of 1 January 1896:

The Ministry did not assume its duty of leading the House, and Mr Higgins graphically described the position of affairs by stating that the House was 'bushed'; while Mr Shiels compared the situation to a rudderless ship drifting hither and thither.

BUSH is also used as a verb in the expression TO BUSH IT, meaning to camp out or to put up with hardships. The term was used as early as 1827 when W J Dumeresq in *Fourteen Journeys Across the Blue Mountains* wrote:

Not being provided for bushing it, in these early forests, we made up our minds to return.

This is an interesting quotation because in it Dumeresq uses the English expression FOREST, used in Australia only for dense stands of timber, whilst at the same time easily slipping into the vernacular of BUSHING IT, a term unknown in his native England.

TO GO BUSH originally meant to leave the city and head for the outback, but in modern parlance it simply means to disappear.

In 1978 when artist Brett Whiteley carried off the triple Archibald, Wynne and Sulman art prizes the *Weekend Australian* the next day carried the story on the front page under the headline:

BRETT WHITELEY MAKES ART
HISTORY—THEN GOES BUSH

The paper was not inferring that he had literally taken off for the country; merely that he had dropped out of sight to avoid reporters and critics.

The term can even be used for a mental dropout. Patrick White used it in this form in *Riders in the Chariot* (1961) when he wrote:

Alf Dubbo now went bush, figuratively at least, as far as other human beings were concerned.

The term has even been exported to New Caledonia where the French community use *la brousse* for woods and forests. They also use the term *aller la brousse* which in translation means TO GO BUSH.

An interesting term still widely used is BUSH LAWYER, describing a layman who fancies he knows a fair bit about the law and is not backward in expressing his pseudo legal views. Such a person invariably talks a lot and 'lays down the law' at the slightest provocation. In a *Lecture on J P Fawkner* in 1896 H G Turner dealt with the origins of the term:

For some years he (Fawkner) cultivated and developed his capacity for rhetorical argument by practising in the minor courts of law in Tasmania as a paid advocate, a position which in those days, and under the exceptional circumstances of the Colony, was not restricted to members of the legal profession, and the term Bush Lawyer probably takes its origin from the practice of this period.

Another common expression is BUSH WEEK as in the common chant of derision, 'What do you think this is? BUSH WEEK?'

The expression frequently crops up in Australian fiction such as *The Pearling Master* by Tom Ronan (1958):

What's the strong of pulling up in the middle of the block? What do you think this is? Bush Week?

The term BUSHRANGER started out in Australia as a perfectly innocuous description of a man with some official task in the bush, such as an English ranger.

In 1798 Matthew Flinders used the English term of WOOD RANGERS when describing such officials, but by 1805 the term

BUSH had replaced WOODS in general usage in the colony so that when George Cayley wrote to Sir Joseph Banks in that year he used the term BUSH RANGERS thus:

> If the Bushrangers will always bring plants from the remote parts of their tours, I can form a good idea of what distance they have been.

However, some confusion must have arisen in this period on the meaning of the term as from the turn of the century the word BUSHRANGERS was also used to describe escaped convicts who turned to highway robbery and theft. James Elder used the term as early as 1801 to describe an escaped convict named Williams, whilst the *Sydney Gazette* of 2 February 1805 was to report:

> On Tuesday last a cart was stopped between this settlement and Hawkesbury, by three men whose appearance sanctioned the suspicion of their being bushrangers . . . they did not, however, take anything out of the cart . . . from whence it may be hoped they prefer the prospect of being restored to society to any monetary relief that might be obtained from acts of additional imprudence that could at best but render their condition hopeless.

On 16 November 1806, the *Sydney Gazette* again turned its attention to the subject of BUSHRANGERS when it published the following account of their depredations:

> BUSHRANGERS. As the daring spirits of these desperate offenders occupies much serious attention at the present moment, we enter into the following particulars . . . Five sheep have disappeared in the course of one night, notwithstanding every vigilant exertion of the stock keepers and guards . . . Night and day they have been harassed by their daring visitors, their huts plundered as well as their flocks, and their provisions carried off.

From that period, BUSHRANGER seems to have disappeared as applying to official rangers, but persisted through most of the nineteenth century as a description of all kinds of desperadoes and highwaymen—the most famous of the tribe being Ned Kelly.

Modern communications brought an end to bushranging as an occupation; but if the BUSHRANGERS themselves died out, the word lingered on in the language with a new meaning, which persists to the present day. The term BUSHRANGER is now widely applied to any person (or enterprise) which exploits or overcharges the public. Thus Dymphna Cusack in *Say No to Death* (1951):

> Bushrangers aren't they? Ned Kelly was a gentleman compared with most of the landlords around here.

Some left-wingers tend to use the term for ALL capitalists, good or bad, and this is neatly summed up by Kylie Tennant in *Foveaux* (1939):

Bud Pellager ... had taken to a mild and lucrative form of bushranging as owner of a garage on the Main Western Highway.

In the early colonial days the bullock wagon tracks that meandered across the countryside in haphazard fashion were BUSH ROADS. This later gave way to an expression BUSH TRACKS, still in use for almost any track or path not properly formed but roughly defined by common usage of vehicles or walkers. Thus *The Reader* of 2 April 1864 referred to:

... the roads from the nascent metropolis still partook mainly of the random character of 'bush tracks'.

Another interesting piece of nineteenth century slang for any outback road so bad that coaches and buggies stuck in it was GLUE-POT. The London *Daily News* in 1892 reported on this aspect of life out back as follows:

The Bishop of Manchester (Dr Moorhouse, formerly Bishop of Melbourne), whose authority on missionary subjects will not be disputed, assures us that no one can possibly understand the difficulties and the troubles attendant upon the work of a Colonial bishop or clergyman until he has driven across almost pathless wastes or through almost inaccessible forests, has struggled through what they used to call 'glue-pots', until he has been shaken to pieces by 'corduroy roads', and has been in the midst of forests with the branches of trees falling around on all sides, knowing full well that if one fell upon him he would be killed.

Finally there is the long-used expression SYDNEY OR THE BUSH, meaning 'all or nothing'. Originally it was used in the context of a man who gambled on making a fortune and living a life of ease in the city, with the penalty for failure being the need to seek a more difficult livelihood in the outback. E Shann in *An Economic History of Australia* (1930) summed up the expression in this way:

'Sydney or the Bush!' cries the Australian when he gambles against odds, and the slogan betrays a heart turning ever towards the pleasant coastal capitals.

Nowadays the expression is used for any risky adventure such as expressed by Richard Beilby in *No Medals for Aphrodite* (1970):

'Here we go', Turk murmured grimly, climbing in behind the wheel. 'It's Sydney or the Bush! Keep your fingers crossed.'

Chapter Eighteen

ON THE SHEEP'S BACK

You'd own the place was beggered – since the country carried sheep.

Harry Morant

For more than a century Australia's wealth was derived chiefly from export earnings of wool—hence the term that the country was RIDING ON THE SHEEP'S BACK.

The wool industry was such a vast enterprise, spread over an enormous area of the continent, that it was inevitable that it should spawn a language of its own, especially as there were no Old World precedents for the form the industry took in the Antipodes.

The original nineteenth-century slang term for sheep was JUMBUCK, this being Aboriginal pidgin-English. There are varying explanations for its origin, the most popular being that it was derived from an Aboriginal word meaning JUMP UP. This was disputed by a Mr Meston, writing in the *Bulletin* on 18 April 1896. He claimed that JUMBUCK was derived from JIMBA, JOMBOCK, DOMBOCK and DUMBOG all Aboriginal words meaning a white mist preceding a shower of rain, to which a flock of white sheep bore a strong resemblance.

The earliest recorded usage of the word was in 1824 when a letter cited by Ramson contained this sentence:

To two Brothers of mine, these monsters exposed several pieces of human flesh, exclaiming as they smacked their lips and stroked their breasts, 'boodjerry patta! murry boodjerry!—fat as jimbuck!!' i.e. good food, very good, fat as mutton.

In 1843 John Hood in *Australia and the East* used the term:

These useful blacks were put upon the foot of the 'jimbucks', and with equal success.

In 1851 John Henderson in *Excursions and Adventures in New South Wales* referred to them as follows:

He thought proper to leave his flock of jimbucks (as they call the sheep).

In 1845 C Griffith in *Present State and Prospects of the Port Phillip District of New South Wales* wrote:

The following is a specimen of such eloquence: 'You pilmillally jumbuck plenty sulky me, plenty boom, borack gammon,' which being interpreted means, 'If you shoot my sheep I shall be very angry, and will shoot you and no mistake.'

In 1855 W Ridley in *Transactions of Philological Society* also referred to the word though erroneously ascribing to it an English origin, when he wrote:

When they adopt English words ending in mutes, the blacks drop the mute or add a vowel: thus, jumbugg, a slang name for sheep, they sound jimbu.

JUMBUCK has long been obsolete in everyday usage, only being kept alive by its inclusion in the words of 'Waltzing Matilda'.

Another term for a sheep was YOE (possibly derived from EWE) and this is still in use in rural areas by older hands, no doubt being sustained a little by the inclusion in the popular song 'Click Go the Shears' whose chorus includes the lines:

The ringer looks around and is beaten by a blow,
And curses the old snagger with the bare-bellied yoe.

It was in the woolshed that the greatest linguistic inventions occurred. The key area of all woolsheds was the BOARD where the sheep were shorn, and from this derived many auxiliary terms including BOSS-OF-THE-BOARD (for the overseer); CLEARING THE BOARD (to complete shearing) and RING THE BOARD (the title claimed by the top shearer of that season). Other woolshed terms included: FLEECY (for the man who picked up the fleeces); BROOMIE or SWEEPER (for the man who continually swept the floor of stray pieces of wool); TARBOY (for the lad who dashed around dabbing tar on sheep cut by the shears); TICK-JAMMER (for the man who baled the wool); DRUMMER (the laziest or slowest shearer in the shed); COBBLER (a sheep with wrinkled, matted wool difficult to shear); PINKING (to nick the flesh of the sheep with the shears); TO TOMAHAWK (to cut a sheep deeply with the shears); the GUN or THE RINGER (the top shearer of the shed); the SNAGGER (a learner-shearer); ROSELLAS (sheep shedding their wool); A RUN (a two-hour spell of shearing); to CUT IN (the start of the season) and CUT OUT (the end of the season).

The above are but a short selection of some of the more widely used terms of the shearing shed. Most still survive within their particular environment and it is interesting to note that that is where they have remained. Although most of these terms have been in use over a very long period they have not been adapted into the general language of the average Australian—even as slang terms.

Cattle preceded sheep into the inland areas of Australia but did not prove to have the same money-spinning propensities as the golden fleece of the sheep. However, the cattle men were just as prolific as the sheep handlers in their invention of words. Of these perhaps the term BULLOCKY to describe the bullock driver was the most enduring and most widely used. Other terms of the cattle industry include DUFFING (cattle stealing); DUFFER (cattle stealer); SCRUBBER (cattle that have run wild in scrub country); MUSTER (round-up of stock); POLEY (a de-horned or hornless animal); PODDY (a calf); MOONLIGHTING (rounding up cattle at night—a term which has now passed into general use to describe a man holding down two jobs at the one time).

This is not the place to cover the slang terms which have arisen in the many other rural industries of the nation, but perhaps mention should be made of one important adjunct to both sheep and cattle men—their dogs. Several distinct types of dogs have been developed in Australia for specific rural purposes and they have been assigned specific names. Best known are the KELPIE, evolved in the 1870s for sheep handling and the cattle dog widely known as the BLUEY.

Rural terms are always a trap for anyone fresh from the city (the BIG SMOKE). I well remember hearing a new announcer from the city make a terrible hash of his first attempt to read a stock report over radio station 2DU at Dubbo. Nobody had bothered to explain to him beforehand that the contraction X-bred on the market sheets meant crossbred, nor had he been told that a EWE (a female sheep) was pronounced YOO. As a result, he launched into the reading of a long stock report which came over the air with numerous references to *ex-bred eewees* much to the merriment of the listening (rural) community and the great embarrassment of the station management.

Chapter Nineteen

THE MAN ON THE LAND

Farmers around the world have a reputation for being a terrible bunch of whingers. In Australia the phrase was tailored to describe the pastoralists as a 'grizzle of graziers'.

A K Holland, 1978

The earliest tillers of the Australian soil were solid English yeomen and farm labourers, not unskilled in the problems of an English farm, but certainly ill-equipped to conquer the vast and unfriendly spaces of the Antipodes. The number of gentlemen farmers was pitifully small, and they had little to draw on in the form of skilled labour, so that agriculture was at subsistence level for the first half-century of the colony's existence.

It was only in the 1830s and 1840s, when the vast inland was being carved up in the wake of the findings of the inland explorers, that the small landowners of England, and the gentlemen farmers, were attracted to the colony in sufficient numbers, and with adequate capital, to provide a base for exploiting the vast acreages which seemed ripe for the plucking. Much of the soil proved less bountiful than first imagined but the success stories outweighed the failures and the flow of settlers continued unchecked well into the twentieth century.

Before the various land acts of the 1830s and 1840s there were vast areas of arable land in Australia to which no title, other than that of nebulous Crown Land, was attached. These lands were said to be BEYOND—meaning outside the proclaimed areas which the administration of the day had proclaimed open for settlement and for which they could provide protection and some services. Men who ventured beyond this rather ill-defined line on a map did so at their own peril and could not expect any help from the authorities if they encountered trouble from the Aborigines or from their fellow countrymen.

Such men went out BEYOND the established lines of settlement and SQUATTED there. They established RUNS for their stock and ruled their holdings at the point of a gun, employing ex-convicts as private armies to guard the stock against thieves (white and black).

Such men became known as SQUATTERS, an American term which was taken over and adapted in many ways to the Australian scene.

In 1830 J Betts in *An Account of the Colony of Van Diemen's Land* described the SQUATTERS of Tasmania in the following terms:

The means of rooting out a class of people called 'Squatters'. These were generally emancipated convicts, or ticket-of-leave-men, who, having obtained a small grant, under the old system, or without any grant at all, sat themselves down in remote situations, and maintained large flocks, obtained, generally, in very nefarious ways, by having the run of all the surrounding country.

Another writer of the period, W H Breton, in 1833 described the early SQUATTERS as follows in *Excursions in New South Wales*:

There are likewise in the colony certain persons called 'squatters' (the term is American) who are commonly, it may be said always, of the lowest grade. These men established themselves on some unlocated spot, where they cultivate enough land to supply them with grain, and not unfrequently pilfer whatever else they require, from the neighbouring farms.

A lot of the odium attached to the word SQUATTER arose from the methods they used to acquire their holdings. They not only resorted to violence, where necessary, to grab and hold land they wanted, but were suspected, not without cause, of stealing their neighbours' cattle and sheep. The *Sydney Gazette* of 28 April 1835 summed it up very well when it said:

In every part of the country squatters without any reasonable means of maintaining themselves by honesty, have formed stations, and evidently pursued a predatory warfare against the flocks and herds in the vicinity.

The earliest description of SQUATTERS invariably refers to them as ex-convicts or disreputable types, but the picture quickly changed in the late 1830s when the wealthier families of the colony realised what handsome pickings were to be had in the interior if one could secure enough paid labour to do the dirty work. As early as 1840 Governor Gipps was to report on the changing status of the SQUATTOCRACY when he wrote to Lord Russell:

A very large proportion of the land, which is to form the new district of Port Phillip, is already in the licensed occupation of the Squatters of New South Wales, a class of persons whom it would be wrong to confound with those who bear the same name in America, and who are generally persons of mean repute and small means, who have taken unauthorized possession of patches of land. Among the Squatters of New South Wales are the wealthiest of the Land, occupying with the permission of Government thousands and tens of thousands of acres; Young men of good Family and connexions in England. Officers of the Army and Navy, Graduates of Oxford and Cambridge are also in no small number amongst them.

From the very beginning the SQUATTER was an object of hatred and envy. He had few friends (apart from other squatters) and many who wished him no good. Geoffrey Dutton in 1973 summed up very well the general feeling which exists even to the present day against the big landholders of the last century:

For those outside the acres of the mythical run, there are, or were, only two sorts of squatters: bloody bastards and just plain bastards. Squatter—thoroughbred—troopers is the national cliche. Squatters feeding poisoned flour to the Aborigines; squatters locking honest selectors out of the best land; squatters eating the heart out of the country; squatters living it up in London; squatters doing nothing for government or the arts or their lowly fellow-Australians. There is a lot of truth in this, particularly with reference to that legion of hungry Scots-Australians who (with some shining exceptions) have sat tight as whisky corks on the millions they have made out of the land.

By 1845 it seems, everyone was getting into the act and SQUATTING was becoming the favourite pastime of the colony. A speech by the Rev J D Lang, reported in *Phillipsland* of 11 February 1846, made these points:

In whatever direction one moves out of Melbourne, whether north, east, or west, all he sees or hears is merely a repetition of this colonial note—'I squat, thou squattest, he squats; we squat, he or you squat, they squat' ... Exeunt omnes. 'They are all gone out a-squatting.'

Although it is more than a century since the era of the SQUATTER, the term still crops up in modern usage as a pejorative term. In 1976 Xavier Herbert made this stinging comment:

Of course Waltzing Matilda is close to Malcolm Fraser's heart. He's a squatter isn't he?

In time the SQUATTERS became known as PASTORALISTS and their descendants go by yet another name—GRAZIERS. If the SQUATTERS, the PASTORALISTS and the GRAZIERS were at the top end of the social ladder in terms of status, then at the very lowest end of the social scale in the farming community was—and still is in some areas—the COCKY (sometimes COCKIE). This originally was a term of contempt for a small, inefficient farmer, but later a more general description of unsuccessful farmers or BATTLERS. More specifically the term COW COCKY was applied to dairy farmers.

COCKY is derived from COCKATOOER, a contemptuous term used (mainly in Tasmania) in the very early colonial period to describe the small landholder.

Mrs Meredith in her book *My Home in Tasmania* (1852) referred to the term and its meaning:

A few wretched-looking huts and hovels, the dwellings of 'cockatooers', who are not, as it might seem, a species of bird, but human beings; who rent portions of this forest . . . on exorbitant terms . . . and vainly endeavour to exist on what they can earn besides, their frequent compulsory abstinence from meat, when they cannot afford to buy it, even in their land of cheap and abundant food, giving them some affinity to the grain-eating white cockatoos.

Rolf Boldrewood in *Squatter's Dream* painted a somewhat different picture of the COCKATOOER when he wrote:

Fancy three hundred acres in Oxfordshire, with a score or two of bullocks, and twice as many black-faced Down sheep. Regular cockatooing.

Later the term was amended to COCKATOO. In 1863 M K Beveridge in *Gatherings Among the Gum Trees* included this verse:

> Oi 'm going to be married
> To what is termed a Cockatoo—
> Which manes a farmer.

In *Station Life in New Zealand* (1867) Lady Barker gives an interesting explanation of the term as follows:

These small farmers are called cockatoos in Australia by the squatters or sheep-farmers, who dislike them for buying up the best bits on their runs; and say that, like a cockatoo, the small freeholder alights on good ground, extracts all he can from it, and then flies away to 'fresh fields and pastures new' . . . However, whether the name is just or not, it is a recognised one here; and I have heard a man say in answer to a question about his usual occupation, 'I'm a cockatoo'.

Even Anthony Trollope mentioned them in *Australia and New Zealand* (1873) though he made a mistake when he referred to cockatoos (birds) scratching the land as this is not their habit. He wrote:

> The word cockatoo in the farinaceous colony has become so common as almost to cease to carry with it the intended sarcasm . . . It signifies that the man does not really till his land, but only scratches it as the bird does.

Valerie Desmond in *The Awful Australian* (1911) had very little good to say about anything Australian and she included the COCKATOOS in her sweeping condemnation as follows:

> . . . But to the cockatoo (small farmer). There is little to be said for him. He spends most of his time growling . . . He is, as a matter of fact, mostly well to do, but the way he lives it is to be hoped will never in its sordidness be known to the other half of the world. His wail for cheap railway freights and seed wheat ceaseth not, and though he has learned to call himself the backbone of the country he is really a national calamity. In the back country he is little better than his dog.

In due course, in typical Australian fashion, the word COCKATOO shortened to COCKY, but the description remained the same. C E W Bean in *On the Wool Track* (1910) provided an amusing tongue-in-cheek definition of a COCKY:

> A 'cocky' is a small farmer. He usually selects himself a three-hundred or five-hundred acre holding, clears it, fences it, pays for it, ploughs it, sows wheat in it—and then goes to bed to wait for his crop. The next morning he gets up and finds the paddock white with cockatoos grubbing up his seed. He is there to plough and sow and reap —cockatoos. And that, they say, is how he got the name of a cockatoo farmer—a cocky.

Inevitably the word developed offshoots. To take up farming was to go COCKYING, a person who assumed a position of leadership in the community (or group) is a BOSS COCKY (this term is still widely used), fencing wire was known as COCKY'S FRIEND and Golden Syrup was known as COCKY'S JOY.

In the convict era the term COCKATOO had an entirely different meaning referring to a convict who had served time on Cockatoo Island, a prison in Sydney harbour reserved for intractable prisoners.

The term COCKATOO also has long referred to a lookout, and this usage is derived from the fact that, when feeding, cockatoos always post one or more sentinels to warn the flock of pending danger. This usage of the word was recorded as early as 1828 when P Cunningham in his *Two Years in New South Wales* wrote:

It being a common trick (among convict work gangs) to station a sentinel on a commanding eminence to give the alarm, while all the others divert themselves, or go to sleep. Such are known here by the name of 'cockatoo-gangs', from following the example of that wary bird.

This usage of the term COCKATOO has continued to the present day, now being used to describe lookout men posted by two-up schools, starting-price betting establishments and similar illegal activities. Lawson Glassop in *Lucky Palmer* (1949) described a typical (human) COCKATOO thus:

> Snedden, the 'cockatoo', a little ratfaced unshaven man with stooped shoulders, whose job was to watch for the police.

In between the wealthy (but despised) SQUATTERS, PASTORALISTS or GRAZIERS on the one hand, and the lowly BATTLER and COCKY on the other, was a whole legion of ordinary farmers going about their daily business of raising stock and planting crops. In another chapter STATUS DOWN ON THE FARM an attempt is made to sort out a kind of rural pecking order for all these men of the land.

Chapter Twenty

SOME BUSH CHARACTERS

Me 'an me dorg
'ave tramped together.
In cold weather,
An' 'ot.
Me an' me dorg,
Don't give a bugger,
Whether we works,
Or not.
        A Swagman's Lament

Previous chapters have dealt with various types of farmers—
the owners of the Australian soil. But of course, they are not the
only humans to share the vast emptiness of the outback with the
crows and cockatoos. The Australian BUSH has always been a
refuge for a whole range of human types who have found city life
too uncomfortable or spiritually and mentally unrewarding,
and who have chased all sorts of personal rainbows in the
interior of the land of their adoption or birth. Usually they
haven't found the elusive pot of gold at the end of the rainbow,
but they have contributed in numerous ways, not the least in
enriching our language, to the development of the nation.

Some of these escapists from the cities have become farm
workers, either on a permanent basis or as itinerants, drifting
around the continent in an aimless fashion. A few have become
hermits and solitary bush dwellers avoiding all human contact.
Of such men it is said that they HAVE KANGAROOS IN THEIR
TOP PADDOCK.

Another type of LONER who, if not exactly a hermit, did
not seem to encourage human companionship, were the

SWAGMEN (or SWAGGIES). Once trudging the inland roads in their thousands, their numbers have been reduced to a handful now by the march of civilisation and the high cost of shoe-leather.

The politicians of the land have long resisted the idea of making the popular song 'Waltzing Matilda' the national anthem of Australia, mainly because they consider it un-dignified to attach such a title to a song which glorifies any outback itinerant (SWAGMAN) who turns out to be a stealer of sheep (JUMBUCK) and who when caught by the police (TROOPERS) suicides by jumping into a pond (BILLABONG). But the SWAGMEN of yesteryear were far more real, and closer to the national ethos, than any of the characters of events depicted in alternate candidates for the title of National Anthem.

The term TO SWAG was used from the 1840s as meaning to 'tramp the bush'. Later it came to refer to the bundled possessions carried by a SWAGMAN (or SWAGGIE). Thus T McCombie in *Australian Sketches* (1861) wrote:

There was the solitary pedestrian, with the whole of his supplies consisting of a blanket and other necessary articles, strapped across his shoulders—this load is called the 'swag', and the mode of travelling 'swagging it'.

In 1896 Henry Lawson in *When the World Was Wide* wrote of the lonely life of the SWAGMAN:

> *I suppose he's tramping somewhere,*
> *Where the bushmen carry swags,*
> *Cadging round the wretched stations*
> *With his empty tucker-bags.*

The term BLUEY was also used for SWAG (hence the expression HUMPING HIS BLUEY) because the SWAGMAN'S bundle invariably was wrapped in the standard blue-grey blanket of the time.

The SWAGGIES in their seemingly eternal trudge around the barren landscape of the continent were said to be WALTZING MATILDA, to be ON THE TRACK, to be ON THE WALLABY, to be HUMPING THEIR BLUEY or simply to be travelling SHANK'S PONY (on foot).

Although SWAGGIES were sometimes referred to as SUNDOWNERS they resented this term because of its de-rogatory associations. By general consensus the true SUNDOWNER was the tramp who turned up at an outback station just before sundown, ostensibly seeking work but hoping he wouldn't find it. Because of the lateness of the hour he was usually given some food (TUCKER) and by sunup, when work was to be done, he had vanished from the scene.

The *Sydney Morning Herald* of 12 August 1893 described the tribe as follows:

> Numbers of men who came to be known by the class name of 'sundowners', from their habit of straggling up at fall of evening with the stereotyped appeal for work; and work being at that hour impossible, they were sent to the travellers' hut for shelter and to the storekeeper or cook for the pannikin of flour, the bit of mutton, the sufficiency of tea for a brew, which made up a ration.

Farming, like any other calling, is an occupation calling for skill, and where skill is involved there must be learners—or apprentices. In Australia the farming apprentices are called JACKAROOS or, if they are female, JILLAROOS.

The name JACKAROO (the early spelling was JACKEROO) came into use in the 1860s as a slang term applied to young Englishmen of good breeding who came to Australia and worked on stations, without pay, to learn the rudiments of farming. He has been compared with the American TENDERFOOT and his role in station life was summed up in the verse:

> *To do all sorts and kinds of jobs,*
> *Help all the men Jacks, Bills or Bobs,*
> *As well as he is able.*
> *To be neither boss, overseer, nor man,*
> *But a little of all as well as he can,*
> *And eat at the master's table.*

In other words he was the NEW CHUM, the COLONIAL EXPERIENCER (a clumsy term quickly discarded) and the equivalent to the New Zealand CADET or the American TENDERFOOT.

The origin of the word JACKEROO is obscure. One theory is that it was a corruption of the word Kangaroo, another that it was derived from the English term JOHNNY RAW whilst the theory has also been advanced that it was derived from TCHACEROO, a Queensland Aboriginal word meaning a bird. As early as the 1850s squatters were referred to as JACKY RUES—though this was a nickname that did not persist—and the term JACKAROO may have derived from that source.

Starting as a noun the term was quickly verbalised, as were so many other words of the Australian bush, so that if reference was made to a man going JACKAROOING it was clearly understood that he was about to GO BUSH to start his apprenticeship on some outback station.

Men who went JACKAROOING didn't exactly have an easy life. In 1894 the *Sydney Morning Herald* wrote of them:

'Jack-a-roo' is of the same class of slang; but the unlucky fellow—often gentle and soft-handed—who does the oddwork of a sheep or cattle station, if he finds time and heart for letters to any who love him, probably writes his rue with a difference.

The term JILLAROO didn't come into use until World War II years when the shortage of male labour in rural areas forced farmers to employ young women in jobs traditionally held by men.

Although initially used to describe unpaid apprentices, both JACKAROO and JILLAROO later came to refer to (mainly younger) paid station hands.

Another distinctive Australian term for a rural worker is BOUNDARY-RIDER, the name given to the employee assigned to patrolling on horse the often vast fenced boundaries of the station to prevent stock straying. The word originally was used on sheep stations (or RUNS) but later spread to cattle stations.

There are even Government BOUNDARY-RIDERS—men employed to constantly patrol the New South Wales section of the dingo fence which stretches along the borders of Queensland, NSW and South Australia for some 9700 kilometres—claimed to be the longest man-made object on earth (it is four times the length of the Great Wall of China). But the term BOUNDARY-RIDER will probably disappear from the language in a few years as the followers of this occupation appear to be a dying breed. In an article on the dingo fence in the *National Times* in 1978, Adele Horin disclosed that at that time there were only fifteen men in the whole of Australia who listed their occupation as BOUNDARY-RIDER on their annual income tax returns.

Chapter Twenty-one

STATUS DOWN ON THE FARM

The wider the brim the smaller the property.

Bush Proverb

The mystique of land has always been so strong in Australia that it is not surprising that a lot of the aura surrounding the ownership of soil should have transferred itself to the men who attempt to wrest a living (not always successfully) from the vast hectares of the continent. The attention which the very large city or town population pays to the quite small rural community in Australia is due to several factors which may be summarised as follows:

1. The very major historical role played by the man on the land in the development of the continent in the nineteenth century.
2. The heavy emphasis placed on rural activities, personalities and problems by the early poets and writers generally and by such influential media as the *Bulletin.*
3. The dramatisation by the media of the 'booms' and 'busts' of rural life and the constant focus on disasters such as bushfires, floods and drought.
4. The natural curiosity of city dwellers about the more adventurous pioneering activities of their rural cousins.

The image that the city dweller has of the 'Dad and Dave' type of man on the land is stylised, and certainly glamorised, and is one that bears little relation to reality. Nor is it easy to dispel such notions by portraying reality which is as elusive as the myth. The fact is that there is no rural stereotype that one can point to and say, 'That is a typical man of the land'. The farmers of this country are as diverse as the hectares they hold.

Because of this it has never been easy to measure status in rural terms since so much depends on personalities, on farming activities in various districts and even on seasonal and geographic factors. Thus a man who owns 40000 hectares of poor country in a marginal rainfall area might command far less respect (or status), than a more successful (in the financial sense) farmer holding 400 hectares in some lush area.

In chapter 19 entitled THE MAN ON THE LAND, we have seen that the two extremes in the Australian scene were on the one hand the SQUATTERS (who in turn became PASTORALISTS and later still GRAZIERS), and on the other hand the lowly BATTLERS and COCKIES. In between, of course, there were (and are) any number of general successful FARMERS. Perhaps the real measure of their success in coming to grips with the harsh Australian environment is that they have not attracted any nicknames—derogatory or otherwise. They remain just FARMERS whether they grow wheat, rice or sugar cane or whether they run modest herds of cattle or sheep. The cattle breeder may be singled out by being referred to as a cattleman whilst the sheep man may be referred to as a WOOLGROWER or a FAT LAMB PRODUCER, but it seldom goes beyond that.

The only sensitive area in this matter of names to fit rural occupations seems to be in the pig breeding field. Many farmers seem to think that the term PIGBREEDER a derogatory one and go to great lengths to disguise their occupation. In 1975 Geoffrey Dutton brought this to light when he wrote:

Recently on a television programme I referred to myself as a pigbreeder. I was surprised a few days later when the owner of a well-known pig stud congratulated me on using the words 'Pigbreeder'. Apparently many of those farmers who grow pigs hide the fact away, like the smell from a badly-run piggery, and refer to themselves as graziers. Farmers. Graziers. Pigbreeders. All three are frequently the same man on the land, and he may be a dairy farmer as well. But the history of disunity goes back many years. The cockies, of course, always copped it, jeered at for the very virtues that made them hang on to their precious selection.

Professor A A Congalton's study, *Status and Prestige in Australia* (1969) provided an interesting insight into how Australians classify the man on the land in terms of social status. Those who participated in the survey placed GRAZIER at the top of their list in the farming category followed fairly close by GENTLEMAN FARMER (defined for the survey as one who is well established, and does not supervise directly the work on his property). Then came LARGE FARM OWNER (defined as one who supervises work on his own land but seldom works actively on it). Further down the list were well established SHEEP FARMERS, DAIRY FARMERS, FARMERS and FARM MANAGERS. Well down the list were TENANT and SHARE FARMERS, SHEARERS, FARM LABOURERS, JACKAROOS, DROVERS and SHEPHERDS with migratory FARM LABOURERS and seasonal LABOURERS at the tail end.

One term which had to be omitted from the tables was SQUATTER because of some confusion on the part of those participating in the survey as to the actual meaning of the word. Some considered the term to mean a person of considerable prestige and scored SQUATTERS up with (or above) GRAZIERS, whilst others thought of a SQUATTER in very unfavourable terms and assigned very low status ratings.

One possible explanation of the confusion is that in post-war years the term SQUATTER has been used indiscriminately around the world—usually in a pejorative sense—to refer to persons who illegally occupy vacant slum properties due for demolition.

The term PITT STREET FARMERS or COLLINS STREET FARMERS was not in widespread use at the time Professor Congalton compiled his study. These terms are widely used to refer, usually in a derogatory manner, to Sydney and Melbourne business and professional men who buy and operate farms on an absentee basis for purposes of tax minimisation. It would be interesting to know whether their fellow Australians rate such men up with the GENTLEMEN FARMERS or much lower down the social scale. The survey also did not take into account another rural phenomenon of the 1970s—the creation of tens of thousands of small HOBBY FARMS (ranging from 5 to 45 hectares in size) around the fringe of capital cities and larger inland towns.

Professor Congalton's survey, whilst interesting, had its limitations since the participants primarily were city (Sydney) dwellers. Their view of status in the countryside would not necessarily square with the views held by the men on the land themselves on this subject.

In more than half a century of living in rural communities or in large towns in a rural setting, I have had the opportunity to make wide contact with all sections of the farming community, and I have observed that within their ranks there is a very distinct and clearly defined social pecking order. This is manifest in many subtle forms at such rural activities as Agricultural Shows, Picnic Races and Field Days.

The pecking order differs from district to district, depending on the rural activities undertaken in the area, but I would venture to suggest that in western New South Wales it runs something like this:

1. SHEEP STUD BREEDERS (and there are sub-classifications of status here with Merino Stud breeders ranking well above other breeders, i.e. of Border Leicesters).
2. CATTLE MEN
3. WOOLGROWERS
4. FAT LAMB PRODUCERS
5. WHEATGROWERS
6. COTTON GROWERS
7. MIXED FARMERS
8. ORCHARDISTS
9. DAIRY FARMERS
10. VEGETABLE GROWERS

I would stress that this list would vary considerably in other areas of Australia and in some districts would have additions. At the moment however, no status at all seems to attach to the wealthiest of all primary producers—the marijuana growers!

Observant readers will note that in the status listing above I do not use the term GRAZIER at all, even though this is number one on Professor Congalton's list. This is because GRAZIER is not a word in general usage in rural areas, though it appears a favourite of some contemporary authors and newspaper writers and columnists. It even extended to the political arena after 1975, when Malcolm Fraser, a farmer, became Prime Minister and was promptly labelled by his political opponents as the CRAZY GRAZIER because of his rural background.

There are several farming associations which incorporate the word GRAZIER in their title and the widespread publicity which such organisations gain in the media in pushing farmers' claims probably accounts for the general community usage. However, I have yet to hear a farmer use the word in referring to a fellow farmer. In my experience, men on the land tend to show much more interest in what their fellow farmers actually *do* (i.e. grow wheat, raise fat lambs, breed cattle) rather than in applying such general terms.

The relatively modern usage of GRAZIER by (city) writers is shown by the fact that Baker does not even mention the word in *The Australian Language*, nor have I been able to find it in any other reference work. In a search for its origins I was rather surprised to find that it is a very old English word. *Lloyd's Encyclopaedic Dictionary* of 1895 defines it thus:

One who grazes or pastures cattle; one who raises and deals in cattle.

This did not deter Professor F H Gruen in *Australian Society* (1965) from referring to a 'grazing elite' and claiming a distinction between GRAZIERS and other FARMERS. Professor Gruen added:

Prominent graziers are often descendants of the large squatters of the nineteenth century; their holdings have become much smaller—both in area and sheep numbers—but they are still usually above average in size. The main distinction is not so much property size or wealth; it is to be found more in their mode of living and leisure activities.

As support for his claim that GRAZIERS are a class apart from farmers, Professor Gruen quoted a 1958 survey which showed that leaders of rural associations with the word GRAZIER in their title had significantly higher educational standards than leaders of other farming organisations.

Chapter Twenty-two

COBBERS, DIGGERS AND MATES

When our ideal of 'mateship' is realised,
the monopolists will not be able to hold
the land from us.

Henry Lawson, 1894

The concept of MATESHIP is so deeply imbedded in the Australian psyche that I'm devoting a separate chapter to the three words, almost entirely masculine in expression, which have been used at one time or another to express the idea. These, of course, are COBBER, DIGGER and MATE. Of this holy Australian trinity the word MATE is the most important not only because it has survived the longest in usage but also because it seems part of the MATESHIP concept itself.

The best definition of mateship that I have encountered was given by Thomas Dodd and quoted in the *Australian Worker* (1926):

What is a mate nowadays? Somebody you can rely on—through thick, thin and middling; past hell and high-water. Like the mariner's compass he always points north to you. In any trouble, you know what he will do, without argument; because, since he is your mate, it is exactly what you would do yourself. Your mate is indeed yourself in another fellow's skin—perhaps your better self, perhaps your worse self; but always the same old six-and-eightpence, even when he measures up to 13/4, or down to 5/2. Seems contradictory, doesn't he?— Your mate. He is! My Australian oath he is! Look at my mate! Take it from me, there never was such a dogmatic, obstinate, prejudiced, pig-headed son of a twisted mallee root since mates were discovered. Yet I stick to him; I can't get rid of him; he is inside my skin; he's me, bother him!

MATE is one of those words which have many meanings in general use wherever English is spoken, but in Australia its use has overtones not found elsewhere.

In its commonest usage in Australia as referring to a close (male) companion or associate it has ancient links with England. The word is a corruption of Middle English MAKE, meaning a companion. Byron in *Prisoner of Chillon* uses the term almost as would an Australian:

> *It seemed like me to want a mate,*
> *But was not half so desolate.*

The nearest equivalent to the MATESHIP concept of Australia however, seems to be the now (almost) obsolete north of England term MARROW. This word is perhaps a corruption of the French MARI from the Latin MARITUS (a husband) and *Floyd's Encyclopaedic Dictionary* of 1895 defines it as:

A match, a mate, a partner; one of a pair.

and again as a verb transitive:

To associate with, to equal, to fit exactly, to match.

This is interesting when we compare the definition of MATE given by Professor G A Wilkes in *A Dictionary of Australian Colloquialisms*:

MATE: A working partner; an habitual companion, a fellow-participant in some corporate activity (always a man).

Considering the extensive use of the word in general Australian speech, it has been neglected to a surprising degree by the linguists. Edward E Morris does not mention it at all in his *A Dictionary of Austral English* (1898), though it was widely used in the nineteenth century, whilst Sidney J Baker made only two passing references to it in *The Australian Language*.

In the English sense of a MARROW, the term MATE was perhaps first recorded by C Griffith in 1845 in *The Present State of Port Phillip* when he noted:

Two (bushworkers) generally travel together, who are called mates; they are partners and divide all their earnings.

In 1847 in *Settlers and Convicts*, Alexander Harris recorded:

It is quite surprising what exertions bushmen of new countries, especially mates, will make for one another . . .

Donald McLean in *The Roaring Days* (1960) summed up the essence of *MALE*-NESS in the mateship concept well when he wrote:

My mate is always a man. A female may be my sheila, my bird, my charley, my good sort, my hot-drop, my judy or my wife, but she is never my mate.

The mateship concept has been so deeply entrenched in bush lore that it inevitably attracted the attention of the Freudians who did not hesitate to proclaim that the term had distinct homosexual overtones. Thus, Max Harris in *The Angry Eye* (1973):

Historians have come to accept fairly calmly the notion that the Australian national philosophy of 'mateship' emerged from what was perhaps the world's only homosexual social ordering of things.

In recent years Australians have tended to become increasingly sensitive about the possible connotations of the mateship concept. For instance, when in 1977 Australian test cricketer Jeff Thomson was asked by a London photographer to stand closer to David Hookes for a photo, he protested:

We're Aussies, mate, not poofters.

The word is also widely used in Australia as a salutation: 'Good day, mate', 'How are yer, mate?', 'Good on yer mate'.

The word can also be used in a neutral way, 'Haven't a clue, mate', and even in a menacing form, i.e. 'I'll remember that. You'll keep mate.'

It is interesting to note a change taking place in the meaning of the word MATE, as so often happens when a slang word remains in currency over a long period. Jonathan King in his *Waltzing Materialism* (1978) noted some cold new nuances in the word MATE and claimed that instead of being, as before, an expression of close friendship and affection, it was increasingly taking on a new meaning akin to the American SUCKER or MUG. King claimed that the word was now being used more and more in an unfriendly or even menacing form such as 'Get out of the way, mate', 'Don't bug me, mate', or 'Listen mate, if you don't shut up I'll knock your block off.'

COBBER is an Australian word which preceded MATE but its origin is obscure. Sidney Baker thought it derived from Suffolk dialect TO COB, meaning 'to like someone' or from the Cornish COBBA (a person), but Eric Partridge believes it is of Yiddish origin from the word CHABER (a comrade).

Although not listed in Edward Morris' *Austral English*, it had widespread currency in the nineteenth century. Almost all references to it then use it in the same form as MATE to signify a close friend, a pal. However, there was one interesting departure from this in 1895 when the *Bulletin* published a jingle which contained the lines:

> *Oh, she's good iron, is my little clinah;*
> *She's my cobber an' I'm her bloke.*

This is one of the rare usages of any of the MATESHIP words as extending the term to females. The usage almost always was masculine.

Although COBBER has been obsolescent since World War II, It experienced a limited revival in the 1960s when Barry Humphries resurrected the word and put it in the mouth of his creation Bazza McKenzie.

DIGGER had extensive usage in Australia in the mid-nineteenth century when it applied generally to all gold miners. It also was in general use in New Zealand from about the same period but there applying to (Kauri) GUM-DIGGERS.

In *Austral English* Edward Morris gives a couple of interesting extensions of the word. One, DIGGERDOM, is attributed to W Howitt in *Two Years in Victoria* (1855):

Diggerdom is gloriously in the ascendant here.

He also provides two quotations to indicate that the word at one time had a feminine counterpart DIGGERESS—now long obsolete:

The digger marching off, followed by his diggeress, a tall, slim young woman, who strode on like a trooper . . . open carriages driving about, crowded with diggers and their diggeresses.   W Howitt in *Two Years in Victoria* (1855)

> *I'm tired of being a diggeress,*
> *And Yearn a farmer's home to grace.*
> J Rogers in *New Rush* (1864)

In the nineteenth century the word DIGGER was not synonymous with MATE or COBBER. It was simply a description of a person—a gold miner, but this changed in World War I. Dr Bean in his *Official History of Australia in the War 1914–18* says that the term DIGGER became common amongst Australian and New Zealand troops in 1917, displacing the former COBBER (comrade) and MATE as a form of address. Bean says that during the third battle of Ypres (in France) it came to denote an Australian private, much as the word TOMMY denoted the ordinary British soldier.

One version of the revival of the word DIGGER in World War I places it as far back as 1915 when Sir Ian Hamilton, commander of the Gallipoli forces instructed his troops to 'dig in' to prevent themselves being driven back into the sea. The troopers obeyed, no doubt with much grumbling, and started calling themselves DIGGERS. This version seems to have some factual ground as it is based on a letter written by Hamilton to General Birdwood which contained these lines:

There is nothing for it but to dig yourselves right in and stick it out ... You have got through the difficult business, now you have only to dig, dig, dig until your are safe.

Like many other Australian words DIGGER is often used in shortened form DIG: 'Good on yer, dig.'

John Pringle in *The Australian Accent* quoted the perfect Australian put-down contained in a note written by a parliamentarian and handed up to a loquacious colleague in mid-speech. The note simply said:

Pull out, dig. The dogs are pissing on your swag!

Chapter Twenty-three

MY COLONIAL OATH!

Profane swearing prevails throughout the interior of New South Wales to an extent hardly conceivable but by those who have actually witnessed it.

H W Haygarth in
Bush Life in Australia, 1848

From the earliest colonial times, visitors to these shores have been complaining (without effect) about the excessive amount of bad language used by Australians in their everyday speech.

Given the nature of the origins of the colony, and the type of men who were transported here in the first half-century of its existence, perhaps the excessive use of foul language is not all that surprising. But, once established, it became an ingrained habit which has lasted well into the twentieth century.

On the other hand, the authorities have at times seemed overly sensitive on the question of what really constitutes bad language and the court records of the nation abound with absurdities in this field.

Away back on 9 January 1832 the *Sydney Herald* reported a court case in which one William McLoughlin was charged by his master with 'excessive insolence'—his crime apparently being that he used the word DAMN to the gentleman concerned. In those far-off days DAMN was considered a pretty strong swear word and even the *Sydney Herald* couldn't bring itself to print the term in full so that its report of the case read:

. . . on being desired to make a Welch rabbit, he exclaimed, 'You're a d——d pretty fellow, ain't you? I'll see you genteely d——d first.'

The court was so appalled by this linguistic excess that it imposed a sentence of fifty lashes on the unfortunate McLoughlin.

In 1882 another Sydneysider who was charged with having used 'profane language' was somewhat luckier when he appeared before the court. The prosecution in that particular case alleged that the accused had said:

My God, you are a Parramatta native.

The bench didn't consider this term particularly offensive and dismissed the charge.

One of course should be careful to judge such offences within the framework of the society in which they were committed. Throughout the nineteenth century DAMN was considered an offensive swear word never to be uttered in the presence of ladies, and when allowed in print to appear as D————N.

Anthony Trollope was considered quite daring when he allowed the word to appear in this form in his novel *The Prime Minister* (published in the 1870s). He had the villain of the novel, Ferdinand Lopes use the swear word in the presence of his sweet young wife and she was suitably shocked.

. . . it was to her a terrible outrage . . . The word had been uttered with all its foulest violence, with virulence and vulgarity. It seemed to the victim to be the sign of a terrible crisis in her early married life.

There is an old bush ditty dating back to the nineteenth century which goes like this:

> *Damn the teamsters, damn the track*
> *Damn Coolgardie, there and back,*
> *Damn the goldfields, damn the weather,*
> *Damn the bloody country altogether!*

Anon

If such ditties were in use today it is almost inevitable that another four-letter word beginning with *F* would be substituted for DAMN and in my view it wouldn't be nearly as effective in getting the point across.

In the Colonial period bullock drivers were held in awe by the rest of the community for the breadth of their vocabulary (and profanity) when addressing their teams. Charles R Thatcher in 1864 summed it all up nicely:

> *If nice expressions you would learn*
> *Colonial and new,*
> *Some bullock driver who is bogged*
> *Is just the man for you.*

In 1900 a bullock driver named W Evans was unlucky enough to be heard by a policeman as he tried to urge his team to greater effort. The upshot was that he appeared in court on the unusual charge of using obscene language to his bullocks. And what is more, the bench found him guilty and passed down a sentence of four days gaol!

The bullock teams (and their colourful teamsters) have long passed from our midst but the tradition of using expletives to express indignation lingers on. The most hard-swearing of the Colonial bullockies would have been proud of the Melbourne football spectator (quoted by Professor Ian Turner in 1973) who hurled the following comment at a player who had offended his sensibilities in some way:

> You rotten, bloody, poofter, commo, mongrel bastard.

If we are to believe author Thomas Kenneally, Australians use bad language with deliberate intent. In 1978 he expressed the view that:

> . . . Australians are a profane and bawdy race . . . it even goes to the extent of being consciously earthy and profane.

Louis Stone summed it up rather nicely in *Jonah* (1911) when he wrote:

> If smokin' cigarettes, an' spittin', an' swearing was 'ard work, they'd all die rich men.

Gilbert Probyn Smith in his famous *Open Letter* to John Norton, delivered this stinging rebuke:

> Your articles are couched in trenchant language, it is true, but surely you can spare the public the brutal, coarse words you use. 'Damn', 'Bloody', 'God Almighty', 'Bludger' etc. are the words most familiar with you now. As an educated journalist and linguist also, does it not strike you that you are cultivating a style at once brutal and not a worthy contribution to the craft you belong to?

Perhaps in time the English will get used to the idea that Australians swear a lot. When the Australian play *Innocent Bystanders* opened in London in 1975, B A Young the theatre critic of the *Financial Times*, wrote:

> The writing is very lively and the characters drawn in the appropriate cartoon style for farce. The Australian dialogue is full of obscenity, but somehow, in that accent it hardly seems offensive. The Australians are becoming as good at laughing at themselves as the Jews.

It might well have been that in the nineteenth century, the use of bad language was entirely a male prerogative, but it seems the Ockerinas of the nation are fast catching up.

In 1975 the National Women and Politics Conference was held in Canberra and some of the sessions developed into slanging matches between various groups of women.

Mrs Cathy Bauman, a grazier's wife from Dingo, in Queensland, returned home with her ears burning from the language used by her fellow countrywomen. She later told the press:

> We were horrified at the swearing. Some of the words were atrocious. The men might use that language when they are out working, but they make a point of not using it around the house. Maybe we are behind the times, but we don't use those words out here ... Country women will need to sharpen up their debating skills before the next conference, but we'll leave the bad language to the urban folk.

The word BUGGER is widely used in Australia as both a noun and a verb with some quite original extensions. C Hartley-Grattan perhaps best summed the word up in *Introducing Australia* (1942) when he noted:

> The word bugger is used in numerous forms and contexts. 'Oh, bugger it all', 'I'll be buggered', 'Buggered if I will', 'Bugger him', 'Go to buggery', 'The silly bugger', 'I'm all buggered up'. And triumphantly containing all the favourite words, 'bugger the bloody bastard'. English people profess to find Australian men foul-mouthed.

There are few other variations that Hartley-Grattan missed such as 'the toast is burnt to BUGGERY', 'I don't give a BUGGER' (I don't care), 'I'll give him BUGGER-ALL' (I'll give him nothing), 'I feel as miserable as BUGGERY'.

Senator Don Chipp, the leader of the Australian Democrats, has a much-lined face. When, in 1978, he said in a television interview that he had a BUGGERED-UP FACE viewers everywhere had instant rapport, especially when he went on to confess that a woman had once told him his face looked 'like an unmade bed'.

Perhaps the last word on BUGGER though should go to Tom Ronan who in *Packhorse and Pealing Boat* (1964) related this gem:

> She had started life at Beagle Bay Mission and on the Bishop's arrival proudly informed him: 'Me properly bloody Catholic bugger, all the same you'.

ARSE is a good old Anglo-Saxon vulgarism for the buttocks, but it has been used in many other forms in England and Australia. Grose's *Classical Dictionary of the Vulgar Tongue* (1823) provides this long-obsolete definition:

> ARSE. To hang an arse; to hang back, to be afraid to advance. He would

lend his a-se, and sh-te through his ribs; a saying of anyone who lends his money inconsiderately. He would lose his a-se if it were loose; said of a careless person. A-se about; turn around.

ARSEY VARSEY. To fall arsy varsey, i.e. head over heels.

Grose mentions the much older, and commoner usage of the term 'To hang an arse', meaning to be 'tardy, sluggish or dilatory'. For example:

> *For Hudibras wore but one spur;*
> *As wisely knowing, could he stir*
> *To active trot one side of's horse,*
> *The other would not hang an arse.*

Hudibras

Americans use the politer form of ASS in this sense ('get off your ASS') but Australians have put the word to a much wider variety of uses: ARSE-up (to be upside down); to get the ARSE (to be dismissed from one's job); to be ARSED out (to be thrown out); to ARSE around (to indulge in horseplay or pranks); to have plenty of ARSE (to be brash, over-confident); to be ARSEY (to be unduly lucky); to ARSEHOLE (to dismiss someone peremptorily); to be given the big ARSE (to be ignored); an ARSE Bandit (a homosexual). Sidney Baker also lists a World War II usage of FLAMING ARSEHOLE, a term used for the large red circle painted on Japanese aircraft.

The word is also extensively used in Australia as a purely pejorative term: 'He's nothing but a flamin' big arsehole'. The expression 'The arsehole of the Universe' has also been applied to various communities (usually isolated and lacking amenities) which are out of favour with the user of the term. It is also widely used by Australian travellers to describe overseas cities or towns they intensely dislike. Calcutta (in India) seems to be the prime recipient of the phrase in recent years.

The last word on this expression however, should go to Athol Thomas who, in an article in the *Bulletin* in 1978 related how he had once wandered into the Port Hotel in Wyndham, in Western Australia, where he encountered a waterside worker wearing grubby shorts, boots without socks and a black singlet.

'So you are up here to write about us,' the wharfie said after getting acquainted, adding, 'Put this in, mate, Cambridge Gulf is the arsehole of the world and Wyndham is 65 miles up it.'

The prevalence of four-letter words in the present day Australian vocabulary is perhaps best summed up in the following two quotes.

Personally, I don't mind if people call me four-letter names because these are Australian household words used by ministers, radio announcers and even the Australian Confucius, Bob Hawke.

David Wang, Melbourne City Councillor, 1976

Almost everyone over the age of seven knows the four-letter word for sexual intercourse, and a perfectly good and decent word it is.

Harry M Miller, 1970

The widespread use of bad language has been the subject of condemnation almost from the arrival of the First Fleet, and few have dared to speak up in support of profanity. One rare example of this was cited by Column 8 of the *Sydney Morning Herald* in 1978 when it quoted a research paper on Armed Robbery, from the Bureau of Crime and Statistics, which noted that in most cases victims offer no resistance. The report however, also went on to note that:

... in four cases, abuse from the victim, couched in foul or Anglo-Saxon language, caused the robber to withdraw.

THE SUNBURNT ——— STOCKMAN

The sunburnt ——— stockman stood
And, in a dismal ——— mood,
  Apostrophised his ——— cuddy;
'The ——— nag's no ——— good,
He couldn't earn his ——— food ———
  A regular ——— brumby,
    —;'

He jumped across the ——— horse
And cantered off, of ——— course!
  The roads were bad and ——— muddy;
Said he, 'Well, spare me ——— days
The ——— Government's ——— ways
  Are screamin' ——— funny,
    ———!'

He rode up hill, down ——— dale,
The wind it blew a ——— gale,
  The creek was high and ——— floody.
Said he, 'The ——— horse must swim,
The same for ——— me and him,
  Is something ——— sickenin',
    ———!'

He plunged into the ———creek,
The ——— horse was ——— weak,
  The stockman's face a ——— study!
And though the ——— horse was drowned
The ——— rider reached the ground
  Ejaculating: '———?'
    '———!'

W T Goodge, 'Hits; Skits; and
Jingles' (Sydney, 1899)

THE GREAT AUSTRALIAN ADJECTIVE

In terms of historical fact, Australians have been using the word BLOODY so long and so repetitively that it is no longer a Great Adjective.

Sidney J Baker in **Australia Speaks,** 1953

The word BLOODY has for so long been called the Great Australian Adjective that it will come as a distinct shock to many true blue Ockers to learn that it didn't originate on these shores but is an import along with Japanese transistors and Russian caviar.

Grose's *Classical Dictionary of the Vulgar Tongue* (1823) claimed it was of Irish origin and noted that it was a favourite word used by thieves in swearing, as in BLOODY RASCAL and BLOODY EYES. Grose also noted that BLOODY BACK was a jeering appellation for a soldier, alluding to his scarlet coat.

Since there were plenty of Irish convicts and plenty of Redcoats in New South Wales in the convict period, it is not surprising that the word was an early import from the Old World, probably arriving with the First Fleet.

Having arrived on Australian soil the word soon gained wide currency and by the middle of the last century visitors were commenting (unfavourably) on its usage. William Kelly in *Life in Victoria* (1859) offered this apology for using the word in the book:

I must be excused for the frequent use of this odious word in giving colonial dialogues, because general conversation amongst the middle and lower classes in the Antipodes is always highly seasoned with it.

In the same year (1859) F Fowler wrote in *Southern Lights and Shadows*:

Your thoroughbred gumsucker never speaks without apostrophising his oath and interlarding his diction with the crimsonest of adjectives.

Willard R Espy in *Words at Play* (1975) puts it this way:

Some Englishmen still consider bloody a bloody indecent expletive, though nobody knows why. Etymologists assure us the word is not, as once supposed, a degenerate form of such oaths as God's blood or by our Lady. Transplanted to Australia, it has thrived without embarrassment. Australian troops stationed in Newfoundland during World War II sang this bloody awful song:

> *No bloody sports, no bloody games;*
> *No bloody fun with bloody dames;*
> *Won't even tell their bloody names;*
> *Oh, bloody, bloody, bloody!*

In 1898 Sydney *Truth* commented:

Bloody has been so completely vulgarised and has descended so low, that it can never be picked up again.

One of the first authors to use the great Australian adjective in print to any degree was C J Dennis and he was able to get away with it because he used it in a patriotic ditty produced during World War I and, as everyone knows, you can get away with blue murder in the name of patriotism:

> *Fellers of Australier,*
> *Blokes an' coves an' coots,*
> *Shift yer bloody carcases,*
> *Move yer bloody boots.*
> *Gird yer bloody loins up,*
> *Get yer bloody gun,*
> *Set the bloody enemy*
> *An' watch the bugger run.*

The *Bulletin* is generally given the credit for naming 'bloody' as the Great Australian Adjective (in 1894) explaining that it called it this:

... because it is more used and used more exclusively by Australians than by any other allegedly civilised nation.

A later editor of the *Bulletin*, the great A G Stephens,

however once became so enraged over the prevalence of use of the word BLOODY that he dashed off the following letter to the *Sydney Morning Herald* (28 March 1927):

There is a common word often heard on the lips of men in common talk, and shocking and disgraceful talk it is . . . This vileness exists in other Australian cities, and in some British and foreign cities, but really we have never heard it as bad as we hear it in Sydney . . . Thoughtlessness, carelessness and horrible custom allow it to go without interference and without reproach . . . The literary jesting with the word by such Australian writers as Goodge and Dennis, however excusable, is not the most creditable feature of their writings . . . The constant use of the word by thousands of Sydney residents is vile . . . We do trust that this public protest will help to remove a public blot on the life of Sydney.

It is interesting to note that Stephens in his letter didn't actually name the word, perhaps being well aware that it wouldn't be permitted in the august columns of the *Herald* at that time despite its common currency in the community.

Stephens' letter provoked some response, including one letter which was even more mysterious in its failure to name an offending word:

. . . there is an even worse word, a low disgusting word, which has come into common use of late.

Another correspondent, signing himself 'Disgusted Aussie', wrote:

Twenty years ago foul mouths were something to note, but now the everyday conversation of the bulk of the toilers is an endless hellsbroth of blasphemy, blood and sewage.

One wonders what would have been the reaction of 'Disgusted Aussie' had he been transmitted by a time machine a half a century onwards and sat down to a screening of *Don's Party*!

Despite its widespread usage, it was only in the years following World War II that Australian newspapers allowed the word BLOODY to creep into their columns, and then in a fairly guarded manner such as when directly quoting some noted personage who had used the adjective.

To get around this self-imposed censorship newspapers (and authors) used the dash —— or sometimes B—— or resorted to the euphemisms BLANK or BLANKETY. For example, this report of 1900:

Correspondents in South Africa pay a unanimous tribute to the great Australian blanky, and state that, in curse-language, the man from this blank continent is laps ahead of Tommy Atkins. When an occasion arrives for extra special profanity, the Cornstalk or Gumsucker is deputed to meet the case, and he never fails. Even mules and bullocks which have become absolutely impervious to the indigenous curse, wake up suddenly when the Australian attacks with his exotic objurgation.

Migrants to Australia have not been slow in adopting (or adapting) the Great Australian Adjective. In some cases it is the first Australian word they learn when they go out into the adjectival workforce. Bill Wannan in *Fair Go, Spinner* (1964) quotes the comic verse 'The Italian Cocky's Lament', telling the woes of an Italian farmer in Queensland. The opening verse goes:

Queensland blooda rotten, your country verra dry;
Me never make a fortune no matter how me try.
One day verra cold; next day verra hot;
Then come a thunder storm and drown da blooda lot.

Through sheer weight of usage the word gradually lost its offensive nature, even in the courts of the land.

In January 1939 a man was charged in Newtown Court, Sydney, with having used indecent language in that he used the word BLOODY. The magistrate, R C Atkinson, ruled that the word might be sometimes offensive, but that it was not indecent, and he allowed the prosecution to change the indictment to one of use of offensive language, whereupon he convicted the culprit and fined him one pound.

In 1942 Mr Justice Halse Rogers in the Sydney Divorce Court commented:

The word bloody is so common in modern parlance that it is not regarded as swearing.

However, up in Lismore (NSW) in 1944 there was a police magistrate who had not heard of the rulings of the Newtown magistrate or of Mr Justice Halse Rogers, or else he disagreed with them, because he proceeded to fine a Hindu who used the word to an impounding officer and who was charged with using indecent language.

On the other hand, in a case in the Sydney Quarter Sessions Appeals Court in 1948, Judge Stacey ruled that the word BLOODY *plus* an upward gesture of the thumb was neither offensive nor indecent.

In mentioning these cases Sidney Baker refers to an interesting comment by an (unnamed) English Judge:

If vulgar and uneducated people were debarred from using the word bloody their conversation would be seriously impeded. Judge Scobell Armstrong said (in Plymouth) yesterday, 'I have been reminded that bloody is a good old English word.' Judge Armstrong added, 'Properly used, it is. Educated and refined people whose heads happen to come into contact with a door lintel sometimes use it. But the vulgar and uneducated use bloody—not sometimes, but always—as a forceful adjective for the purpose of emphasis.'

Although the court records are littered with examples of men and women being convicted for use of the great Australian adjective, the penalties imposed for such offences invariably have been extremely light. However, when a member of the Federal Parliament, Hugh Mahon (1858–1931), in 1920 described the British Empire as '. . . this Bloody and Accursed Empire', he was expelled from the Parliament for seditious and disloyal utterances.

The word has had plenty of usage in Parliament, possibly because our politicians are of such low standard, especially in the field of expression, that they are incapable of inventing witty substitutes. Sometimes they use the word despite themselves out of sheer habit. For instance Mr C H Webb, Labor Member of the House of Representatives in 1970 seems to have had an unfortunate slip of the tongue when he proclaimed:

I never use the word 'bloody' because it is unparliamentary. It is a word that I never bloody well use.

The Federal Minister for Transport in the Whitlam Government, Mr Charles Jones, on the other hand, was proud of the word. In 1973 he made a pronouncement on the forthcoming budget which stated, in part:

There is going to be some bloody mammoth changes—some mammoth changes which the Budget will disclose. Bloody mammoth changes, that is the only way you can describe them. I think Frank Crean has done a bloody good job to stand up to the pace. Bloody oath, he has done a marvellous job in standing up to the bloody pace . . .

When Mr Jack Kane was being prepared to be photographed after his election to the Senate in 1970 he volunteered this comment to the photographer:

Look, I'll take my bloody braces off . . . got to look like a man of action.

In March 1978 *Rydge's*, the Australian management magazine, was able to report something of a breakthrough in that the word 'bloody' was likely to appear for the first time in a television advertisement in Australia.

The magazine reported that Ross Quinlivan of George Pattersons (an advertising agency) for years had been trying to have the word included in advertisements as a typical Australian expression. General Motors-Holden however, had turned down its use as a slogan boosting its radial tuned suspension 'She handles like a bloody beauty', and the makers of a certain brand of beer turned their face against the use of the term, 'It's a bloody good drop' in their advertising.

Quinlivan had better luck with the Australian Army, reported *Rydge's*, as he had been able to persuade that institution that the great Australian adjective was just the word it needed to boost recruiting, and an advertisement was built around an actual quotation by a young recruit at an Army camp. When asked what his family thought about his joining the army, the young soldier told an agency researcher: 'My old man just kept saying it's a bloody miracle.'

Rydge's added an unhappy (but all too familiar) footnote to the story when it revealed that the Federation of Australian Commercial Television Stations (FACTS), which vets all commercials, had objected to the use of the word 'bloody' in the advertisement so it could not be used after all.

In Australia the word 'bloody' is used mainly for emphasis and sometimes with considerable effect as several well-known stories indicate. For example, Frank Clune in *Rolling Down the Lachlan* (1935) relates the following amusing tale:

A new-chum selector, tired of finding his gate open, hung up the following sign:
KINDLY SHUT THE GATE
But finding no difference at all, he crossed out the 'kindly' and left:
SHUT THE GATE
The amended inscription, however, had less effect than the first. So he went to a neighbour digger who knew his Condobolin onions better than himself. And this digger says, says he 'Orl you gotta write up is:
"SHUT THE BLOODY GATE!"'
The selector did so; and there has never been trouble since.

The story is told of the waitress at a country hotel who, at breakfast time, poked her head around the door and shouted ''ands up all youse who wants bloody cornflakes!'

Len Evans, the food and wine authority, in one of his columns, told a slightly different version which he claimed happened to him at an outback Queensland hotel in the good old days when guests were served with an early morning cup of tea.

On that occasion, Evans related, the serving wench staggered into his room, obviously much the worse for wear from a heavy evening before. Banging the cup down on the bedside table, she said, 'I hope youse have sugar.'

'No I don't,' said Evans.

'Well then,' replied the lass calmly, 'youse better bloody well not stir it then.'

Chapter Twenty-five

BASTARDS ALL

BASTARD will have to be abandoned — and not before time. What's so devastating about calling someone a pack-saddle, an old French pack-saddle at that? This is the original meaning of the word.

Max Harris, 1978

It has been said that the language of Australians is peppered with the three indispensable Bs—BASTARD, BLOODY and BUGGER.

Whilst BLOODY is certainly the most commonly used of these unpleasant linguistic triplets, BASTARD is the most important, if only because of its many nuances and the risks that visitors take in using it incorrectly.

BASTARD, of course, is a very old Anglo-Saxon word used in a pejorative sense to refer to one who is illegitimate. In most parts of the English-speaking world it is still used in that sense, and it comes as a distinct shock to visitors to Australia to find that here the word has many alternative usages—even as a term of affection. ('He's not a bad sort of ol' BASTARD')

The well known bush philosopher Michael Sawtell once summed up very well the various nuances to the word 'bastard' when he wrote:

It is utterly false to talk of the Great Australian Adjective. We should talk of the Great Australian Noun . . . If we wish to express our contempt for a man, we say 'He's a proper bastard', meaning, he is vile. If we wish to praise him, we say: 'He's a good bastard', meaning that he is a good fellow. The sergeant was correct in calling the Japs bastards. He wished to express his contempt for them. I know they are all God's children, but some of His Children are bastards.

Francis James also expressed it nicely in 1973 when he explained:

There are two types of people, bastards and bloody bastards, but all men should be mates.

Judge A B Piddington, in *Worshipful Masters* (1929), related the following anecdote to illustrate the differing interpretations that can be placed on the word 'bastard':

In an assault case at Armidale (NSW) Assizes he (Wilfred Blacket, KC) was cross-examining a prosecutor named Lonsdale—brother of a well-known member of State and Federal Parliaments:

Counsel: Now, Mr. Lonsdale, didn't you grossly insult my client before he hit you?

Witness (*surprised*): No!

Counsel: Didn't you apply a very abusive term to him?

Witness (*still 'guessing'*): No!

Counsel: Now, sir, didn't you call him a bastard?

Witness (*readily*): Certainly I did.

Counsel: Well, wouldn't you be greatly provoked if a man called you a bastard?

Witness: No! (*then ponderingly*) I would if he called me a w——'s bastard, because that would be a reflection on my mother!

In his very amusing verse *Gumleaves and People*, published in 1967, Len Fox summed up very neatly the average Australian attitude to bastards:

Bastards sitting in their offices
And bastards trying to boss you around
Bastards up there in Canberra
You expect those bastards to be bastards
    But what gets me
Is having bastards all around you
Bastards on your own side who turn out to be Bastards.
I guarantee if they started a society
To rid the earth of bastards
In six months the bastards
Would take it over.

The 'Bastard from the Bush' is a poem that has had a considerable circulation in one form or another since Henry Lawson first penned it towards the end of the last century. Originally it was a very bawdy poem indeed and was circulated only privately, but one time when Lawson needed money he cleaned it up and published it under the title of 'The Captain of the Push'. The original Lawson version is not known to exist and the underground copies that have circulated over the years have differed considerably both as to the story and the salacity of the language. One fairly well known version contains the following toned-down verse which gives a fair summary of the style of the original:

'Now, look here,' exclaimed the Leader to the Bastard from the Bush.
'Now, look here—suppose the Bludgers let you come and join the Push,
Would you smash a bloody copper if you got the git alone?
Would you stoush a swell or Chinkie—split his garret with a stone?
Would you have a moll to keep you, and chuck up work for good?'
'Yes, my oath!' replied the Bastard. 'My bloody oath I would.'

Perhaps the most widely publicised use of the word BASTARD occurred in 1966 when President Lyndon B Johnson visited Australia. His motorcade through Sydney streets came upon crowds of Vietnam war protesters who hurled themselves on the roadway in front of the Presidential car. The then Premier of New South Wales, Robin Askin, who was riding with the US President in the motorcade thereupon tended this piece of advice to the accompanying police officers:

Run the bastards over.

Commenting on this incident (in 1971), Mr Don Chipp (then Federal Minister for Customs and Excise), told a meeting of the American Chamber of Commerce in Canberra:

I would like to think that men of goodwill of my generation have more in common with the agonised student movement than with some of the extreme nigger-flogging reactionaries of the establishment complete with their 'run-the-bastards-down' philosophy.

The word has caused all sorts of problems with foreigners who do not appreciate the Australian overtones. Patsy Adam Smith in *Folklore of the Australian Railwaymen* (1969) relates the following amusing story:

There was a Welsh fellow with us, a lay preacher, and . . . a ganger called him a Welsh bastard. It was friendly you know. But Taffy didn't know and told us that he had evidence of the marriage of his parents. The ganger got heated and said if he himself didn't mind being called a bastard why was this Welsh bastard complaining and with that Taffy up and jobbed him.

Writing in the *Australian* in 1972, Richard Zachariah reported a slightly new twist to the use of 'bastard' as an insult:

A friend of mine inadvertently cut across another motorist in a Melbourne street recently. Pulling up at the next set of lights, he prepared himself for a storm of insults. He took all the expletives without a whimper, but the final insult still hurts to this day. Summoning all his hatred, the enraged motorist spat out: 'You foreign-looking bastard.'

The ultimate 'put down', using the word BASTARD was given in H D Williamson's *The Sunlit Plain* (1958):

'Have you ever heard of a bloke being one of Nature's gentlemen?' I says. 'Why, yes,' he says, grinning all over his fat mug. 'Well,' I says, 'you're one of Nature's bastards.'

And the insult can be extended from people to places with remarkable ease. Thus Ion L Idriess in *The Broken Years* (1974) quotes the 1915 diary of Bill Gammage:

Of all the bastards of places this is the greatest bastard in the world.

And the word can be used in an entirely different sense to mean 'It's a terrible thing'. For example, Lawson Glassop in *We Were the Rats* (1944):

It's like one of your mates going out on patrol and not coming back. It's a bastard, but you can't do anything about it.

Despite the fact that BASTARD is such a commonplace word in the language of Australians, police still tend to regard it as obscene—if directed at them. In 1978 Hugh Lunn reported in the *Australian* on a demonstration in Brisbane in which a young woman was arrested for 'assaulting a police officer'. Lunn recorded that as a man near her struggled for breath in a headlock because he wouldn't face police cameras, she shouted: 'You are choking him, you bastards.' 'Slap a charge of obscene language on her too,' said a very angry policeman surrounded by press, and holding his temper. 'Aren't you puritans?!' she said.

Even on the political front there seem to be clear distinctions on the use of the term. Addressing the Canberra Branch of the ALP in 1974 the then Prime Minister Gough Whitlam had this to say:

I do not mind the Liberals, still less do I mind the Country Party, calling me a bastard. In some circumstances I am only doing my job if they do. But I hope you will not publicly call me a bastard, as some bastards in the Caucus have.

However, in 1975 Gough Whitlam extended the term a little when he described the Queensland Premier, Joh Bjelke Petersen (not at all affectionately) as a BIBLE-BASHING BASTARD.

In 1970 the Premier of South Australia, Don Dunstan,

considered it necessary to squash some rumours that were flying around the City of Churches in these words:

I am not a half-caste, I am not Melanesian, and I am not, in the technical sense, a bastard.

A slight twist to the bastardisation of the language was provided in 1978 when Desmond Keating of Crawley, Western Australia, in a letter to the *Australian* wrote:

Would it not be a good idea for the Aboriginals of the Aurukun and Mornington Island communities to request the Queen of Queensland to lean on her Top Banana there and straighten out the bastard?

The word can even be used as a simple adjective BIG as in the phrase:

He run up a bastard of a bill at the hotel before they turfed 'im out.

Australians seemingly have such attachment to the word BASTARD that on occasion they carry it with them into the last moments of their lives. For example, Harry ('Breaker') Morant, the rebel Australian Bushman who was one of the Australian contingent to the Boer War, was court martialled by a British military court for committing atrocities on Boer prisoners, and was sentenced to death. When he faced a British firing squad in Pretoria, South Africa, on 27 February 1902, his last defiant words were:

Shoot straight you bastards. Don't make a mess of it.

A sidelight on the word BASTARD is that initiation ceremonies at Australian colleges and institutions have long been known as BASTARDISATION. From time to time they have drawn severe criticism from outsiders shocked by some of the apparent excesses of the ceremonies. For instance the Hawkesbury Agricultural College, in New South Wales, which has a long history of bastardisation, has one particularly revolting practice in which first-year students are required to parade fully clothed through knee-deep pig swill. These exercises are known as the MOTT STAKES and the participants are referred to as MOTTS—after a form of bacteria which lives in faeces. After a student has completed the course to the satisfaction of senior students he (or she) is said to have gone through MOTTING.

In his book *Bastards I Have Met* (1972) Barry Crump listed an imposing twenty-six types of bastards that he had met in his wanderings in New Zealand and Australia. The list itself is quite instructive: Actual Bastard, Bad Bastard, Clever Bastard, Dozey Bastard, Enigmatic Bastard, Filthy Bastard, Good

Bastard, Hard-case Bastard, Intellectual Bastard, Jovial Bastard, Kinky Bastard, Lazy Bastard, Miserable Bastard, Nasty Bastard, Officious Bastard, Poor Bastard, Queer Bastard, Rude Bastard, Situational Bastard, Temperamental Bastard, Unlucky Bastard, Vain Bastard, Weak Bastard, Xenial Bastard, Young Bastard, Zealous Bastard.

Observant readers will have noted that in compiling this list, Barry Crump worked his way right through the alphabet from A to Z, so the list is to that extent artificial. However, some of the types described by the author in his tales of bastardry are found in fair numbers both in New Zealand and Australia. The adjectives BAD, CLEVER, FILTHY, LAZY, MISERABLE, OFFICIOUS, POOR, QUEER, UNLUCKY are quite frequently used in descriptions of bastards to be found all over the continent.

Australians take the word so seriously that they have even formed The Antedeluvian Order of Old Bastards, a fairly loosely knit organisation with chapters in all capital cities (and some country towns). The irregular meetings of these chapters seem given over to much liquor consumption and considerable emphasis on stories in the vein of 'Bastards I met recently . . .'. Members carry around in their wallets visiting cards proclaiming they are regular Old Bastards, and some even wear lapel badges advertising this strange piece of information—no doubt to the great astonishment of new arrivals in the country exposed for the first time to one of Australia's more unnerving and bizarre institutions.

In February 1979 there was considerable political upheaval in Canberra when the Minister for Finance, Mr Eric Robinson, resigned from cabinet on the grounds that he could no longer work with THAT BASTARD, meaning the Prime Minister Malcolm Fraser. Mr Robinson four days later withdrew his resignation but not before the press had had a field day on the event during which it was widely recorded that a number of his parliamentary colleagues referred to Mr Fraser as THAT BASTARD. A few weeks later the columnist of the *Sydney Morning Herald* was able to report a new variation on the language as follows:

A possible new entry in the Australian Oxford Dictionary? A Toukley resident went to his corner shop to find the usually cheerful owner in a bad mood. He asked her if anything was the matter. Through clenched teeth she replied: 'I've had a FRASER of a day'.

Chapter Twenty-six

AUSTRALIAN INSULTS

Paul Landa, the NSW Minister for Planning and the Environment, told a University of NSW graduation audience last week that five years ago he had been called a 'commo, poofter, black, dago bastard.' All these things, the minister said, had become socially acceptable. Now, he said, he is being described as a 'leftist, middle-class, trendy academic.'

From the Overflow Column in the **National Times,** 1977

Homo sapiens is certainly the most aggressive animal to inhabit this planet and his pugnacity takes many forms. Where his physical aggression is restricted by social forms, he has to rely on verbal assaults on anyone who earns his displeasure, so that insults form a very substantial proportion of the vernacular of almost all languages.

Australians however, seem to have taken the insult further than most other people to the extent that their everyday language seems to reflect an aggressiveness of an extraordinary high degree. Australians are much given to name-calling, much of it being of a highly offensive nature to those on the receiving end, whilst phrases such as 'May all your chooks (fowls) turn into emus and kick over your dunny', or 'He was as flash as a rat with a gold tooth', or 'Up you for the rent, sport' (an extension of the old-time British 'Up You' insult) go beyond mere inventiveness. They are a new linguistic art form in which Australians seem to excel.

Sidney J Baker in *The Drum* (1959) pointed out that Australians had many strong aversions including BLUDGERS, TOP OFFS, SQUIBS, LAIRS and POOFTERS. Baker however, advanced the novel theory that the main aversion of Australians was noise. Not the traditional high decibel reading noises condemned by environmentalists, but NOISY INDI-VIDUALS. Baker explained his theory this way:

The Australian's sensitivity to aural assaults is amply disclosed in his language. He has little enthusiasm for the EARBASHER, the SKITER and the PUNISHER, he barely tolerates BULL ARTISTS and other purveyors of MEADOW MAYONNAISE, COWYARD CONFETTI and GUYVER, he feels marked distaste for the person who PERFORMS or DOES HIS BLOCK, he has only disapproval for the WHIPPER OF CATS and the WHINGER, but most of all he reserves a deep contempt for the person who BUNGS or STACKS ON AN ACT. To him, the bunging or stacking on of acts is incontrovertible evidence that the personal control which he esteems in all men has been lost.

Examples of the common practice of using insults emerge in the most unexpected places. In the Bundaberg, Queensland, Magistrate's Court in 1977, Stipendiary Magistrate R Tully described a defendant, a young man who appeared before him on a drink-driving charge, as A CLOWN, A CLOT, A RATBAG, A NIT and A DICKHEAD.

The young man appealed against his conviction and in 1978 three judges sitting as the Court of Criminal Appeal in Brisbane dismissed the appeal and said that the Magistrate was not biased in using these expressions, but had merely been expressing an opinion formed on evidence before the court. The judges however, considered that Mr Tully's language was inappropriate for anyone sitting in a judicial capacity.

In a subsequent interview with the press, Mr Tully defended the language he had used and said that he had trained for eight years as a member of Rostrum (a public speaking organisation) where he had been taught to use the language of the people he was talking to. He explained:

If you're talking to a politician you use reserved language and correct English. If you're talking to a mob of hoons you have to get down to their level before they can understand.

One of the most interesting Australian linguistic inventions is the word NONG—meaning: dill-brained, stupid, an ass or oaf.

Sidney Baker did not record it in *The Australian Language*, though he did list it in *The Drum* (1959), noting that it referred to a simpleton or fool.

The *Oxford English Dictionary* suggests it might have had its origin as far back as 1700 when NIGMENOG was an English expression for SILLY FELLOW.

Professor Wilkes, in *A Dictionary of Australian Colloquialisms*, records the nineteenth-century usage of a similar term NING-NANG as being a horse couper's term for a worthless thoroughbred.

Whatever its origins, it does not seem to have had much usage prior to World War II, and the term NONG or NING-NONG is believed to have first gained widespread currency amongst Australian forces serving in New Guinea during the War. After the War it passed, like so many other words of army origin, into general community usage.

The expression gained some publicity in 1953 when a motorist was charged in the Brighton Court in Melbourne with having used unseemly language. Giving evidence for the prosecution, a detective said that the defendant had said to him and to another police officer: 'Why don't you look where you are going, you nongs!'

After some discussion in the court on the meaning of the term NONG, during which the Bench, the prosecuting officer and counsel for the defence disclaimed any knowledge of its origin or meaning, the case was dismissed.

Commenting on the case, Sidney Baker said the word had first been drawn to his attention in 1944 by the noted Australian zoologist Dr A J Marshall who had claimed that the word NONG was the equivalent not only of DILL but also of DROOB, DRIP, DRONGO, DOPE and DUMBELL. According to Baker, Marshall claimed the word was a form of genial criticism, and that its offensiveness was to be measured rather by the susceptibilities of the addressee than by the intent of the speaker.

The insulting term SLOB (meaning a person who is either 'soft' or is stupid or a lout or all three) is certainly not of Australian origin, though it is fairly widely used here. However, in 1974 it gained some official recognition—rare for a derogatory slang word—when the Traffic Accident Research Unit of the NSW Department of Motor Transport conducted an extensive TV and Press advertising campaign designed to reduce drink-driving accidents. The advertisements were focused on a character known as 'The Slob' and in its advertisements the definition of SLOB was: 'a man who drinks six middies or more in an hour and then attempts to drive'.

Many slang words have originated in the armed forces and then been given a new lease of life on Civvy Street—sometimes in their original sense, sometimes with new meanings.

BONKERS is one such word. Of (British) naval origin, Eric Partridge defines one who is BONKERS as being 'slightly drunk, light-headed; naval—hence crazy'.

It is not mentioned by Sidney Baker or by Professor Wilkes,

but I have found it to be in fairly widespread use in recent years, as referring to someone slightly crazy. It is used synonymously with 'around the bend', 'off his cracker', 'mad as a cut snake' and similar expressions. When asked in February 1978 about her future political prospects Senator Susan Ryan (then aged 35) replied:

> The idea of being in the Senate until I'm 65 would drive me bonkers.

In the last century the derogatory term HUNGRY was universally applied to anyone who was mean, or grasping. It was a particular term of abuse for station owners who refused to give food to swagmen (SWAGGIES or SUNDOWNERS). The term could even be applied to the station itself, rather than the owner. Thus Henry Lawson in *Two Sundowners* (1902):

> They came to a notoriously 'hungry' station, where there was a Scottish manager and storekeeper.

An interesting Australian term in widespread use is KNOCKER, meaning a person addicted to fault-finding or disparagement. Australians are highly critical of KNOCKERS, which seems to me to be an act of linguistic self-flagellation since it is rare to meet an Australian who isn't one.

Jack Moses in *Beyond City Gates* (1923) had this to say of the breed:

> The 'knocker' of his home town is, on this line of deduction, a 'knocker' of his Empire; a destroyer of thought, labour and enterprise.

Max Harris in *Australian Civilisation* (1962) commented on KNOCKERS as follows:

> It is said that Australians are 'knockers'; that is, they gain pleasure from seeing superiority in talent, intellect or energy reduced to the scale of average mediocrity.

As Max Harris has noted, STIRRERS are a slightly different breed from KNOCKERS, but they are just as prevalent in the community and to STIR THE POSSUM, meaning to liven things up, to deliberately create a disturbance and MAKING WAVES has long been a favourite Australian pastime.

Sydney businessman and founder of the Australia Party, Mr Gordon Barton, in 1972 disclosed in an interview in the *Sydney Morning Herald* that he had been offered a seat in the Senate if he would 'stop stirring the possum' on the Federal political level.

The term has even been used to describe a Catholic Mission in a Sydney parish. Ruth Park in her *Poor Man's Orange* (1949) used the term in this way:

A mission was like a tonic. It stirred the possum in the people, and for months afterwards they could still feel the enthusiasm.

Another derogatory expression is RUBBISH. To RUBBISH a person or idea in Australia is to disparage or dispose of him (or it) in a contemptuous fashion. Thus David Ireland in *The Industrial Prisoner* (1971):

They rubbished him every chance they got, why should he always go back for more?

A person who is flashily dressed, or dressed in poor taste, is said to be dressed up 'like a pox doctor's clerk'. The former Federal Labor politician Mr Al Grassby and the former South Australian Premier, Mr Don Dunstan are two prominent personalities who have attracted this appellation as a result of dressing rather less conservatively than their fellow Australians.

An article in the *Nation Review* in 1973 said of Mr Dunstan:

Good money was laid among the better class working men that he (Mr Dunstan) would, on this auspicious occasion, come up with an outfit to be the envy of every pox doctor's clerk in the land.

Barry Humphries, hiding behind his Barry McKenzie creation in 1974, delivered this serve:

If Al Grassby wants to convert me or any other clean-living Australians into getting dressed up like Lord Muck and getting round kitted up like a flamin' pox doctor's clerk, old Grazza's going to have his time cut out.

Even the Traditional Christmas spirit is not allowed to dampen the traditional Australian pastime of directing epithets at those activities which arouse the ire of their fellow countrymen. For instance the December 1978 bulletin of the Randwick-Coogee (NSW) Legion Ex-service Club contained the following unseasonal comments:

It would be nice to find the insect, microbe or germ who is pinching the decorations off the Christmas tree on the stairway with a broken leg, arm or (preferably) neck and, after the creep's sojourn in hospital, we would be able to charge it with theft.

In this brief sentence the writer managed to introduce four insulting terms: INSECT, MICROBE, GERM and CREEP, as well as use the slang term PINCH, meaning to steal.

In Australia you may call a man a BASTARD or even a BLOODY BASTARD, and reasonably expect nothing except a return of the compliment. But beware of calling any Australian a BLUDGER. It is the deadliest insult that can be offered in the

Antipodes, and anyone who uses it loosely must be prepared to defend his person from assault from the person to whom it is directed.

The term BLUDGER is of unknown origin but has a long history on our shores. Originally it was used to describe a low grade brothel bully or a prostitute's pimp, but it was taken over by the Australian army in two world wars and its meaning was considerably widened to include anyone not pulling his weight, not doing his fair share of the work, or of living off someone else's exertions.

In the 1970s it was a pejorative term widely used in the community to describe people (usually young) who preferred to take the dole rather than work. The term DOLE BLUDGER became an accepted ritual word, popular with politicians and newspaper editorial writers. Thus the NSW Chief Secretary, Eric Willis MLA in the Legislative Assembly in 1971 said:

> The only people who would benefit from full pay on workers' compensation would be 'genuine loafers, shirkers or bludgers'.

As with most words of this type, the meaning alters with the passage of time. For example Richard Cornish in *The Woman Liluth* (1975) refers to someone having 'bludged some furniture' (meaning begged).

The shorthand version of BLUDGE can be used either as a verb or noun. To avoid paying for something or to live by someone else's exertions is to BLUDGE (v) whilst a job requiring no particular exertion is known as 'a good bludge'. Thus Donald Friend in *Gunner's Diary* (1943):

> I've been three weeks in hospital with measles. Ah—that's not a bad bludge.

Writing in *Darkest Adelaide* (1911), C W Chandler gained no friends in the City of Churches when he proclaimed:

> . . . that bludging has been reduced to a fine art in Adelaide cannot be gainsaid. Here the bludger is an institution . . . There is no need to send missionaries to China or India's coral strand—we have so many Heathens nearer home.

The sensitivity of Australians when called BLUDGERS was illustrated in March 1978 when the Federal Parliament referred to its Parliamentary Privileges Committee for investigation of an editorial in the Melbourne newspaper *Sunday Observer* which under the heading POLITICAL BLUDGERS had said, in part:

> . . . Many of our so-called leaders proved themselves lazy, two-faced

bludgers at the opening of Federal Parliament in Canberra . . . Until now not one newspaper has bothered to point out the outrageous antics of these powder-puff thespians of the Parliamentary stage.

The Privileges Committee subsequently reported that the editorial reflected on members of the House in their capacity as such and therefore constituted a contempt of the House of Representatives.

The Committee reached this decision after taking evidence from Mr P S Isaacson, managing director and editor-in-chief of Peter Isaacson Publications Pty Ltd, owners and publishers of the *Sunday Observer*, and Mr A L Armsden, who was editor of the paper when it published the editorial. The Committee found both men guilty of contempt of the House.

In the case of Mr Isaacson it recommended: 'In view of his expressions of regret made before the committee and his publication of an adequate and acceptable apology, no further action be taken.'

Mr Cameron said: 'In the case of Mr Armsden, the committee recommended that in this particular instance his demeanor and actions were not worthy of further occupying the time of the House. The allegations contained in the editorial were examined by the committee. It was satisfied that they were without foundation.'

Chapter Twenty-seven

WOGS, DOGS, BOGS AND LOGS

To be a true Australian you have to dislike everybody from anywhere else.

Barry Humphries

From the time the First Fleet dropped anchor in Sydney Cove in 1788, the new arrivals considered the original black inhabitants as their natural inferiors and applied derogatory names to express their attitudes.

At first the Aborigines were known as NATIVES or BLACKS but these terms were soon replaced by the more derogatory term NIGGER—a complete misnomer because the Aborigine is not a negro. But the name persisted throughout the nineteenth century and well into this century. As the *Argus* put it in 1891:

The natives of Queensland are nearly always spoken of as 'niggers' by those who are brought most directly in contact with them.

And as black activist Bobbi Sykes put it at a much later date (1973):

A black with money is still only a rich nigger.

In this century the term NIGGER has almost dropped out of currency to be replaced by the equally offensive words ABO and BOONG. When a little more emphasis is considered necessary, the Aborigine will these days invariably be referred to (by whites) as THAT BLACK BASTARD.

In its infamous manifesto of 1887 the *Bulletin* even went so far as to proclaim that Aborigines weren't Australians. The logic of this is hard to understand but the manifesto itself was crystal clear in its intent:

No nigger, no Chinaman, no lascar, no kanaka, no purveyor of cheap coloured labour, is an Australian.

In parts of Australia things haven't changed all that much in the past couple of centuries, at least so far as name-calling is concerned. Writing in *Nation Review* in 1977, Julianne Schultz reported as follows a visit to a certain hotel (which she named) in an outback Queensland country town:

> . . . the publican (whom she also named) was talking to his assembled cronies. 'Guess who's in town,' he roared, 'Idi Amin and two smartarse solicitors from Brisbane. What do you mean who's Idi Amin, Sugar Ray Robinson of course. Those smartarses are going to come and visit me. Well, they might be able to force me to serve the boongs, but there's no saying how much I'll charge. I'll charge the coons ten bucks a bloody beer if they want to drink here and then they won't come back. You guys all want another drink—on me.'

For those who want to avoid such racist tags, there is a difficulty in arriving at an acceptable name when referring to Aborigines. When John Ducker, the Secretary of the NSW Labour Council, referred to Aborigines as 'blacks' at a meeting of the Council in 1978 he was immediately challenged by Joe Poole, organiser of the Australian Railways Union who objected to the term and suggested that the Secretary should refer to Aborigines as 'coloured people'.

The report of the meeting noted that:

> Mr Ducker replied that he had once spoken with a leader of the Northern Land Council on the matter.
> 'I asked him what term he preferred—Aboriginals, first Australians, coloured people, blacks or whatever.
> He asked me: 'What colour is my skin?'
> I replied: 'Black.'
> He said: 'Then that's what you should call us.'
> 'I will not apologise for calling blacks what they call themselves,' Mr Ducker concluded, before embarking on a discourse on manufacturing industry.

Racial prejudice turns up in the most unexpected places, even in commercial reports. A report on the sugar yield at Bundaberg, Queensland, in 1890 contained this fascinating paragraph:

> The First White is a clear, dry, beautifully grained sugar; the Second White, though not so clear, is quite dry and would rate in the highest class; the First Yellow is dry, well granulated and apparently as perfect as such sugar can be made; the Second Yellow is a very excellent sugar for domestic purposes, far removed from the Dark Brown, or 'Ration sugar'. (suitable for Kanakas)

Sometimes a product with a name which can have an alternate meaning can be on the market for long periods without any comment, until some controversy throws its undesirable word associations into the spotlight.

One such product is an organic meat and bone mixture which for many, many years was marketed by a Sydney firm under the curious name of 'Abo Fertilizer'. The symbol used to promote the product was a boomerang!

The product escaped the attention of black power militants until 1976 when a complaint that the name was racist was lodged with the Commissioner for Community Relations, Mr Al Grassby. Mr Grassby said he would investigate the complaint, adding:

> It has been around a long time, but I suppose it would be just as noxious to Aboriginal people as Dago or Pom Fertilizer would be to other groups.

When a newspaper columnist contacted the manufacturers of the product he was told that the word ABO did not refer to Aborigines at all, it stood for the company slogan ALWAYS BUY OURS. When asked why the boomerang symbol was used with the product, a company spokesman said: 'A boomerang is our symbol—it's very Australian.'

No doubt the publicity inspired the manufacturers to question the wisdom of continuing to use such a name, but other products with equally dubious name associations still remain on the market. For instance, every time I go into a supermarket I am confronted with COON cheese. How long would that product last on the market in other parts of the world—say England—where the term COON is a very derogatory one indeed?

The word COON is not extensively used in Australia, at least not by white Australians. It is however, sometimes used by Aborigines to describe other Aborigines of whom they disapprove.

A few years ago a white friend of mine was discussing with an Aboriginal acquaintance named Fred, a forthcoming social event involving a large gathering of Aborigines from various parts of the state. Fred, who was one of the organisers of the event, expressed concern at the likely behaviour of some known trouble-makers, and gloomily observed: 'There will be a lot of COONS there, you know.'

Somewhat surprised by the use of the word, my friend commented: 'You mean a lot of BLACKS are coming?'

The irony was lost on Fred, who replied. 'Yes, there will be a lot of blacks, but there will be an awful lot of coons, too.'

Racial bigotry probably reached its zenith in Australia in the last half of the nineteenth century, and the target comprised members of one race, the Chinese, who flocked into the country in their tens of thousands in the wake of the gold rushes. Because they were so different from the other (white) settlers they attracted the attentions and suspicions of the community as no other minority group has before or since.

The Chinese were branded as CHOWS, CHINKS, PADDIES, OPIUM SMOKERS, SLIT-EYES, QUANGS and just YELLOW BASTARDS.

For some reason the Chinese took particular exception to the nickname PADDY. J Inglis in *Our Australian Cousins* (1879) records:

> Their (the Chinese) usually placid temper seems to be ruffled when the boys take to calling them Irishmen. What there is between Pat and John which calls forth such manifestations I know not, but a Chinaman here is mortally insulted when you call him Paddy.

Englishmen have long been called POMMIES (or the shortened version POMS) by Australians, to the very considerable irritation of those on the receiving end of this name-calling. In some cases the term is used without malice: 'He's not a bad bastard for a POM'; but on other occasions it is directed in a distinctly derogative manner: 'He's a right proper POMMIE bastard, he is'.

The origin of the term is in much dispute, the two favoured versions being:

(a) That the term POM or POMÈ had its origin in the convict era, P.O.M.E. being the initials of PRISONER OF MOTHER ENGLAND. Supporters of this theory cite the fact that the letters were carved on the walls of Port Arthur gaol in the 1830s.

(b) That the term POM or POMMY is a contraction of POMEGRANATE, the theory being that Englishmen were so named because their rosy cheeks resembled this typical English fruit.

In 1978 the South Australian Attorney General, Mr Duncan, took the insult a stage further when he described the visiting English morals campaigner, Mrs Mary Whitehouse, a NOTORIOUS POM. Had the Attorney General described the good lady as a POM it probably would have passed unnoted, but his addition of the word 'notorious' caused considerable controversy and prompted the *Australian* to pen an editorial entitled 'A Stinkardly Insult' in which is pointed out that it is insulting to call a person 'notorious'. The editorial cited the case of Ben Jonson who called someone 'a notoriously, stinkardly bearward'—a bearward being a person who publicly exhibits bears. The editorial then went on to pose these interesting questions:

> . . . did Mr Duncan mean she was worse because she was notoriously English? Would he find her less offensive if she were notoriously Australian? Would she be even better if she were notoriously South Australian? Mr Duncan (presumably of Scottish descent) treads a tortuous semantic path.

POM (or POMMY) is still the most common word which Australians use to describe Englishmen. Usually without malice, but there is certainly nothing friendly in another (increasingly) common expression directed at Englishmen—a KIPPER. Michael Saclier, from the Research School of Social Sciences at the Australian National University in 1973 explained the term thus:

> . . . the term KIPPER (instead of Poms). . . is used by many Australians and is self-explanatory. For the less observant, it derives from the statistically proven similarity between the Englishman and his favourite breakfast food—both are spineless, two-faced and smell.

Of course the Poms don't always take these aspersions without challenge. Sometimes they hit back with some effect, as English journalist Jean Rook did in 1977 when she wrote of Mr Ian Sinclair, the Federal Minister for Primary Production:

> Mr Sinclair's attitude to the Pom is typical of his nation—thin-skinned, green as a gum tree with jealousy, and bloody-jawed as a Botany Bay shark if roused.

Of course, the Aborigines, the Chinese and the English haven't been the only victims of Australian racial name-calling. Every migrant minority has had to suffer tags of unpleasant nicknames with perhaps the large Italian community being singled out for the most offensive—DAGO, WOP and EYETIE.

Donald Horne in 1971 summed up the whole sorry story this way:

> . . . the . . . bigoted history of Australian immigration policy, in which at first convicts hated free settlers, and then Aussie workmen hated Pommy bastards who might pinch their jobs and then everybody hated Wops, Frogs, Huns, Chows, Japs and anybody else for whom they could think of as a one syllable name.

Public figures have learned to be careful in utterances on race, being well aware that indiscreet expressions can blow up in their face if reported in the press. A double standard therefore exists under which political figures mouth platitudes that offend no one in public, but privately give vent to racial utterances of the most appalling nature.

Very few are prepared to say in public what they say around the bar with their mates. One such individual was the late Sir William Yeo, one time President of the RSL in New South Wales. Sir William was a blunt, outspoken individual who did not give a damn whom he offended. When, at an RSL conference in the 1960s, he publicly expressed the view that all foreigners, and particularly those of Eastern or Middle Eastern extraction, were 'wogs, dogs, bogs or logs' there was a clamour from other delegates to dissociate themselves from these (publicly) damaging views. It wasn't that the other delegates necessarily disagreed with Sir William's viewpoint; it was simply that they were terribly upset by their utterance with the press present. In their eyes Sir William had committed an unforgivable gaffe by saying in public what most of them thought privately.

The practice of name-calling on a racial basis is not unknown in the parliaments of the land. In the House of Representatives in 1975 Dr R T Gun (Labor) addressed Mr J W Bourchier (Liberal) as follows: 'Why don't you shut up, you great poofter?'

Whereupon Mr Bouchier replied: 'Come around here, you little Wop, and I will fix you up.'

In 1977 the advertising agency for Thai International, the Thai airline, took advantage of some less desirable Australian traits to promote the airline. An advertisement which they ran in the Singapore edition of the *Straits Times* featured a photo of a singlet-clad Australian with a large (and typical) beer gut, cigarette in mouth, flinging food into a frypan and surrounded by tomato sauce and other distinctly Australian condiments. The text under the photo read:

Get into it, They came from Europe to begin a new life. The Dagos, the Balts, the Wops.

And they brought with them a love of fine food that would do little to change the Australian's love of the meat pie. If you go to Sydney you'll see they're still wallowing in the tide of tomato sauce. If you love fine food—give yourself a fair go. Give Australia a miss and get into it on Thai International. And if your flight can't avoid a stop in Australia— stop on board. Thai International. Twice a week into Sydney: And out of it—fast.

The racist attitudes of many Australians are one of our less desirable exports. In an article in *Nation Review* in 1978 Merv Rutherford and Tom Kelly related some of their experiences on a recently concluded trip to northern Sumatra. Arriving at a place called Samasir, they were met by a local youth aged about 17 who enquired whether they were Australians. When they said yes, he responded with: 'Beauty bottler mate, no bloody worries cobber, good munga here, mate'.

He said he had picked up his particular brand of English from previous Australian visitors. And to demonstrate his versatility in the language of Oz, he hailed two attractive local girls who just then walked past. The young guide challenged them: 'Hey, you spunky, you wanna good man?' When the girls kept on walking, he yelled: 'Hey you chow wog, what are you? Don't you speak English, or what?'

Chapter Twenty-eight

WOT'S IN A NAME?

'Wot's in a name?' she sez . . . An' then she sighs
An' clasps 'er little 'ands, an' rolls 'er eyes.
'A rose,' she sez, 'be any other name
Would smell the same
Oh, w'erefore art you Romeo, young sir?
Chuck yer ole pot, an' change yer moniker!'

The Sentimental Bloke By C J Dennis

Australians certainly didn't invent the practice of applying nicknames to individuals. Through the centuries tall men have had to bear up under the nickname of LOFTY (or its foreign language equivalent), men of short stature have been labelled SHORTY or TOM THUMB, whilst the red-headed lads automatically have attracted the nickname of CARROTS or BLUEY. However, in Australia nicknames have been taken far beyond the limits found in other lands, and it would seem that the average Australian has a perfect mania for applying a tag or nickname to every object around him, both living and inanimate.

Quite early in the Colonial period the inhabitants of the various states were assigned collective nicknames, some of which persist today.

QUEENSLANDERS are Banana-landers or Banana-benders.

NEW SOUTH WELSHMEN were Cornstalks (though in an earlier period this was a term applied to all young Colonial men and women).

VICTORIANS were known as Cabbage-patchers (believed to be derived from the small size of the state rather than for any propensity for growing these vegetables).

SOUTH AUSTRALIANS were invariably known as Crow-eaters (taken from the Piping Shrike featured in their coat of arms). Also known as Pie-eater.

WESTERN AUSTRALIANS are Sand-gropers (they in term derisively call the inhabitants of all other states 'Easterners').

TASMANIANS invariably are known as Islanders or Taswegians. Tasmanians retaliate calling the residents of other states the MAINLANDERS.

In 1974 the *Bulletin* turned up an interesting example of some extreme local Tasmanian xenophobia from the little resort of Bruny Island, some 6½ kilometres from Hobart. The *Bulletin* recorded that when one of the staff of the Tasmanian Opposition Leader, Max Bingham, visited Bruny Island, he was stopped by a suspicious local who asked him: 'Are you a *mainlander?*'

And by that he didn't mean someone from across the Bass Strait. To the enquirer, a MAINLANDER was someone all the way from Hobart!

Australians have the habit of handing out nicknames to fit personal characteristics. Some examples:

BROWN SUGAR (because he's coarse and unrefined).

MIRROR (A name given to an executive much given to procrastination and saying 'I'll look into this').

THE ALL-NIGHT CHEMIST (A talkative individual so named because he 'never shuts up').

HURRICANE LAMP ('He's not too bright').

FLICKERING CANDLE ('Who is even dimmer than Hurricane Lamp').

BILIOUS BILL (A union representative so named because when confronted with a complaint invariably replied: 'I'll bring it up at the next meeting').

THE BARRISTER (A man who is always at the bar).

DANDRUFF (Who was so weak he allowed himself to get the brush-off wherever he went).

THE RIFLEMAN (Who was always 'shooting through' when there was work to be done).

RUST (A perpetual cadger of lifts, so named because he would get into everybody's car).

HYDRAULIC LIFT (name given to a light-fingered gent who would 'lift' (steal) anything).

Some of these nicknames are devastatingly accurate. I once knew a Police Superintendent who throughout his working life carried the embarrassing nickname of CRIME ('Because crime doesn't pay'). The nickname had been assigned to him by his fellow officers in his early days on the force because of his excessive free-loading habits and, as he never ceased cadging, the nickname followed him from posting to posting throughout his long career.

In *Australia Speaks* Sidney Baker quoted an anonymous verse in circulation around the turn of the century which managed to include seventeen Australian nicknames (mostly abusive) in its six short lines:

> *Wowsers, whingers, ratbags, narks,*
> *Silvertails, galahs and sharks,*
> *Knockers, larrikins, and chromos,*
> *Bengal Lancers, bludgers, homos,*
> *Botts and polers, spielers, lairs,*
> *Advance Australia—you are theirs!*

Bill Scott in the *Complete Book of Australian Folklore* mentions the following nicknames he has met in his travels: Dungy, Bottler, Battler, Sinbad (from his habit of exaggeration), The Parrot, Walkie-talkie, Fish, Aspro, Big Red Mick and Little Red Mick, Onions, The Moaner, Knocker, Dusty (Miller, of course), Stuffer, Dingy (Bell), Bendy, Old Ek-ek (from the noise he made when he laughed), Zombie, Punchy, Slug, Emu-head, Hooky, Val Egg, and The Bony Herring.

He also quotes from Stan Boyd's *Notebook* a partial list of names current around the Coen and Cooktown areas of Queensland in the period 1873–1896. These include: Dick the Needle, Tom the Thread, Billy the Whip, Four-ton Jack, Billy the Pup, Dick the Dog, The Jumper, The Maggot, Lovely Les, Billy the Bludger, Pretty Boy, Twenty Foot, Wednesday Bob, Blue Bob the Bastard, Paddy the Fenian, Dick the Devil, the Great Australian Bite, The Nip, The Strangler, The Burner Off, Red Ned, Mick the Rager, The Sand Groper. Twenty-five to Six, Legs Eleven, The Blue Tongue, The Human Bat, Toothbrush.

The bullock drivers of the outback not only gave their animals nicknames, but they also appended names to their wagons. Edward S Sorenson in *Life in the Australian Backblocks* (1911) wrote of the practice as follows:

> The bullocky takes as much pride in his wagon as a captain does in his ship, and, like the ship, the wagon is always she . . . Each wagon bears a name fancifully painted on the sides. Some I have met with are: Margaret Catchpole, Gipsy Queen, Currency Lass, The Never Get Stuck, Dancing Girl, Sarah Bernhardt, Rose of Beauty, Flirt, Marie Corelli, Mary Ah Foo, and The Eulo Queen. There are Freetraders, Protectionists, Democrats, Republicans, and Home Rules wheeling about in dozens; also Wombats, Wallabys, Brumbys, and other animals.

One happens upon peculiarities at times in bullock nomenclature. One teamster called his pets Villain, Rascal, Vagabond, Scoundrel, Demon, Vampire, Monster, etc; and another's team was named after prominent politicians, with Barton and Kingston in the pole and Reid and Lyne in the lead.

Joseph Furphy ('Tom Collins') in his *Such is Life* illustrates the problem that confronts writers in trying to make sense of Australian idiom:

At the Blowhard Sand-hill, on the night of the 10th, I camped with a party of six sons of Belial, bound for Deniliquin, with 3,000 Boolka wethers off the shears. Now, anyone who has listened for four hours to the conversation of a group of sheep drovers, named, respectively, Splodger, Rabbit, Parson, Bottler, Dingo, and Hairy-toothed Ike, will agree with me as to the impossibility of getting the dialogue of such dramatis personae into anything like printable form. The bullock drivers were bad enough, but these fellows are out of the question.

Members of the clergy have not been exempted from the old Australian tradition of bestowing nicknames on individuals at the drop of a hat. Arnold Haskell recorded the following amusing incident to indicate that even bishops were not considered immune:

In a country hotel in Queensland the vicar was lunching with his bishop who was undertaking a pastoral tour. The waitress approaches and turns to the vicar, 'What will you have, Les?' The bishop raises his eyebrows mildly, surprised at the familiarity; but it is his turn now. With a beam she says, 'And what will little Robin Redbreast have?'

Even the Almighty hasn't escaped the attention of the '*names*' in our midst as HUGHIE has long been the name assigned to God in the outback, especially when it rains. There are some interesting examples of this usage in Australian literature:

The clouds burst. 'Send her down, Huey!' cried the man in the wheelchair, raising clenched fists and flinging back his head.
Osmar White in *Under the Iron Rainbow* (1969)

Miners and prospectors would turn out and yell to a dull, dirty sky clouded with red dust: 'Send her down! Send her down, Hughie!'
K S Prichard in *The Roaring Nineties* (1946)

'All you want to do is get married and have kids,' he said. 'Don't worry about the money. Hughie looks after that, my boy.' The Corporal was diverted. 'Who's this Hughie?' he said . . . 'Ah,' Gell said, affecting a gravity which was not altogether false. 'You don't say "God", you see, because nobody believes in God but everybody believes in Hughie. I dunno—it's just a thing you hear the boys say.'
Seaforth MacKenzie in *Dead Men Rising* (1951)

Even my own home town of Dubbo has not escaped the attention of the nation's nicknamers. In Sydney these days a person (particularly if from the country) who is a bit dense or otherwise considered objectionable is branded a DUBBO. ('He's a right old DUBBO is that one.') The term, in Sydney at least, appears to have replaced the former derogatory expressions of BUSHWACKER, COUNTRY BUMPKIN or HAYSEED.

The Australian propensity for using nicknames can cause confusion in many areas, not least the Police Courts where interpreters of colloquialisms would seem essential if we are to judge by the following 1971 transcript of a case involving bikies:

Question: Who was in what car?

Answer: I was in the GT with Snot, Scurvy, Goliath and Tramp.

Q: And who was in the other car?

A: Dingo, Doggy, Dirty, Doug and Glug.

Q: You have told us you left with a number of firearms, including a sawn-off shotgun, a pistol and several rifles. What was the purpose of going to the house?

A: To say 'Hi'.

A commuter train which travels from the Blue Mountains to Sydney in the mornings, returning in the evenings, has long been known as THE FISH (legend has it that one of the early drivers of the train was named Fysh). Perhaps inevitably, a slightly later train catering for shoppers has long been known as THE CHIPS.

Perhaps not so many Sydneysiders are aware that the silver commuter train which runs from the Central Coast to Sydney is known as the '80-wheeler'. This piece of linguistic information came to light in 1978 when Sergeant K J Ferguson, Vice President of the NSW Police Association, told the annual conference of the Association that the 'threat of the 80-wheeler' was held over the heads of policemen working in the Central Coast area if they did not toe the line laid down by their immediate superiors' Sergeant Ferguson explained that policemen who lived on the Central Coast wanted to work at local stations, not be forced to commute into the city for work. He said one patrolman who had booked a friend of the local inspector had been forcefully reminded that if he continued such indiscretions involving friends of the Inspector, then he 'would be facing the 80-wheeler'—meaning that he would be transferred to a city station.

New slang words and expressions at times originate and gain acceptance in unusual circumstances. For instance in 1978 graffiti reading RALPH THE BONG started to appear on walls around Sydney. Intrigued by this, the columnist of the *Sydney Morning Herald* sought an explanation from readers, and this was quickly forthcoming.

The columnist learned that a BONG was, in Chinese terms, a hideously unlucky dragon. A BONG is also a bolt used in rock climbing, but the graffiti on Sydney walls had nothing to do with either meaning of the word.

The *Herald* columnist was assured that the word had originated at the North Sydney school Shore, where for some time it had been applied to anyone with low mental ability. Early in 1978 someone applied the term to a student named Ralph and expressed the opinion in graffiti on a school wall. The phrase was quickly picked up and RALPH THE BONG spread far beyond the walls of the school to become a slang term as well as a piece of apparently meaningless graffiti.

This claim however, did not go unchallenged. The ink was hardly dry on the newspaper reporting it before four sixth form students from Barker College (another Sydney boys' college) descended on the editor to claim that RALPH THE BONG has originated at *their* school (not Shore) and that to them a BONG was a pipe for smoking marijuana.

'Garbo' is an Australian invention to describe a garbage collector and a very expressive word it is too. At Christmas time each year the garbage collectors and their compatriots under arms, the ever-dwindling race of night-soil collectors, burst into poetic fervor and leave Christmas cards and leaflets in household letterboxes around the nation. (Hoping of course that the following week the householders will remember them with a tip or a few cans of beer.)

In the *Complete Book of Australian Folklore* (1976) Bill Scott revealed that for some years he had been collecting the pieces of quaint Christmas verse from the Dunnymen and the Garbologists of the nation, and he reproduced a few samples from the period 1967–1972 in his book. The authors of these terrible pieces of doggerel from the 'wanderers of the day' and the 'pilgrims of the night', as Bill Scott described them, are not above using euphemisms when describing their own daily activities, and the cards illustrated in the book were signed variously by 'Your Sanno Man', 'Your Cleansing Man', 'Your Sanitary Man' (a lack of imagination here), 'The Rovers of the Day' and 'Your Garbologist Man'. None of the cards illustrated used the good old term GARBO which the rest of us use when describing our local garbage collector. Evidently the GARBOS aren't all that keen on their own nickname.

Politicians of course have always been fair game when it

comes to nicknames, and the longer they are in office the more names they tend to accumulate.

The doyen of Australian politicians, the late Sir Robert Menzies perhaps collected the two longest-lasting sobriquets: PIG IRON BOB and MING THE MERCILESS.

The first he acquired in the years immediately prior to World War II when he authorised shipments of scrap iron to Japan in defiance of waterside workers' bans and general public disapproval. The name PIG IRON BOB was hurled at him so often at political rallies over the years that it almost became a term of affection in the end. His other nickname MING THE MERCILESS was not so kindly meant, and referred to his alleged ruthless methods of dealing with critics within his own party. But, in the end, even MING was a term lacking in approbation. In 1969, a letter writer in the *Sydney Morning Herald* referred to the wrangling and bickering then taking place within the Federal Liberal party and uttered this cry:

I sigh for the days of old Ming, that great White Father, who promised us nothing and made sure we got it.

The Queensland Premier Joh Bjelke-Petersen gained the nickname THE FLYING PEANUT because (a) he was a peanut farmer and (b) he used a state-owned aeroplane to make extensive outback tours of Queensland.

Senator Margaret Guilfoyle quickly earned a reputation for toughness when she was appointed Minister for Social Security in the Fraser Government formed after the 1975 Federal election. And just as quickly, in typical Australian fashion, she picked up the two unenviable nicknames of ATTILA THE HEN and THE IRON BUTTERFLY.

When the tough-minded Senator Reg Withers was dismissed from office as Minister for Administrative Services in 1978, following an adverse finding on him by a Royal Commission headed by Mr Justice McGregor, it was revealed that the Senator's nickname in Parliamentary circles had for some time been THE TOECUTTER. It was further revealed that his press secretary, Mr Russell Schneider, also had a reputation for toughness around Parliament and that the pair often were referred to as TOECUTTER AND SON. The nickname derived from a group of Melbourne criminals who in the 1970s gained this gruesome title because of their unpleasant habit of using bolt cutters to amputate the toes of rival gangsters, or members of the gang with whom they had had a falling-out.

In February 1978 when the well-known cartoonist Larry Pickering introduced a new cartoon series 'The Ishbondogla

Gang of Narrabundah Low' (school) in the *Weekend Australian* newspaper the very first thing that he did was to assign nicknames to his various characters: FOUR-EYES (Malcolm Fraser), TITCH (Tony Street), SWOTTO (Bill Hayden), CHOOK (Gough Whitlam), PIGGY (Phillip Lynch), NICKERS (Margaret Guilfoyle), EYEBROWS (Bob Hawke), THE MASCOT (Sir William McMahon), FEATHERS (Andrew Peacock), BUBBA (John Howard), BIG AL (Al Grassby), SNOWY (Sir John Kerr), GAWKS (Doug Anthony), STINKER (Jim Killen), HARPIC (Joh Bjelke-Petersen).

Nor did the *Weekend Australian* consider it necessary to append a glossary to the new cartoon series. Although the nicknames assigned to the characters by Pickering were not nicknames usually associated with the various political figures, the newspaper must have considered that its readers would quickly adapt to the wordy appendages supplied by their cartoonist.

Not all Australians appreciate being given a nickname, particularly if it is derogatory. In March 1978, Robert Haupt wrote an article for the *Australian Financial Review*: 'The Battle for Beekman Place', in which he claimed that the Australian Consul-General in New York, Mr Peter Barbour, former head of ASIO, was known around the Consulate as THE SPOOK.

This brought an immediate response from members of the Consulate Staff in New York, twenty-nine of whom signed a letter branding as blatantly untrue the claim that Mr Barbour was known as THE SPOOK. The letter went on:

We all know Australians are not slow to award nicknames, particularly to superiors, but the Consul-General has acquired no nickname of any kind.

Many Australians would consider that any executive who did *not* acquire a nickname must be a distinctly colourless individual, so perhaps the letter in defence of the Consul-General was really a backhanded compliment!

In 1976 an Adelaide citizen named Colin Herring took an action which most Australians would regard as extreme when he changed his name to Sub-Paragraph Three. In a letter to an Adelaide newspaper in 1977 he explained the reason for this unusual action as follows:

I changed my name from Colin Bede Herring to Sub-Paragraph Three on September 1, last year, at the South Australian bureau of births, deaths and marriages.

Sub-Paragraph Three has stuck in my mind since I left the taxation office. It was a paragraph that referred to all taxation officers.

Sub-Paragraph Three, and I just can't remember what Section, read: 'All officers are reminded that they are not permitted to place their banana skins and/or Coke cans in the waste paper bins provided, for they are for the paper shredding machine only.'

When I have a child it will be called Sub-Paragraph Four, if it is a boy, or if it is a girl I will call her Sub-Paragraph Three, Sub-Section One.

Chapter Twenty-nine

WOWSERS

It would be hard to exaggerate the traditional importance
of 'wowsers' in Australia or, more generally, of the strong
Australian urge to restrict the activities of other people.

Donald Horne **The Lucky Country,** 1964

If there is one really original Australian insult it must surely be
the word WOWSER, a term of abuse that has been used for
almost a century to attack those who in other parts of the world
would be described as KILLJOYS, COMSTOCKS or
PURITANS.

John Norton, the founder of the muck-raking newspaper
Truth claimed to have invented the word. He first used it as a
headline in *Truth* on 8 October 1899 and it has been claimed that
he made it up from the initials of one of his slogans: WE ONLY
WANT SOCIAL EVILS RIGHTED.

However, in later years Norton gave conflicting evidence on
the origin of the word. On one occasion he claimed that he had
invented it at a meeting of the Sydney City Council, of which
Norton was an alderman, when another alderman who stut-
tered badly was trying to pronounce a word beginning with 'W'.
In this version, Norton shouted, mockingly, 'Wow! Wow! Wow!
—you're nothing but an old Wowser!'

Yet another version has it that it came into being in the 1870s
in Clunes (Victoria) where hot-gospellers became known as
'Rousers'. This version has it that a member of the Town
Council, who had difficulty pronouncing his rs had referred at a
public meeting to 'Wowsers'—and the name stuck.

Whatever its origin, once it came into being, John Norton
seized upon it and used it with considerable effect, to discredit
his political and religious opponents.

In the Sydney City Council in 1899 he referred to a fellow alderman as:

... the white, woolly, weary, watery, word-wasting wowser from Waverley.

When asked to define the term, Norton once replied:

Everyone knows right well what the word Wowser really means ... a single, simple word that does at once describe, deride, and denounce that numerous, noxious, pestilent, puritanical kill-joy push—the whole blasphemous, wire-whiskered brood.

On another occasion Norton gave the following definition of the word:

Everyone knows right well what the word Wowser really means and what a Wowser is. Even among sectarian savages and smellful saints of the dirty dickeys, soiled shirts, stale singlets, and stinking socks, the real meaning of the word Wowser is as well known as the meanings of such Words and phrases as larrikin and hooligan, bludger and wop, Johnny Woodser, Johnny Warder, Dicken, 'I don't think' and 'I should smile'.

There have been various attempts to define the word WOWSER, amongst them the following:

William Holman MLA, (1910):
A wowser ... is a man who, being entirely destitute of the greater virtues, makes up for their lack by a continuous denunciation of little vices.

John Scaddan, Premier of WA (1912):
A wowser is ... a person who is more shocked at seeing two inches of underskirt than he would be at seeing a mountain of misery.

Randolph Bedford MLA:
Australia has a word for the Anthony Comstocks, a word that should be used the world over to describe a killjoy, and that word is WOWSER.

Eugene Gorman QC (1960):
Wowser is a simple, satisfying, succinct, single word which aptly distinguishes the whole race of windy, watery, cantankerous, snuffling Chadbands, Stigginses, Holy Joes and Scripture-spouting sneaks, hypocritical humbugs, and unctuous, dirty-minded rotters, who spend their time interfering with the healthy instincts and recreations of healthy-minded, honest humanity.

The Sydney *Daily Telegraph*, in a 1937 editorial, even went so far as to express the opinion that:

... If Australia had given nothing more to civilization than that magnificent label for one of its most melancholy products—the word WOWSER—it would not have been discovered in vain.

There are even different types of wowsers, based on religious orientation, as Donald Horne noted in *The Lucky Country* (1964):

Catholic 'wowsers' were less likely to inveigh against drinking and gambling than Protestant 'wowsers' but they led the field in inveighing against any except a particular use of sex.

The term is known well beyond the borders of Australia. When the Canadian Prime Minister, Pierre Trudeau visited Australia in 1970 he commented:

You have wowserism; we have Toronto. You have Poseidon; we have inflation.

OCKERS AND OCKERINAS

An ocker is a mythical Australian creature like a unicorn or a bunyip. The only person who has ever seen one is Mr Max Harris every time he shaves.

Barry Humphries, 1977

It is perhaps only poetic justice that Australians, who have for so long been so busy appending names to everybody else, should collectively have been branded with the unflattering term OCKER.

The word OCKER has been around a long time as a nickname for OSCAR, but it acquired new meaning in the 1970s when it was used to describe the uncultivated, rough raw Australian male in much the same way that the English describe oafish individuals as ALFS.

The experts have had some trouble with both the origin and meaning of the term OCKER. The editor of the *Australian Pocket Oxford Dictionary*, Professor Grahame Johnston admitted in a 1976 interview that he had had six letters suggesting different etymologies of the word, one of them going back to the Middle Ages. The dictionary finally came up with the following fairly cautious definition:

OCKER. Boorish person; person who is aggressively Australian in speech and behaviour, often for humorous effect. (Orig. Uncertain; perh. orig. a nickname for persons with such surnames as O'Connell and O'Connor, or alt of Oscar).

Despite its origins, it seems that its current popularity is due almost entirely to the portrayal in the early 1970s on Australian TV by comedian Ron Frazer of a character name Ocker.

Professor Wilkes in *A Dictionary of Australian Colloquialism* records the first use of the term in print in 1971 when it cropped up in George Johnston's *A Cartload of Clay*:

The big man would be a good player, a vigorous clubman, a hearty participant in the companionship of the club bar. He was a type Julian had sometimes talked to him about, what the boy called an 'Ocker'.

Professor Wilkes notes use of the term in the august pages of the *Sydney Morning Herald* in April 1974:

That image, of the RSL itself as a sabre-rattling elitist organisation with an over-privileged influence on governments, and of RSL members themselves as beer-swilling, 'pokey-playing' Ockers, has, executives believe, faded if not totally evaporated.

Other examples quoted by Professor Wilkes include:

Peter Porter (1974): The new Australian boorishness is known as Ockerism, from a slob-like character called Ocker in a television series —the embodiment of oafish, blinkered self-satisfaction.

Ron Frazer (1975): Back in the Ocker days, guys would come up to me in their thongs and shorts and with a can in their hand and say, 'Y'know, mate, I know a guy just like that Ocker character'.

Max Harris (1975): The resurgence of an aggressive Australian ockerdom was coincident with the first election of the Whitlam Government and the discovery of a 'new nationalism'.

The excessive use of adjectives is not confined to verbal communication in Australia. It tends to spill over into the written word. In 1978 the Letters Editor of the *Sydney Morning Herald* was moved to complain that excessive amounts of 'Ockerism' popped up in letters from correspondents, making them boring and repetitive. He commented:

Too many letters are full of rip-offs, hassles, whingers, bludgers, fair-goes and fair cracks of the whip.
It is not so much that they are unintelligent but rather that they do not make for very interesting reading.
Ears are assaulted every day by such expressions. We want the Letters columns to provide a relief for the eyes.

The *Sydney Morning Herald* Column 8 in 1976 recorded an unusual example of alliteration reported by a Sydney man who approached an airline booking clerk in Albury seeking a seat on the plane to Sydney, only to be informed: 'Sorry, Ocker, the Fokker's chocka.'

Not everyone dislikes OCKERS; it seems that some even seek them out. In 1978 the proprietors of the sex magazines *Ribald* and *Bawdy* needed extra staff. They took large display advertisements in several daily newspapers which outlined the types of jobs vacant and then went on to note some special qualifications which applicants needed, including:

> . . . we want good honest 'Ockers' for these positions, no drunkards, 'fairy princesses', tantrum throwers or wowsers.

In 1975 a new dimension was added to the word when a schoolgirl, Sandra Mackey, in a Sydney radio quiz was asked to define the word OCARINA (a small musical instrument). She brought the house down (and created a new Australian word) when she defined Ocarina as a 'female Australian'.

The new word (spelt OCKERINA) was soon taken up and gained wide currency. On 27 July 1975 the Sydney *Sunday Telegraph* was able to comment report on a new-found species as follows:

> Ockerina of the week was surely the woman on the Eastern Suburbs bus, studying a race guide while slurping down a meat pie.

Chapter Thirty-one

BAZZA McKENZIE

The image of Australians in the minds of many Englishmen may well be more influenced by a satire like **The Wonderful World of Barry McKenzie** than by the activities of Australia House.

Richard Woolcott,
Department of Foreign Affairs, 1972

If any single individual is to be blamed for exposing the Ocker image to the wide, wide world it is the brilliant satirist Barry Humphries.

The Ocker was there, of course, long before Barry Humphries came on the scene. But Humphries took him, lovingly shaped him in a marketable form and presented him to the world in the form of Barry ('Bazza') McKenzie, the ultimate send-up of the bronzed Oz.

The Adventures of Barry McKenzie initially appeared in comic strip form in the English satirical magazine *Private Eye* in the 1960s and attained such a cult following that he eventually appeared in a book, although for a time Australian censorship laws kept the character out of his native land. Eventually it attained the ultimate accolade of being made into two quite terrible films which were in such deplorable taste that naturally they made a lot of money.

Bazza McKenzie was the eternal innocent being ripped off in London by greedy Poms, and at the same time the uncouth beer-swilling, chundering colonial. He was a smash hit in England because he fitted to perfection the average Englishman's image of an average Australian. He even succeeded in attracting a wide following in Australia, where the populace squirmed uneasily as they recognised the basic truthfulness of this awful character, but seemed hypnotised by the brilliance of the portrayal.

Not the least of Humphries' considerable achievements with the creation of the McKenzie character was the way he manipulated the English language. Indeed, there have been few men who have been able to change the idiom of a country to the extent that Humphries has through the character of Bazza McKenzie, whose vocabulary was both extensive and unusual.

Humphries has gone on record as saying that he obtained most of the unusual words and expressions for his McKenzie character by listening to Sydney taxi drivers. I think he is having us on. I have spent as much time in the front seat of Sydney taxis as Humphries has, and I have yet to hear a cabbie come up with a new word or expression.

I believe the truth is that Humphries, who is one of the great comic geniuses of our age, *invented* most of the slang words and expressions that he put into the crude mouth of Bazza McKenzie. There may have been an odd word or phrase which he resurrected from obscurity, but most of the terms which became known as Bazza McKenzieisms in the 1960s, and which subsequently passed into the currency of the language, were the product of the very imaginative and fertile Humphries' mind. By constant use of these terms in his stage presentations and through the McKenzie strip, book and film characterisations, many of the words and phrases came into wide general usage.

Barry Humphries has a lot to answer for in the linguistic after-life!

The extent to which Humphries managed to project his creation Barry McKenzie as the image of the average Australian is reflected in the resigned quote attributed to a Qantas hostess in 1973:

The Qantas Jetaway low-fare flights . . . are the absolute dread of every flight hostess and steward. We call them the Bazza McKenzie charters.

Some of the expressions which Humphries, mainly through his creation Barry McKenzie, has either invented or resur- rected from obscurity, include:

TO VOMIT: Chunder, Technicolour Yawn.

TO URINATE: Splash the Boots, Point Percy at the Porcelain, Shake Hands with the Wife's Best Friend, Syphon the Python, Water the Horse, Strain the Potatoes, Nip into the old utensil for a liquid laugh, Flog the lizard, Nip out and drain the dragon, Go to the throttling Pit.

SEXUAL INTERCOURSE: Sink the Sausage, Park the Prawn, Spear

the Bearded Clam, Dip the Wick, Exercise the Ferret, to Feature, Dip the Dagger.

SEX ORGANS (MALE): Percy, Python, Dragon, One-eyed Snake, The Old Fella, Beef Bayonet, Pork Sword, John Thomas, the Virile Member.

SEX ORGANS (FEMALE): The Bearded Clam, the Golden Doughnut, Donga.

MENSTRUAL PERIOD: Got the flags out, Red sails in the sunset.

Some of the insults and other expressions coined by Humphries and put into the mouth of Bazza McKenzie or one of McKenzie's mates are worth recording:

'I'll knock yer teeth so far down yer throat yer'll have to put yer toothbrush up yer freckle to clean 'em.'

'Go stick yer head in a dingo's donga.'

'Gawd, I'm as dry as a kookaburra's khyber.'

'Go stick yer head up a dead bear's bum.'

'She bangs like a dunny door in a gale' (speaking of a nymphomaniac).

'Up you for the rent, sport.'

'You smell like an Abo's armpit.'

One of Barry McKenzie's favourite euphemisms for the penis is 'the one-eyed trouser snake', an expression that has now apparently gained international currency. Olive Scott, in the *Australian* in 1977 carried this report in her column:

The *Province*, a morning newspaper published in Vancouver, Canada, this week carried a report from Melbourne about anti-venine as 'an antidote for the venom of all dangerous snakes in Australia', adding: 'However, this does not include the venom of the deadly one-eyed trouser snake, for which there is no known antidote.'
Quite so.

Barry Humphries is also the master of the *double entendre*, a good example being from his *Barry McKenzie Holds His Own* (1974):

'Going back to Oz, mate? What route are you taking?'
'No one, sport, I'm travelling with me Auntie Edna.'

Of course not everybody loves Barry McKenzie. He has his opponents some of whom express themselves in very strong terms indeed. Thus film critic Helen Frizell, in 1974, panned the film *Barry McKenzie Holds His Own* as follows:

Personally, I've had a gutful of watching Bazza (McKenzie) and his mates boozing away, showering one another with the amber fluid, and doing their Ugly Australian act abroad. And, although some may consider it transcendentally witty for Bazza to vomit into the camera lens, once you've seen this you've seen it, and an almost Technicolour yawn was my reaction. The Ockerish audience seemed to love this, but then the film was made about Ockers for Ockers.

Mr Aly Eyiam, the first Robert Menzies Scholar was also quite disenchanted with the efforts of Barry Humphries. In 1975 he wrote:

The harm done to Australia's image by the film, *The Adventures of Barry McKenzie*, will take at least ten years to repair. Australian clubs in Earls Court have restricted entrance and proudly boast, No Blacks.

In London I realised the world is becoming more a global village, but Australia seems out of it.

An interesting sidelight to Barry Humphries' efforts to project the Australian image abroad was the fact that when *The Wonderful World of Barry McKenzie* first appeared in book form (published in England in 1968) it was banned as obscene, and declared a prohibited import in Australia. The ban was not lifted until 1970. The very same government that had banned the book then decided that it was a cultural object and, through the Film Development Corporation, advanced $250 000 to make it into a film!

Chapter Thirty-two

HAVING A NAUGHTY

One of the commonest words used by Australian men to describe sexual intercourse is 'naughty' which sums up precisely this sort of attitude . . . though they desire sex, they regard it guiltily as immoral and rather dirty. It is a fantastic situation, in which society accepts a stern neo-Victorian morality as correct, transgresses it at every opportunity and then feels guilty about it afterwards.

Craig McGregor in
Profile of Australia, 1966

A few years ago a friend of mine was playing a game of bowls, his opposite number being a Superintendent of Police. The 'Super' was playing a terrible game` and after one particularly poor shot, blurted out to my friend by way of apology or explanation: 'I'm off my game today. You see I had a naughty with the wife this morning.'

When he later related the story to me, my friend was full of wonder that a six foot four inch Superintendent of Police, in the prime of his life, should be so drained of energy by a sexual act in the morning that he couldn't play bowls properly that after-noon.

I must confess that I was more interested in the fact that in this day and age a Superintendent of Police should continue to use the term NAUGHTY for the sexual act. I thought it did much to explain the attitude of many senior police officers of the old school towards censorship and modern problems of sexuality in the community.

Of course Police Superintendents aren't the only ones to use the word NAUGHTY as a euphemism for sexual intercourse.

The word has popped up quite a few times in modern literature, for example:

Until I met Thelma, I always thought that sheilas had to be talked into a bit of a naughty.
Eric Lambert in *Glory Thrown in* (1959)

He put his arm around her, patting her buttock. I smiled, remembering his oft-repeated remark: 'I got a lot of knockbacks but I get a lot of naughties.'
Frank Hardy in *Legends from Benson's Valley* (1963)

These sheilas fascinate me . . . I want them to invite me in for a good old-fashioned naughty.
Geoff Morley in *Jockey Rides Honest* (1972)

I'll give you a new dress . . . and we'll 'ave a bit of a party, and then another naughty, eh?
Xavier Herbert in *Poor Fellow My Country* (1975)

Expressions widely used in Australia as euphemisms for sexual intercourse include ROOTED, SCRAPE, STUFFED, HAVING IT OFF and ON THE NEST.

As all are respectable English words in their own right, great care has to be taken when using them, especially in mixed company, since the risk of misinterpretation is obvious. In his food and wine column in the *Australian* in 1978, Len Evans quoted the following amusing story which he said originated in Singapore:

The Qantas hostess, who, toward the end of a long flight, was serving the last meal.
'Will you have some vegetables, sir? We have broccoli, peas, potatoes and mushrooms.'
'Are the mushrooms stuffed?'
'No sir, just terribly tired.'

Len Evans must also be credited for unearthing what he called the quintessential Australian joke, revolving around a word-play on another of the extensively used euphemisms for sexual intercourse—ROOTED. The joke, as related by Evans in his Indulgence column in the *Weekend Australian* in 1978, involves a Queensland drover who says to his mate:

'Yeah, I'm going down to NSW for me holidays.'
'Aw, yeah—what route are you taking?'
'Aw, I think I'll take the missus—she stuck to me through the drought.'

I agree with Evans that this is a very typical joke—but it is much more than that, and speaks volumes on the attitude of the average Australian male towards women.

Other terms in general use in Australia for sexual intercourse include: BANG, BASH, KNOCK, GRIND, POKE, SHAG, STUFF and NOOKY.

It should be noted that the majority of these expressions imply violence or force, which may explain a lot about the sad relations between men and women in Australia.

KNOCK is a term for sexual intercourse that is almost obsolete in the community, though as late as 1971 Frank Hardy used it in *Outcasts of Foolgarah*:

Well, he's not knocking orf my sister-in-law and that's for sure.

In 1965 William Dick in *A Bunch of Ratbags* also used the expression:

I had caused him to miss out on a knock many weeks ago with Elaine, and he had never forgiven me.

The word KNOCK however, nowadays is used mainly in non-sexual ways, i.e.:

TO KNOCK: To criticise continually.

TO BE KNOCKED OUT: To be rendered unconscious.

TO KNOCK BACK: To reject (originally this was a sexual term for when a woman rejected a man's advances, but now has general non-sexual application).

TO KNOCK BACK A FEW: To have a number of drinks.

TO BE KNOCKED UP: To be tired. (Australian women should beware of using this term when visiting North America where the expression means 'to be pregnant'.)

TO PUT THE HARD WORD ON (or sometimes TO PUT THE ACID ON) has long been an Australian expression for a man seeking sex with a woman outside of marriage, and our literature has many references to it. For example:

I love him, and I found out I wasn't any better than the others when he started to put the hard word on me.
H Drake-Brockman in *Sheba Lane* (1936)

The landlord tried to make love to her, or, as she termed it, 'put the hard word on her'.
Kylie Tennant in *Foveaux* (1939)

If I'd slung a diamond bracelet her way before I'd put the hard word on her, it'd have been a very different story.
Dal Stivens in *Jimmy Brockett* (1951)

Another term, less commonly used is TO CRACK IT, as used by Lawson Glassop in *Rats in New Guinea* (1943):

You wouldn't even crack it with a nymphomaniac.

In its sexual sense the term is probably an offshoot of the expression to CRACK A FAT, i.e. to have an erection. Barry Humphries used this in its colloquial form in *The Wonderful World of Barry McKenzie* (1968) as follows:

Pommy Sheilas? Aw, they're apples I s'pose—but the way I feel now I don't reckon (I) could crack a fat!

To CRACK IT however, is an ambiguous expression as it is more commonly used in Australia in a completely non-sexual context, meaning to succeed in some enterprise, i.e.

Romped home with flying colours in his accountancy exams, but like me, he's never been able to crack it for a decent job.
From *Caddie, a Sydney Barmaid*, (1953)

Keep on with your art, mate. You'll crack it one day, I'm sure of it.
Alexander Buzo in *Rooted* (1973)

Another expression for sexual intercourse that is distinctly Australian is IN LIKE FLYNN, derived from the well publicised sexual prowess of the Australian-born movie star Errol Flynn.

In *The Removalist* (1972) David Williamson used the expression in tandem with a Barry McKenziasm ('threading the golden doughnut') when he had one of his characters explain:

We'll be in like Flynn there tomorrow night. We'll thread the eye of the old golden doughnut—no worries.

The expression SINK THE SAUSAGE as a term for sexual intercourse apparently had a special significance in legal circles in days when many divorce actions centred on adultery by the erring husband. In an article in *Nation Review* in 1973 on divorce reforms then pending, journalist Richard Beckett quoted an unnamed NSW Solicitor as proclaiming:

The sinking the sausage rule still applies.

Jim Ramsay in *Cop it Sweet!* (1977) cites two slang expressions for intercourse which I personally have never heard used but which I pass on for the record:

MORNING GLORY: Fornication before noon.
MATINEE: Fornication in the afternoon.

The term GETTING OFF AT REDFERN has been used as a euphemism for the practice of coitus interruptus, Redfern being the suburban station immediately prior to Sydney Central. When Eric Partridge mentioned this in 1970, a correspondent to the London *Times* immediately pointed out that this was a case of Australian plagiarism. The correspondent claimed that the term GETTING OUT AT GATESHEAD had long been used in England to describe coitus interruptus.

Whilst many Australian slang expressions with sexual overtones are coarse in the extreme, a few have a certain degree of wit. One I like is OFF LIKE A BRIDE'S NIGHTIE, meaning to make a quick exit from the scene or to act promptly. It was used by Christopher Bray in *Blossom like a Rose* (1969):

'Come on youse blokes!' he shouted. 'We're off like a bride's nightie!'

Sometimes euphemisms used for sexual terms are so obscure that even the users are only vaguely aware of their meanings. In *Cinderella Dressed in Yella* (Second Edition 1978) the authors report amongst rhymes of the playground the following ditty:

> *It's only human nature after all*
> *To get your favourite girl against the wall,*
> *And let your accumulation*
> *Meet her accommodation*
> *And increase the population*
> *Of the coming generation*

The authors of the book record usage of this rhyme in Melbourne in 1960 and 1973, and in western Victoria in 1938. One man in reporting the rhyme commented: 'We all knew it, but really had no idea of what "accumulation" and "accommodation" meant.'

Pack rape has been an unpleasant feature of male-dominated societies for thousands of years, so Australians cannot be accused of inventing the practice, but they probably could lay claims to some modern innovations ranging from the ONION to the TRAIN.

ONION is a modern term, not recorded by Sidney Baker, and refers to the practice of bikie gangs in common sexual sharing of one of the girl-followers or of an outsider unwillingly abducted for the occasion. In many instances the girl (or girls) involved apparently participate willingly, so the term pack rape may not always be an accurate description for the ONIONS carried out so frequently on Australian beaches in summer. The origin of the term is obscure, but probably refers to the fact that the girls involved are passed around in a circle of males.

A different kettle of fish entirely is the TRAIN, a subtle form of pack rape achieved by peer group pressures.

The practice came to light in 1977, when the media investigated allegations of continuing mass rapes in the

Queensland sugar cane town of Ingham, which has a very large Italian community. In Ingham there developed over the years an organised system of mass rape known as TRAINS. The system and explanation of the term TRAIN was outlined as follows by Brisbane sociologist Dr Paul Wilson in his book *The Other Side of Rape* (1978):

These more general group rapes started as a social activity at the cabarets which are held every Saturday night in one of the Ingham hotels . . . At such functions the group organisers would decide on the woman for the night. This information would then be passed on to the other members of the loosely defined group through an intricate signalling mechanism. The leader would raise his hand above his shoulder and drop it 10 centimetres in a yanking motion, like the conductor of a train pulling the cord 'Toot! Toot!' This signal would go around the room until all the men intending to participate had so indicated, after the woman in question had been pointed out to them. Hence the colloquial phrase for the rapes developed—TRAINS—a term with more significance than simply the signalling mechanism reminiscent of the cane trains which shunt through the town during the cane season. A variety of derivations set the phrase in a more illuminating context—how women are trained, we want to train your woman, and so on. The coercive manner of securing the woman for the evening's entertainment was quite sophisticated . . .

After studying the fairly long list of painfully crude terms which Australians use to describe the sexual act, one could hope that future generations might prove more wittily inventive if they have to resort to euphemisms. Personally I like the quote which Ross Campbell (in an article in the *Bulletin* in 1977) ascribed to an unnamed scholar who was asked how the students of Paris spent their leisure. According to Campbell, he replied:

Sir, in a venerean ecstasy we inculcate our virile members into the penitissime recesses of the pudends of certain amicabilissime meretricules.

Chapter Thirty-three

GIRLS ARE WEAK, CHUCK 'EM IN THE CREEK

There were these sheilas comin' down through the paddock from the lookout hill, I said to Larry, Get a load of the talent and Larry says Cer-ikey, like, look at the Norks on that, well, they was nearly close enough to hear us so I says Shut up, mate, fair go, and we just sorta stand around lookin' at nothin' but takin' 'em all in as they go past. And I'm not bullin' you, mate, there was this redhead in this terrific green-coloured cozzie, they musta bin over the ol' swimmin'-pool and as she goes past she turns to me and kinda smiles, lookin' through me, like as though I'm a thousand miles away. But seein' me, mate, get it, not missin' a thing.

From **Four Conversations and a Comment** by Alan Seymour, 1962

Visitors to these shores have long been appalled by the chauvinistic attitudes of Australian males towards their womenfolk, perhaps best summed up by the school-yard chant:

> *Boys are strong,*
> *Like King Kong.*
> *Girls are weak,*
> *Chuck 'em in the creek.*

With such a start in the kindergarten, it is little wonder that adult relationships between the sexes are on such a low level.

Whilst countless visitors, and plenty of local amateur psychologists, have devoted thousands of words to the situation, only one that I know has blamed the sorry state of relationships of the sexes in Australia on the language; or, to be more exact, on the fact that Australians, both male and female, fail abysmally to communicate because they haven't acquired the art of small talk.

The person to come up with this interesting theory was the late Sidney J Baker who in his book *The Drum* (1959) devoted quite a bit of space to the problem of communication—or lack of it—between Australian men and women. I think his conclusions make considerable sense, at least to explain the old puzzle as to why at almost all Australian social functions men should herd in a group at one end of the room, with women at the other end.

The explanation, as advanced by Baker:

> . . . The real reason for all this, I feel, is not the selfish hedonism of Australian males, but the fact that, so far as females are concerned, they are almost entirely bereft of non-sexual small talk.

Baker, of course, was not the first by a long chalk to hurl this particular accusation at Australian women. Away back in 1906 the veteran politician Victor Daley made this comment:

> I'd sooner talk to a man than a woman any day. Ten minutes exhausts them.

And almost seventy years on (in 1968) we find Mr Alan Renouf, then permanent head of the Department of Foreign Affairs, make a similar complaint:

> If you find yourself stuck with the wife of an Australian diplomat overseas, she'll talk to you about holidays, about children, but she'll never say anything that will interest you.

But back to Sidney Baker, who felt that the lack of communication between the sexes in Australia was a failure shared by both parties. Baker raises the old 'mateship' concept, mentioned by so many other writers on the theme of Australian sexual relations, but points out that the Australian male is very fearful of losing 'face' amongst his fellows if he should step out of line to make tentative efforts to discourse with women at social functions. Such action, he points out, goes against the traditional masculine view that a male who engages a female in prolonged discourse is either (a) planning to marry her (b) establishing a vantage point to 'put the hard word on her' or (c) has so many peculiarities that he should be written off as a queer.

Baker puts forward the proposition, and I agree with him, that on matters that interest him, such as sport, pub anecdotes, and practical matters, the Australian male can be quite articulate, but that he lacks knowledge of and tolerance for social chit-chat. He further points out that because of his relative isolation, the Australian male has been obliged to make his own rule on many things. Lacking both sources of reference and cultural experience, he lacks the poise and confidence these things can give, and his social rules omit a number of things that are accepted without question in Europe.

Baker then goes on to give the Australian woman a 'serve' in words that certainly will not endear him to the liberationists of the nation, but which certainly do contain a strong element of truth. He comments:

Since Australian females lack practice in conversational exchanges with the opposite sex they, too, are frequently shy. Even at their best their verbal offerings are often shallow and repetitious. They are poor conversational entertainers. They are almost totally lacking in a self-critical sense of humour. Their thinking tends to be of a *non sequitur* variety that would send all but the most complaisant male up the wall. And because of these things, they are usually tense, wary and given to private dreams about knights in shining armour which males rightly scorn. So, because of shyness on both sides, there is little verbal ease between our males and females. And this takes us near to the heart of the problem. Here is a situation that grew out of male diffidence, was sanctified by frontierland courtesy, became static because of female inexperience, and, with nothing to modify it, became fixed into a tradition. If, as a consequence, the Australian male is prepared to wash his hands of the whole affair and confine its correction to manoeuvres on the couch, one can hardly blame him.

How the present unsatisfactory system operates can best be gauged by a quite fascinating report which *Nation Review* published in 1976 on dinners at the Australian country home of the publisher Rupert Murdoch. The report read, in part:

. . . conversation during dinner tends, out of necessity, to involve the women to a greater extent. The fact that they are seated alternately with the men makes it very difficult to ignore them. Perhaps it is due to their greater involvement in the conversation that it becomes noticeably more banal.

If Baker is correct, then there is still a long way to go before the sexes are able to establish a satisfactory social rapport on the continent. This very desirable objective is certainly not helped by the extensive use of slang terms by Australian men when speaking of women (or female anatomy) generally.

The commonest nicknames for women in Australia in the last

century were DONAH and CLINAH but around the turn of the century these gave way to SHEILA, believed to have been derived from the Irish generic name of SHEELA or SHELA applied to any girl. An old bush ballad of the late colonial period included the term:

> *And he bit that rookin' sheila on the stern.*
> *Then the sheila raced off squealin',*
> *And her clothes she was un-peelin';*
> *To hear her yells would make you feel forlorn.*

The name endures for a long period and still pops up from time to time. Thus the *Australian* of 1 September 1975 spoke of:

> ... Fat, lazy and going to seed ... That's yer spoilt Ocker sheila.

Conversation primarily revolving around women's interests sometimes is referred to as SHEILA TALK, thus Henry Williams in *My Love Had a Black Speed Stripe* (1973):

> They talk about love at first sight with sheilas, but with sheilas I don't think it ever lasts like that ... beats me how any bloke can enjoy himself talking with women. Sheila talk has always driven me up the wall.

SHEILA had a long innings but has now almost disappeared from general adult language. However, the word seems to linger on in school-yard rhymes. The authors of *Cinderella Dressed in Yella* (second edition, 1978) report two such examples. The first popped up in the 1960s and was a parody on the Profumo scandal in England. The Antipodean version chanted in the school-grounds of Melbourne well into the 1970s, and long after the original events had been forgotten across the world, was:

> *Half a pound o' Mandy Rice,*
> *Half a pound o' Keeler,*
> *Put 'em together and what have you got?*
> *A pound of sexy SHEILA.*

The second rhyme to use SHEILA is reported from the Melbourne playgrounds of 1973 and catches neatly the mood of the time:

> *Children be good and obey your parents,*
> *And never do anything they say is bad.*
> *Don't smoke and drink but save your money,*
> *And spread paper on the seat of the dunny.*
> *Children remember these words are golden,*
> *And fellas, don't rape sheilas in the*
>   *back seat of your Holden.*

Fowlyard terms have long been used in applying nicknames to women in Australia, perhaps the commonest being CHOOK —a name applied indiscriminately to a domestic fowl and a domestic female ('I'm goin' home to me old chook'). By extension an older, tougher hen (or woman) is known as a BOILER and Sir Reginald Ansett, then head of Ansett Airlines, certainly didn't endear himself to the airline hostesses who were on strike in 1975 when he commented:

I'm not joking. I'm not going to have a bar of them. They are a batch of old boilers sitting on their executive. Frankly I've had them. We can run our airline without people to serve drinks.

At the other end of the scale younger women have long been known as CHICKENS. An older woman is said to be NO SPRING CHICKEN. In more recent times the old nickname has been shortened to CHICK in line with American practice. Not all women appreciate this fowlyard appendage and in 1977 the visiting Canadian sociologist Maureen Baker was driven to comment on the matter as follows:

I've never really thought about it; I just know I hate the way Australian men call all women 'chicks'.
Before I came here a year ago I'd heard about the low status of women in this country but had not realised how true it was. Now I've lived here, I find the situation is even worse.
There exists here, like no other country in the world, a male-dominated society—ockerism at its worst. Women are taught their role is in the home, they certainly don't belong in the pub culture.

Other nicknames for women include BIRD, CROW (an old or very unattractive woman), BAT (an especially unattractive woman). A low-class brothel is sometimes referred to as a BAT House. OLD BAG, SKIRT, SORT, BAROSSA (rhyming slang for girl from Barossa Pearl, a popular white wine), CHROMO (a prostitute), TALENT (a likely prospect for seduction), SCRUBBER (an unattractive or sexually promiscuous woman), TOWN BIKE (a very promiscuous local girl), GRUNTER (another name for a promiscuous girl) and BLACK VELVET (an Aboriginal girl). A woman who refuses to have sex after being wined and dined is called a QUANDONG; the origin of the term is unknown. On the other hand when a woman yields to sex on the first outing with a man, he is said to have scored A HOLE IN ONE.

These terms not only are offensive to women, but also show a distinct lack of originality. The only inventive feminine nickname I have come across is DICKLESS TRACEY (a woman police officer). That may still be offensive but at least it has a certain wit.

An interesting example of masculine attitudes in the upper levels of the political scene was provided in 1977 by Mrs Margaret Whitlam, wife of former Prime Minister Gough Whitlam. Asked whether she had had any influence on her husband's political views when he was Prime Minister she replied in the negative and added:

His attitude is: 'What has the old bag been saying now?'

Terms in general use for women's breasts include BOOBS, KNOCKERS, MILKING MACHINES, NORKS, NUBBIES, TITS, A PAIR and BEE STINGS—i.e. small breasts (an import from America). In 1974 some sort of legal history was made when BOOBS was officially banned as a trade name by Mr Frank Ryan, the NSW Corporate Affairs Commissioner. Mr Ryan refused to register the name for a Sydney shop dealing in women's underwear and bikinis. The owner of the shop subsequently appealed to the Attorney General who reversed the original ban. At the time a Sydney newspaper interviewed Mr Ryan and asked him for his reason in applying the ban. He gave this answer:

The commercial exploitation of the name containing a slang expression descriptive of a portion of a woman's anatomy would generally be undesirable as likely to be offensive to members of the public.

The newspaper then interviewed Mrs Ryan and asked her what she thought of the affair. She said that she had observed to her husband:

You are a pompous old goat. You are likely to go down in history as the man who hated boobs.

The term NORKS is believed to have been derived from NORCO, a brand of butter sold in New South Wales since the wrapping on the butter at one time featured a cow's udder! The term still has wide currency:

Hello, honey, that sweater—one deep breath and your norks will be in my soup.
                    Criena Rohan, *The Delinquents* (1962)

Wow, she's peeled right off. What norks!
          Barry Oakley in *Let's Hear it for Prendergast* (1970)

The Australian insistence on applying a nickname to everything applies not only to women's breasts, but also to their covering. In 1978 the *Rag Trader*, a magazine of the apparel industry reported as follows:

> We heard recently of a new bra. It is called the SHEEPDOG—because it rounds them up and points them in the right direction.

Nicknames given to a woman's vagina include: PUSSY, FANNY, THE BOX, HOLE, HONEYPOT, MUFF, SLIT, SNATCH, GASH, TWAT, CRACK (to CRACK IT is to have sexual intercourse and a CRACKER is a prostitute) and DOT (Hawking the DOT is the act of prostitution).

R Ellis and I Turner in *Australian Graffiti* (1975) recorded an amusing scrawl on the wall:

> I'VE LOST ME VIRGINITY

Underneath was written:

> NEVER MIND, AS LONG AS YOU'VE GOT THE BOX IT CAME IN!

The BOX also has male associations of a sexual nature as the protector worn by sportsmen is known as a RUPTURE BOX. Australian test cricketer Keith Stackpole in *Not Just for Openers* (1974) related the following amusing story:

> Once, I was hit in the box during a one-day match; an agonizing blow that left me crook for four days. A supporter for the opposing team shouted, 'Weak Australian sod, get up'.

It is the belief of males around the world that the taking of alcohol—especially wine and spirits—by a woman, makes her more vulnerable sexually. But only the Australians seem to have taken this bit of homespun philosophy a step further by referring to alcohol as a LEG-OPENER. The expression crops up quite regularly in Australian literature, viz:

> Gotta bit of leg-opener in the back seat of the heap.
> *Bobbin up* by Dorothy Hewett (1959)

> . . . shearers had been known to buy a bottle of Charlie's 'leg-opener' to knock off a sheila.
> *Big Red* by Leslie Haylen (1965)

> The bottle of sparkling burgundy (a disgusting drink, apart from its legendary powers as a leg-opener) . . .
> *Andy* by Geoffrey Dutton (1968)

When trading insults Australians don't hesitate to hit below the belt (literally) without respect of the sex of the recipient. The *Bulletin* told a story of how in 1962 the well known TV personality Dita Cobb appeared in the make-up room of a Sydney TV station clutching her head from a heavy evening before. In walked Bobby Limb, singing at the top of his head.

'Darling,' promised Dita, 'if you don't stop that racket I'll give you a good kick in the balls.' 'Try it,' retorted Limb, 'and I'll give you a good kick in the balls right back.'

Checkmate!

An interesting example of male attitudes to women was provided in a 1977 issue of the Marrickville (a Sydney suburb) RSL Club Journal which produced this report on its (female) staff in a gossip column:

Now for some news about our barmaids—Elaine, for some reason, is now called the Jet Setter. Junie Hall is sporting a new set of fangs. Betty is moving sideways, Jap fashion. Pat has just returned from holidays, having stayed at Petersham Heights. Gai is still going strong with Johnny Walker. Elga has had a facelift. Flo and Edna had such a good time on holidays, I hope to see no swelling of the legs . . . or . . .

In this chapter reference has only been made to terms thought up and used by men about women. But there seems to be in existence a 'secret language' used exclusively by women and to which males are not generally privy. This was brought out in a *Sydney Morning Herald* (1978) book review by Nancy Keesing. The book reviewed was *Words and Women,* by Casey Miller and Kate Smith, and Nancy Keesing ended her review with this comment:

When is someone going to codify and publish the hidden words which some women use almost exclusively in conversation with other women?

Miss Keesing lifted the veil of mystery only slightly when she provided the following examples: 'She's had somethink out' (a partial hysterectomy); 'She's had everythink out' (a total hysterectomy); 'She has old age creeping on' (she has taken an elderly lover); 'She took the cure' or 'She cracked an egg' or 'had an appendicitis' (all euphemisms for an abortion).

Anne Baxter in her book *Intermission* revealed how surprised she was when she first heard a pregnant woman say she was 'three months gone'. She might have been even more surprised had she heard some (predominantly) male expressions for the same condition: PREGGERS, UP THE SPOUT, UP THE STICK (Stick is a euphemism for penis), DUFFED, UP THE DUFF and IN THE OVEN.

Incidentally a fairly original term for a miscarriage in the outback used to be TO SLIP A JOEY.

Chapter Thirty-four

TUCKING INTO THE TUCKER

The quality of a race of beings is determined by two things: food and climate.

Marcus Clarke, 1890

When the early explorers and settlers left the comparative safety of the coastal settlements to venture into inland Australia they faced many problems—not the least being the lack of food suitable for white palates. They found that natural foods, to which the Aborigines had adapted over periods of thousands of years, were completely unsuited for tender stomachs nurtured in the northern hemisphere.

For example, the Aborigines made use of the sporocarp of the plant *Marsilea quadrifolia* (sometimes called clover fern). They referred to it as ngardu which quickly became corrupted to nardoo. They chewed it as a narcotic and ground it to make up a substance not unlike flour. Andrew Jackson, in *Burke and the Australian Exploring Expedition of 1860*, records that when the natives were given a quantity of flour as a gift they at once referred to it as 'whitefeller nardoo'.

The early explorers thought that the nardoo flour would sustain them if their rations ran out, but they were quickly disillusioned on this point as they found that it was an acquired taste which did not sit easily on white stomachs. W Howitt in *Discovery in Australia* (1865) records:

They now began to inquire of the blacks after the nardoo seed, imagining it the produce of a tree; and received from the natives some of their dried narcotic herbs, which they chew, called pitchery. They soon found the nardoo seed in abundance, on a flat, and congratulated themselves in the idea that on this they could subsist in the wilderness, if all other food failed, a hope in which they were doomed to a great disappointment.

A similar tale was told in the diary of H J Wills (1861):

I cannot understand this nardoo at all; it certainly will not agree with me in any form. We are now reduced to it alone, and we manage to get from four to five pounds a day between us.

. . . It seems to give us no nutriment.

. . . Starvation on nardoo is by no means very unpleasant, but for the weakness one feels and the utter inability to move oneself, for, as far as appetite is concerned, it gives me the greatest satisfaction.

Apparently nardoo was something to be eaten only as a last resort in the inland and the white man's feelings about it are perhaps best summed up in Lyndall Haddow's poignant verse:

> On the far Barcoo
>   Where they eat nardoo,
> Jumbuck giblets and pigweed stew.
>   Fever and ague
> And scurvy plague you
>   And the Barcoo rot;
> But the worst of the lot
>   Is the Bel-y-ando spew.

Barcoo rot, referred to in the verse, was another name for land scurvy. Another outback complaint of the last century was Barcoo vomit which Edward Morris in *The Dictionary of Austral English* (1898) describes as follows:

BARCOO VOMIT, n. a sickness occurring in inhabitants of various parts of the high land of the interior of Australia. It is characterized by painless attacks of vomiting, occurring immediately after food is taken, followed by hunger, and recurring as soon as hunger is satisfied.

The name Barcoo is derived from the district traversed by the river Barcoo, or Cooper, in which this complaint and the Barcoo Rot are common.

The term Belyando Spew, incidentally, is named after a river in western Queensland. Belyando Spew was a sickness common amongst shearers in the last century and was marked by severe attacks of vomiting after meals. The incompetence of successive generations of shearers' cooks was long blamed for the complaint but it is more likely that it was caused by a combination of factors: bad food, poor working conditions and the continual bending of the shearer's body throughout his long day.

Whilst white explorers and settlers did learn to consume, if not with relish, the flesh of kangaroos, there were many other species of fauna which the Aborigines regarded as delicacies but which did not sit well on white stomachs. Chief amongst these, of course, were witchetty grubs, snakes and goannas.

Even here white reluctance seems to be breaking down if we are to heed a story in the *Bulletin* in 1978 in which Keith Dunstan revealed that at long last witchetty grub soup was being marketed in Australia—and exported. The enterprising individual behind this culinary exercise is Mr Peter Beattie who runs the Riverboat restaurant at Swan Hill in Victoria. He serves platters of yabbies, Murray crays, witchetty grub soup and at times (despite the objections of environmentalists) snake and kangaroo. His *piece de resistance* is the Squatters Special which consists of beef done in carpet bag style with yabbies and sitting on a bed of damper.

Mr Beattie's chief claim to fame however, is that he was the first man to can witchetty grubs. He obtains these in bulk from sawmills and cooks 500 gallons of soup at a time. This is canned by SPC at Monbulk and business is said to be booming with 60 per cent of the manufacture going overseas to the United States, Japan and Hong Kong.

Those who don't care for witchetty grub soup can always eat their grubs straight. The recommended method is to put a lightly greased shovel over a campfire and cook the grubs on that. They are said to have a slightly cheesey flavour.

Another native delicacy which the white settlers did eventually get around to accepting as an edible food is the yabby, a small crayfish found in inland waterholes (and now found in large numbers in most inland dams). The Melbourne *Argus* of 6 October 1894 gave this description of the yabby:

In the case of small crayfish, called 'yabbies' . . . these may be found all over Australia, both in large and small lagoons. These creatures, whilst nearing a drought, and as the supply of water is about to fail, burrow deeply in the beds of the lagoons, water-holes, or swamps, piling up the excavations on the surface over their holes, which I take, amongst other reasons, to be a provision against excessive heat.

Some confusion can arise here as the common name yabby is also applied to other smaller types of crayfish found by the seaside and used strictly as bait. The *Australasian* on 30 January 1897 had this to say about this particular type of yabby:

The bait used is 'yabby', a small crayfish found in the sand on the beach at low tide. The getting of the bait itself is very diverting. The yabbies are most prized by fish and fishermen, and the most difficult to obtain. The game is very shy, and the hunter, when he has found the burrow, has to dig rapidly to overtake it, for the yabby retires with marvellous rapidity, and often half a dozen lifts of wet sand have to be made before he is captured. There is no time to be lost. In quite twenty-five per cent of the chases the yabbies get away through flooding and collapse of the hole.

Although many of the foods that Australians eat are the same as those found overseas, very often we contrive to give them new names. A typical example is the tropical fruit which is known in most parts of the world as papaya, but which in Australia is always referred to as paw paw (sometimes there is an alternate spelling pa paw).

The original slang word in Australia for food was TUCKER and its use survives even today in the outback. It was derived from the English schoolboy term of TUCK for food bought from a pastrycook and the provincial term TO TUCK IN, meaning to eat.

In Australia the term quickly became to mean food generally and has special meanings in the outback. For example TO MAKE TUCKER, means to earn enough to pay for food.

Thus Wood and Lapham in *Waiting for the Mail* (1875):

We heard of big nuggets, but only made tucker.

And the Melbourne *Argus* of 14 June 1890:

When a travelling man sees a hut ahead, he knows there's water inside, and tucker and tea.

Or Rolf Boldrewood in *A Sydney-Side Saxon* (1891):

I took my meal in the hut, but we'd both the same kind of tucker.

As a natural progression, a food storage bin became known as a tucker-box, an item that has become part of folk legend as a result of being a central part of the song about the dog who shat in the tucker box nine miles from Gundagai. The song was cleaned up by purists and ended up with the dog sitting on (instead of shatting in) the tucker-box.

I thought the term had dropped from usage (in the cities at least) in recent times but in 1976 a book reviewer in the *Sydney Morning Herald* wrote:

People planning holiday camping trips would be well advised to pack a copy of *Wild Food in Australia* (Fontana paperbacks), because you never know when some dingbat is going to leave the tuckerbox behind . . .

Australians certainly didn't invent picnics or barbecues, but from these two activities—sometimes separate, but often combined, they have managed to produce a few new words.

Barbecue has naturally been shortened to BARBIE in the lazy Australian tradition, whilst to barbecue a steak is to CHARCOAL-IT.

The first brands of portable food coolers marked in Australia bore the 'Eskimo' brand so this was immediately shortened to ESKY—a term now in wide use to refer to all brands of such coolers.

From the earliest days of settlement, Australian stomachs have taken a frightful battering at the hands of generations of third-rate cooks, who in the initial period plied their trade in the woolsheds, camps and stations of the nation and who, in more recent times, have transferred their lack of culinary skills to the kitchens of the cafes, hotels and restaurants of the sunburnt country.

It is not without justification that outback cooks from the earliest time earned the nickname of GREASY. This was a term originally coined in outback shearing sheds and transplanted easily to Army cooks in general at the outbreak of World War I.

The GREASIES of the outback were a race apart from their fellow men, and bush folklore abounds with stories of their dreadful culinary deeds, and of retribution effected on them by long-suffering consumers of their products. T A G Hungerford in *Riverslake* (1953) summed it up very well:

'God, cooks aren't people!' Carmichael retorted ... 'I'm going to write a book about greasies one day!'

Although from the mid-nineteenth century the term GREASY seemed to have been the automatic nickname for any shearers' camp cook, the term also had some currency as a term for shearers in general. Thus a report in the *Sydney Morning Herald* in 1963 noted an interesting fact:

A lot of greasies (shearers) get hen trouble. Some shearers' wives reckon we shearer blokes are either too tired, too drunk or too far away.

If an Australian GOES CROOK at someone it means that he is intensely annoyed or angry with that person. But if he has eaten food (or consumed liquor) which doesn't agree with him, he immediately FEELS CROOK IN THE GUTS. To be crook therefore is to be ill or even slightly UNDER THE WEATHER. It is perhaps comforting for the man in the street to learn that even the highest of the land can feel this way on occasion, as witness the remarks of Senator Cotton in 1975:

... I should not eat fish for breakfast ... I just felt crook after having the fish.

We all know exactly what he meant and how he felt.

Chapter Thirty-five

A NATION OF PIE-EATERS

Let others refrain from ridiculing our culture, of
which the meat pie and a beer are traditional parts.

Ald Calpis, Sydney City Council, 1974

'As Australian as the meat pie' is a saying that has been around
a long time, and with some justification, because the consumption of these articles of gastronomic pleasure to so many is
quite enormous. They are to the average Aussie what the
hamburger is to his American counterpart, and what fish and
chips are to the English. Perhaps the explanation behind the
popularity of these three basically plebeian dishes is that they
can all be eaten on the run. Lower-class stomachs it would
appear thrive on mobility during the actual intake.

One should not underestimate the importance of the meat pie
in Australian culture, or its ability to remain in the affections of
the inhabitants of the continent, even when they travel to far-off
climates where the meat pie (as it is known here) is not
obtainable.

On returning to Australia for a holiday in 1975, singer Olivia
Newton-John told airport reporters:

Just give me a meat pie and milk shake. There's nothing like it to
make a girl feel at home.

And the fame of the meat pie has spread far afield, as in the
same year Miss Wong Lai Sin, a visiting Malaysian pewter-
smith, was also interviewed by airport reporters and proclaimed:

I had long wanted to visit Australia and eat a meat pie and see a
kangaroo.

It is perhaps easier to trace the history of the meat pie in Australia than the up-and-down story of what actually went into them—particularly in the early days when improvisation was the rule rather than the exception.

Australia's first pieman of note, William Francis King (1807–1874), migrated from England in 1829 and won fame as a pieman and a remarkable athlete. 'The Flying Pieman', as King was known throughout the colony, was Australia's first long-distance runner and made considerable sums by backing himself for endurance running feats. In between his record-breaking runs he sold apple, kidney, pork and mutton pies, 'laced with delicious hot gravy'. One suspects that they were the larger and more traditional English pies rather than the small compact mass-produced versions of today.

The contents of colonial pies always were subject of speculation on the part of the consumers, and the literature of the day seems to indicate that the many suspicions voiced on the subject were well justified.

Brunton Stephens in *My Other Chinese Cook* wrote of a wily Oriental bush cook:

> *He was lazy, he was cheeky,*
> *He was dirty, he was sly,*
> *But he had a single virtue,*
> *and its name was rabbit pie.*

The ballad however, went on to disclose that the toothsome delicacy had been made from a litter of pups! From this tale came the expression, 'No more puppy, no more pie'.

The following verse from an old bush ballad indicates that when meat was unavailable, other fillings were used for outback pies by resourceful cooks:

> *Fair Australia, Oh what a dump.*
> *All you get to eat is crocodile's rump,*
> *Bandicoot's brains and catfish pie.*
> *Let me go home again before I die!*

Another old timers' dish was the Grabben Gullen Pie, also known as Possum Pumpkin Pie. *Bill Harney's Cook Book* (1960) explained the delicacy as follows:

In the early days, possums were caught, cleaned and cut up, put into a hollowed-out pumpkin which was then roasted until the meat was cooked—a very tasty pie it was, too.

The compilers of *Cinderella Dressed in Yella* (second edition,

1978) report a school-yard rhyme in use in New South Wales in 1955 that went like this:

> ———'s pies are full of flies,
> *With maggots in the middle.*
> *Anything that runs, jumps, walks, crawls or flies,*
> *That's what they put in* ———'s pies.

On the subject of the content of the meat pie it was perhaps left (as usual) for the Premier of Queensland, Joh Bjelke-Petersen, to have the last word (in 1978):

If this keeps up, Queensland will have no option but to take back Waltzing Matilda, Qantas and the lamington—all good Queensland products—and leave Australia to struggle along with the meat pie, which is full of Queensland beef anyway.

The meat pie is not without its detractors, of course—no national dish ever is—but few critics have been as extreme as Lelord Kordel, the American diet authority who in 1976 proclaimed:

The Australian meat pie looks like what little babies do in their nappies.

In 1969 Heinz Bernhard, in a letter to a Sydney newspaper, expressed doubt as to whether present-day meat pies contained any meat at all. They were, in his opinion, just 'encrusted gravy'. And he piled insult on insult with the comment that:

. . . The Australian meat pie has got to be consumed, eaten or sucked in while in a forward leaning position with a list of at least fifty-five degrees.

This brought forth the information from a local piemaker that under the Pure Foods Regulations of the State (NSW):

. . . The meat pie . . . must weigh between 5 and $5\frac{1}{2}$ ounces of which 3 ounces must be filling and one and a half ounces must be meat. The rest is gravy. But some people add sauce to make it more runny.

Loyalty to the meat pie runs so strong Down Under that in 1976 the Federation of Australian Pie Connoisseurs was formed and its first president, Rod Hill, composed a Federation song (to be sung to the music of 'Advance Australia Fair'), the first verse of which went as follows:

> *When Englishmen go out to dine*
> *Roast beef their staple dish,*
> *The Russians all eat caviar*
> *And Eskimos chew fish;*

The French, they say, are fond of frogs;
The Yanks—Kentucky fries:
But dinkum Aussies, one and all
Shout: 'Give us hot meat pies!'
Yes, dinkum Aussies, one and all
Shout: 'Give us hot meat pies!'

In 1978 Keith Dunstan coined a new word when he described Australian pie addicts as a new breed of JUNKIES. Noting that a Melbourne football crowd consumed upward of 40 000 of the delicacies in an afternoon, Dunstan wrote:

There is little harm in a pie junkie. I have friends who won't leave Melbourne because they believe the pies elsewhere would never be the same. Then there is a TV producer here who so believes in Sydney pies that he has them flown over every day by air freight.

Oh yes, I believe it is one of the beautiful cultural skills that a Melburnian junkie learns early—how to eat a pie from a paper bag without dribbling. These esoteric arguments about whether they contain meat or not are hardly important.

Australians take their basic foods very seriously, which is probably why they haven't any slang terms for meat pies as such, though they have allowed themselves to attach nicknames to individual *types* of pies. For example, in a broadcast over the ABC on 1 December 1940 F J Mills related the following story:

A man approached a pie cart in the city the other night, just as the pie cartist was packing up and about to depart.

'Gimme a torpedo or a time bomb, please,' he ordered.

'Sorry mate, sold right out of both,' replied the pie cartist.

'Got any hot islands, then?' asked the customer.

'No, sold out, too,' was the answer.

In relating this story, Sidney Baker commented that the term pie cartist appeared to be a useful one of Australian origin.

In 1978 the pie eaters of the nation were startled when a Queensland firm launched Australia-wide a new type of pie of triangular shape which, they claimed, was easier to eat. The new pies were called STRADDIES so at last the pie had a distinctive name, but only time will tell whether this new trademark is destined to become a household word along with Vegemite and the lamington.

PIE EATER was for a long time a derogatory term for a South Australian. The term is now obsolete and its origin is puzzling since statistics clearly reveal that Victorians have always been the major consumers of pies on a per head of population basis. It is interesting to note that South Australia is the only state where a nickname has been given to the actual manner of serving a meat pie. This nickname—A FLOATER— is used when a meat pie is launched in (or floated on) a sea of thick green pea soup, with the inevitable tomato sauce splashed on the top. After this weird baptismal rite the object—by universal definition a pie—is magically transformed into a FLOATER.

Chapter Thirty-six

POPULAR
AUSTRALIAN FOODS

I suppose it can be regarded as a state of Australian
vulgarity, but I am from time to time addicted to steak and
eggs; it renews my faith in the nation. While you can still
buy steak and eggs, the bloody poofters will never take over.

Sam Orr, 1974

Whilst the meat pie can probably lay just claim to recognition
as the Australian national dish, we should not overlook another
favourite—steak and eggs. It has absolutely no linguistic
connotations but is so deeply entrenched in Aussie culture that
it should not be passed over without mention.

The Australian devotion to steak and eggs was catered for by
Greek cafes which were scattered across the continent in their
thousands in the pre-war years. They are still around, but are
fast vanishing in the smaller towns under the impact of
changing eating and social habits. 'The Greeks', as they were
known, were the standby of the traveller and local alike when
they sought out their favourite dish of steak and eggs. If the
quality was often lacking, the quantity and the service usually
were beyond reproach. Writing in the *National Times* in 1975,
Bill Olson summed up these outback gastronomic outposts as
follows:

. . . and the Greek cafe. Open all day and all night. Steak cut from
drovers' old boots, limp shredded lettuce, one tomato slice, bitumen-
black tea from a pot wadded with generations of sour leaves. Banana
special, fruit salad and ice cream, peach Melba.

Lennie Lower, in his humorous novel *Here's Luck* dealt

seriously with the virtues of steak and eggs as a satisfying meal. He had his hero, Jack Gudgeon, deliver a lecture on the subject to his son Stanley, and this resulted in the couple applying the nicknames STEAK and EGGS to two GIMME GIRLS they subsequently picked up.

The term FRIED EGGS incidentally is also local slang for breasts, and was used as such in the summer of 1978 when an elderly beach inspector at the Sydney suburban beach of Balmoral came across a group of topless sunbathers lying on their stomachs and (according to press reports) admonished them thus:

I'm telling you girls, I don't want to see any more fried eggs around here this afternoon.

The consumption of eggs incidentally is not always without its problems if the cook happens to lack certain standards of hygiene. The problem (and the solution) was outlined brilliantly by George Wallace in his immortal poem:

> *'What will you have?' said the waiter,*
> *reflectively picking his nose.*
> *'I'll have two boiled eggs, you bastard,*
> *you can't put your finger in those.'*

Sausage is certainly not an Australian word, but locals might well claim that the objects that are sold under that title in Australia differ markedly from specimens in other parts of the world, as do their slang terms.

SNAGS and BANGERS are the two most common terms applied by Australians to sausages. Sidney Baker listed SNAGS without giving any explanation of the word.

The origin of BANGER is easier to trace as the word originally meant cattle, and later a dairy farmer or cow hand. In colonial times a BANG was also a brothel, so perhaps the inventive settler combined the terms to give vent to his (often well-founded) suspicions on the contents of sausages.

The unusual nature of some Australian sausages is even known overseas, as in 1978 the English magazine *Weekend* claimed that in Australia one could still buy sausages, called SNAGS made of kangaroo meat. The magazine appropriately titled the article containing this piece of misinformation, 'Fry Me Kangaroo Down, Sport'.

The importance of the lowly sausage on the Australian menu was emphasised by the following report in the Canberra *Times* in 1978:

A Bangers and Mash night will be the next function for members and friends of the Cheese Club.

To come the 'raw prawn' in Australia means to take someone down, but to come to a prawn night is an entirely different matter, though at the prices they sometimes charge at such functions the original interpretation might be the correct one.

A PRAWN NIGHT is an Australian invention, the Down Under answer to the American clam bake. PRAWN NIGHTS have by tradition been associated with RSL Clubs, where they originated in the early 1970s, but can be held anywhere and are merely excuses for the consumption of vast quantities of sea food delicacies.

Concordia News, the bulletin of a Sydney suburban club, in 1974 gave a hint that such events are regarded as a male preserve when it reported:

In October we plan a Gentlemen's night, not to call it Prawn Night, and whilst we have organised the necessary attractions, we still keep it under wrap until next programme. (Any females interested in a Ladies Day? Say, how to make scones, etc?)

Australians by tradition have preferred their food to be plain and filling, which is why they resisted for so long trying the spicier dishes of European migrants. In 1976 the Queensland Premier Joh Bjelke-Petersen got right down to the heart of the matter when he came out in support of a ban on imported cheese, which was said to carry the danger of infection. On that occasion he echoed the sentiment of every true-blue Aussie when he proclaimed:

Just because a few migrants want their spicy tucker, I fail to see why the Australian community as a whole should suffer the possibility of disease.

The traditional Australian (male) resistance to new gastronomic experiences is perhaps summed up best by the following piece by Sydney *Sunday Telegraph* columnist 'Bennelong' in 1976:

A Sydney taxi-driver provided evidence this week that no self-respecting Ocker is safe from the clutches of migrant sub-cultures: 'The missus has just got this French cooking phrase. Last week it was wog—y'know, all that spaghetti sortabusiness. She's always getting phrases, my missus. Good tucker, but. She's a beaut cook. We had chicken last night. Gaw. Y'oughta seen the garbage she put in it. And the plonk! Not according to Hoyle. I reckon. Bloody good feed, but, bloody good-oh!'

No summary of Australian eating habits would be complete without mention of the well-known food additive tomato sauce, of which enormous quantities are consumed by residents of the Lucky Country. Australia didn't invent tomato sauce, of course, as it has long been established overseas as ketchup, but no other race has attacked the sauce bottle with such vigour. As one anonymous Down Under poet put it:

> *Shake, shake,*
> *Shake, the tomato*
> *sauce bottle*
> *First none will*
> *come, but*
> *then a lot'll.*

There is urgent need to research more into the psyche of the tomato sauce used in Australia. There is need to answer the question posed in 1974 by David Dale as follows:

Just who are these tomato sauce freaks? Exhaustive studies have been done of the regular sauce consumer, and now, if you're the sort of person who buys a bottle of tomato sauce every fortnight, your life's an open book. You don't earn much money, don't travel much, mainly watch TV in your leisure time, and don't expect big changes in your social circle. You are unhappy about the political direction Australia is heading. But you do like your brand of sauce. Wouldn't change, unless the price of one of the other brands dropped dramatically ... You put sauce on your steak, your chops, your sausages, your eggs, your chips, your fish fingers and, of course, your pies. Your kids take tomato sauce sandwiches to school, and have even been known to put it on their icecream.

Tomato sauce is no new-fangled addition to the Australian menu as it was well established in the middle of the last century, as evidenced by this piece of doggerel written by Robert Sealy in 1859:

> *Spread not for me, boy,*
> *banquets of the Persian,*
> *Chops and tomato sauce*
> *will very well do.*

The *Sydney Morning Herald* columnist in 1978 recorded the shock waves that swept through patrons (and staff) of a well known Sydney restaurant when a patron ordered *canard a l'orange* and proceeded to swamp it with tomato sauce. An anguished (French) waiter who witnessed this act of sacrilege commented:

Zis glop, glop, glop iz the most obscene thing I hear in Australia.

Chapter Thirty-seven

DISTINCTIVELY AUSTRALIAN

The Captain Cook Bicentenary Celebrations programme . . .
should include a Mammoth International Cook-in, to devise
a truly Australian national dish. Surely we have more to
offer the world than lamingtons, pavlovas and pies?

Cyril Pearl, 1970

The previous chapters have dealt with some of the more popular
foods consumed by Australians from the time of the first
settlement. It is perhaps time now to examine some of the foods
which had their origin in this country, and therefore gave to the
outside world new culinary experiences and added new words to
the English language.

Perhaps the first truly national food developed in Australia
was the damper—the bush bread made of flour and water which
is kneaded and formed into a dough that is baked in ashes.

'Zake', a contributor to the *Bulletin* (4 June 1958) claimed that
the damper was invented by Australia's first baker, William
Bond, who came out with the First Fleet and set up his bakery in
Pitt Street (Sydney). He began selling dampers because the
conventional loaf of bread was beyond the conveniences
available when he first started dough-bashing. The contributor
cited no evidence for this claim, which runs counter to the
generally held theory that damper originated in the bush.

The first written reference to damper was by P Cunningham
in 1827 in *Two Years in New South Wales* (Vol II, p. 190):

The farm men usually make their flour into flat cakes, which they
call damper, and cook these in the ashes . . .

Charles Sturt in *Southern Australia* (1833) also mentions the damper at an early date:

I watched the distorted countenances of my humble companions while drinking their tea and eating their damper.

From then on many accounts of its preparation and admirable properties appeared regularly in Australian literature. One particularly interesting account was penned by C H Eden in *My Wife and I in Queensland* (1872):

At first we had rather a horror of eating damper, imagining it to be somewhat like an uncooked crumpet. Experience, however, showed it to be really very good. Its construction is simple, and is as follows. Plain flour and water is mixed on a sheet of bark, and then kneaded into a disc some two or three inches thick to about one or two feet in diameter, great care to avoid cracks being taken in the kneading. This is placed in a hole scraped to its size in the hot ashes, covered over, and there left till small cracks caused by the steam appear on the surface of its covering. This is a sign that it is nearly done, and in a few minutes the skilful chef will sound it over with his knife, and if he finds it hard will take it out and stand it on its edge to cool. No disagreeable dust or grit ever adheres, and the smell, especially to a hungry bushman, is most seductive.

The damper isn't to everyone's taste and some early travellers in the bush ate it out of necessity rather than preference. Colonel Godfrey Charles Mundy, who was Deputy Adjutant General in the Australian colonies from 1849–1851, later wrote in his book *Our Antipodes* (London, 1852):

Returning from the Cave, at a filthy cabin where we halted for the night, some of us tasted for the first time the Australian bush-bread, a baked unleavened dough, called damper—a damper, sure enough, to the stoutest appetite—whence its name, I suppose, for it is as heavy as lead. Its manufacture is as follows: a wheaten paste is made, kneaded for a short time, flattened out into a muffin-shaped dough, about the size of the top of an ordinary band-box, and an inch or two thick; a part of the hearth-stone is cleared of the wood ashes, the dough is dropped upon it, and the hot ashes raked over it; if not made too thick, the damper comes out done to a turn in about half an hour.

Some controversy has always existed on the origin of the name of the damper. Some writers have stoutly maintained that it owed its name to the explorer Dampier, but the more traditional view is that its name came from the method of damping fire in bush camps in the evening. This was set out in a letter by G V K of Warragul (Victoria) in *The Australasian Post* of September 1958:

The damper goes right back. In the first settlement in Australia there were few matches. Fire was the one source of lighting. Candles, pipes etc. were dependent on the fire.

Last thing at night the fire was made safe. Provision was also made for it to come alight in the morning by the simple method of damping it down. This was done by raking all live coals to the centre (sometimes short pieces of wood being added), and the whole thing damped down by being covered with fine ashes. The air being mostly cut off, combustion was slowed. In the morning the ashes were raked off the coals, a few bits of kindling added, and hey presto, you had a fire.

In baking the damper, a good big fire was first built, and allowed to burn down to a heap of coals. A nest was made in the centre to receive the damper, and again the fire was damped down with fine ashes, which gave an even temperature. The bread thus baked was called damper. I should know, as I was reared at Pine Creek (NT), being born there more than sixty years ago.

On mining camp, with big teams, and on mustering, the camp fire was always damped at night so that we got a quick start in the morning. And our dampers were baked in a damped-down fire.

But perhaps the last word on dampers should go to John Nelson (1844–1922) for his short poem 'To a Damper' included in *The Men of the Fifties* (1938).

> *Here let me lay thee down to rest*
> *Where I have made thy fiery bed*
> *In soft white ash, and let me now*
> *Heap coals of fire upon thy head!*

A fairly close cousin to the Australian damper is the Johnny-cake. The term is American and there refers to a cake made by the Indians of corn and toasted before the fire. The Australian Johnny-cakes are dough-cakes fried in fat, though the term was sometimes used for small cakes baked in the ashes much after the style of the damper. C H Eden in *My Wife and I in Queensland* (1872) refers to them as follows:

Johnny-cakes, though they are smaller and very thin, and made in a similar way to dampers; when eaten hot they are excellent, but if allowed to get cold they become leathery.

H Finch-Hatton in *Advance of Australia* (1885) commented on them thus:

Johnny-cakes are made with nothing but flour, but there is a great art in mixing them. If it is done properly they are about the lightest and nicest sort of bread that can be made; but the efforts of an amateur generally result in a wet heavy pulp that sticks round one's teeth like bird-lime.

Then the *Argus* of 10 March 1894 gave this detailed recipe:

It is also useful to make your damper or 'Johnny-cake', which serves you in place of yeast bread. A Johnny-cake is made thus: Put a couple of handfuls of flour into your dish, with a good pinch of salt and baking soda. Add water till it works to a stiff paste. Divide it into three parts and flatten out into cakes about half an inch thick. Dust a little flour into your frying-pan and put the cake in. Cook it slowly over the fire, taking care it does not burn, and tossing it over again and again. When nearly done stand it against a stick in front of the fire, and let it finish baking while you cook the other two. These, with a piece of wallaby and a billy of tea, are a sweet meal enough after a hard day's work.

Another traditional bush standby in Australia from about the 1870s was bully beef, a tinned corned beef which featured all too regularly in the diet, and was soundly execrated by Australian troops in two World Wars.

Bully beef was developed like so many other products in history to meet a specific need—to keep men alive in Central Australia whilst the Overland Telegraph Line was being constructed by Charles Todd. In *The Territory* (1951) Ernestine Hill tell the story of the invention of bully beef as follows:

Todd's problem was to keep them alive—no cattle stations and never a rabbit out there in 1870. The Government offered £10,000 reward for the first drover to cross the north with sheep or cattle.

In the meantime, bully beef, the famous Australian 'bully' that has travelled the Seven Seas in peace and war, and kept the wolf from the door at the South Pole, made its bow to a grateful world. J V Hughes, of Booyoolee Station, in South Australia, packed the first fibre of it in a tin, and fibre it was, but it was meat. Nicknamed 'red blanket' because of its red label, for two hungry years on the Telegraph Line it was breakfast, dinner and tea for 500 men.

There is a school of thought that the idea and the name was derived from the French bouilli, and indeed it was pronounced bouilli by pedants of the time, but it was originally written 'Booyoolee beef' . . . And every old bushman of Australia will tell you that 'bully for short', the good old tinned dog of the campfires, Number One Tucker, first came to the great, wide spaces in the pack-saddles of Todd's men.

Some words start out as trade marks and gradually become generic terms through constant usage. One such word that deserves to become enshrined in our language in this way is VEGEMITE which seems to have a special place in the hearts (and stomachs) of Australians. That it is an acquired taste is amply demonstrated by the curling of the lip and sudden backing off which invariably is experienced when a non-Australian is exposed to the product for the first time. But once the Vegemite habit is acquired it seems to become an addiction which the user carries with him (or her) to the ends of the earth. Many have been the tales of travellers trapped in remote and uncivilised places sending home for jars of the stuff.

When singer Helen Reddy returned briefly to Australia in 1977 after a long absence abroad she explained the reason for the journey briefly in the simple words:

I ran out of Vegemite.

And no one batted an eyelid. Every true Australian instantly understood her feeling.

When Belinda Green, former Miss World, returned to Australia in 1978 she told reporters that in Los Angeles the Australian colony was a tightly knit group. She added:

Every now and then we would hold a gumleaf mafia meeting with Vegemite provided for whatever Aussies were in town.

Perhaps it was reports such as these seeping back to the United States that prompted the Holiday Inn at Ventura, Southern California in 1977 to put Vegemite on the menu as a means of making their Australian guests feel more at home. The reaction of their American guests to the strange substance unfortunately has not been recorded.

Vegemite, which is a pure concentrated yeast extract produced in the form of a concentrated (dark brown) cream, was first commercially produced in 1923, so several generations of Australians have been exposed to its unusual form and taste. It won some kind of fame during World War II when the Australian Army recognised its nutritional value, and purchased substantial quantities for the troops in 7 lb tins, 8 oz tins and half-ounce ration packs. The mind boggles at the thought of 7 lb tins of the stuff, and one is tempted to ponder on the thought of resourceful diggers hurling the stuff at Japanese bunkers instead of hand grenades as some kind of new secret weapon. The War Archives unfortunately are silent on the subject.

One presumes that the management of Kraft Foods are very happy indeed with the national and even international image of Vegemite.

Firms who produce rival products by no means share this enthusiasm. In an article in the *Financial Review* in August 1978, Valerie Lawson disclosed that the Sanitarium Health Food Company, the makers of Marmite (a rival yeast extract product to Vegemite) were very unhappy about the way Vegemite received continual publicity as the ultimate all-Australian food. The article disclosed that Marmite actually beat Vegemite on to the market in the 1920s but had lost ground since then. The article disclosed that in the 1930s Marmite was so successful that a competitor had brought out a rival product called PAWILL and had promoted it (unsuccessfully) under the slogan *'Marmite but Pawill'*. Such a dreadful pun deserved the oblivion that befell the product.

The article went on to note that the Kraft-made Vegemite in 1978 controlled 90 per cent of the Australian market and that Kraft was sending 2000 six-packs of Vegemite a year overseas to nostalgic Australians in all corners of the globe.

Another distinctive Australian product is Golden Syrup, a syrup refined for raw sugar, which still survives on the supermarket shelves. Few of the present-day generation however, know that for half a century or more it was known as 'Cocky's Joy', and before that as 'Kidman's Joy' or 'Kidman's Blood Mixture'—a somewhat backhanded tribute to Sir Sidney Kidman, the 'Cattle King', whose penny-pinching ways led him to supply the substance to his stockmen in place of the much more expensive jam.

The CHIKO ROLL is an Australian invention which has taken its place alongside the humble meat pie as a favourite take-away food since it was first invented and marketed by the late Frank McEnroe in the early 1950s. When McEnroe, a former caterer, died in March 1979 at the age of 70, it was recorded that more than 56 million Chiko rolls were then being consumed annually by Australians, with a million more being exported each year to Japan.

No chapter on distinctive Australian foods would be complete without mention of the lamington. Originally slang for a homburg hat, as worn by Baron Lamington, a Queensland Governor (1896–1901), the word now has an entirely different meaning and refers to a small plain cake, oblong in shape about 7 centimetres long by 5 centimetres wide and 5 centimetres deep, dipped in chocolate icing and then rolled in desiccated coconut. The inventor of this delicacy is unknown, but it is consumed in considerable quantities by Australians including the highest of the land, if we are to believe the following comment (in 1974) by a Prime Ministerial aide following reports that the then Prime Minister, Gough Whitlam, was sulking his way towards a resignation:

The absolutely certain indicator of Gough's state of health and humor is his massive ingestion of cream cakes, especially lamingtons. Today he has been consuming them at a great rate.

In *Nation Review* (1977) John Hepworth made these interesting comments on the lowly lamington and its place in our society:

Apart from the dreaded Pavlova, the only part of the Australian national cuisine which could fairly be considered to be a truly original contribution to the dining tables of the world is the even more dreaded Lamington. I think one could say without fear of any serious challenge that nothing quite like the Australian Lamington is known anywhere else on earth. Which surely makes the effort of a dedicated group of citizens in the cataplexic Melbourne suburb of Camberwell—knocking up near on a quarter of a million of the prickly little buggers (and flogging them off to the grateful public) in a day and a half—a matter worth public comment and national pride . . . It should be nationally known—and we should dip our lids—that the mothers and fathers of the 1st Camberwell South Scouts in Melbourne town have, in a day and a half, made and sold no less than 19,040 dozen Lamingtons to raise funds for the troop. By my pocket computer, 19,040 dozen means precisely 228,480 Lamingtons. They are going to apply to have the tally included in the Guinness Book of Records. And by God, so it should be: if they get knocked back on this it will be time to mount the barricades.

The Pavlova is often credited with being a distinctive national dish, but we must tread carefully here because across the Tasman, New Zealanders have made similar and very vociferous claims to being inventors of the dish. Let us simply say that the Pavlova is of Australasian origin, which will satisfy everyone.

This dish, which is basically a light meringue covered liberally with cream and passionfruit or strawberries, is a prime favourite with young and old. It is a pity that such a distinctive Australian dish was not given a more national title rather than being named after some far-off Russian ballerina.

I am informed that an attempt to export the Pavlova to England in the early 1970s failed initially because the English would not have a bar of the passionfruit topping. When the passionfruit was removed and replaced with strawberries the position changed dramatically and sales rocketed!

Another dish, a sweet called Peach Melba, named after our own Dame Nellie Melba is found all around the world and was created by the famous chef Escoffier when he was at the Hotel Savoy in London.

Chapter Thirty-eight

GETTING ON THE GROG

Drunkenness, the fruitful parent of every species of crime, is still the prevailing vice of the colony.

Sir George Gipps,
in **Quest for Authority in Eastern Australia**

There were only two things in plentiful supply in the early years of the Colony of New South Wales—the lash and rum. And most of the inhabitants had more than their fair share of both, but like Oliver Twist, they still cried for more if we are to judge by the old 'Convict Rum Song'.

> *Cut yer name across me backbone,*
> *Stretch me skin across yer drum,*
> *Iron me up on Pinchgut Island*
> *From now to Kingdom Come.*
> *I'll eat yer Norfolk Dumpling*
> *Like a juicy Spanish plum,*
> *Even dance the Newgate Hornpipe*
> *If ye'll only gimme Rum!*

The NORFOLK DUMPLING referred to above incidentally, is not some new Australian gastronomic delicacy but the slang expression of the day for a term in the hell-hole of Norfolk Island. The Dance of the Newgate Hornpipe, of course, was the hanging from the gallows.

Dr George Mackaness in his *Life of Vice Admiral William Bligh* commented:

The population of Sydney (circa 1806) was divided into two classes, those who sold rum and those who drank it.

Rum played such a vital role in the early years of the colony that it was the accepted currency of settlement; and when Governor Bligh endeavoured to break the officers' monopoly on the rum traffic he was ousted in the famous 'Rum Rebellion' of 1809.

Nor is the primary school entirely safe from the evil influences of the liquor trade if we are to believe the following 1974 report from the *Australian Church Record* describing the perils of 11-year-olds in NSW State Schools:

The girls had their first cooking lesson. The tasty morsel to be cooked was rum balls. Whether rum essence or the real jungle juice scarcely matters. Small girls were to be introduced to this highly desirable alcoholic flavour. Perhaps it is part of the modern approach to cooking, which is to saturate almost everything in some form of alcohol and give it a French name.

The report refers to rum balls, which I rather fancy is an Australian invention. I would be happy to be corrected on this point, but I haven't seen them elsewhere in my wanderings around the globe and feel that this is another potential export the Department of Trade might care to investigate more thoroughly.

Despite the fact that so much social activity in Australia is centred on drinking, the inhabitants of this hot and thirsty continent have never got around to distinctive Australian names for their collective watering holes. All the names they have applied to liquor outlets have been traditional English words, though it is a curious fact that their use has not always synchronised with usage in the 'Old Dart'.

In the early colonial days the licensed premises were invariably inns—a word rarely used today except in describing multi-storey motels. In the outback the illegal seller of spirits was the bush shanty, and this did give rise to the verb TO SHANTY (to drink habitually) and SHANTY-KEEPER. These terms were short-lived.

INN gave way to HOTEL which still survives, though the more trendy English term of PUB has taken over since World War II. The only linguistic deviation has been the term RUBBEDY (slang for Pub).

A very interesting rural expression which had wide currency at one time was 'to tie up a dog' or 'to chain a pup', meaning to obtain drinks on credit from a publican. If a drinker subsequently reneged on such a debt it was said 'the dogs are barking'. As late as 1937, a publican who was leaving the district inserted an advertisement in the *Bathurst National Advocate* which in part proclaimed:

... He particularly requests that all dogs tied up at the hotel be released. This reservation specially applies to Kelpies, Alsatians and other large breeds.

The expression is not now in use, probably because flint-hearted publicans of today rarely extend credit.

What many visitors to Australia do not appreciate at first is that the continent is divided into six states with different sets of liquor laws—sometimes widely diverging in character and enforcement.

Some states have very peculiar licensing laws for restaurants, some being fully licensed and permitted to sell and serve liquor, while others have licences which do not permit them to sell liquor, but allow them to open and serve bottles of drink brought in by customers. Overseas visitors often observe that one of the stranger sights to be witnessed in Australia is that of well-dressed males (and sometimes females) entering restaurants with brown paper wrapped parcels under their arms, the shape of the packages clearly proclaiming their contents to be bottles.

Restaurants who have to operate under this archaic system have to signal the fact to intending customers that they aren't allowed to *sell* liquor—they can only serve the customers' liquor, a very nice distinction. They do this by putting signs in their windows and in their advertisements comprising three simple initials BYO. This must be a great puzzle to the visitor who cannot be expected to understand that this simply means BRING YOUR OWN (grog).

It is also not at all unusual for printed invitations to parties these days to carry the BYOG catchline, and even canvas carry bags imprinted with the BYO initials are now on sale at many speciality shops.

Visitors from overseas find this so confusing that locals sometimes feel the need for special interpretation. For instance, *This Week in Sydney*, a weekly guide to Sydney restaurants, shops and tourist spots in 1978 introduced a special note as follows under the heading BYO:

A note for the international visitor on the subject of wine (booze, grog or plonk in the vernacular). Many restaurants have a full liquor service (licensed restaurants) while others have licences which allow patrons to bring their own, hence the terms BYOL: bring your own liquor. BYOW: bring your own wine, BYOG: bring your own grog, or stripped to essential simplicity: BYO.

The BYO label was given a slightly different twist in the Northern Territory in 1978 when the Noonamah Hotel on the outskirts of Darwin displayed the rules for a contest which ended with the letters BYOF. The *F* stood for frog and the rules related to the Top End's first Frog Swallowing Contest.

The contest incidentally was easily won by a Darwin mechanic, Ted Stanton, who, with the aid of a bottle of mint sauce, had no difficulty swallowing six live frogs.

The current favourite slang expression for beer is THE LIQUID AMBER, but this is used indiscriminately with SLOPS, TURPS, GROG or PISS for beer and other alcoholic drinks.

From SLOPS comes the term to BE ON THE SLOPS (to be on a drinking bout). The term was even used by the Queensland Minister for Prisons, Mr Herbert, in 1978, when referring to weekend detention of prisoners at Brisbane gaol:

> . . . they have been on the slops all day and come into gaol to dry out.

Another slang expression for liquor is GROG and this too, has its chain of associated terms such as GROGGING ON or ON THE GROG. This actually is the earliest of the slang terms for liquor—and one that has persisted to the present day—as it was noted as far back as 1819 when G W Evans in *A Description of Van Diemen's Land*, wrote:

> . . . grog fever is the only prevailing disease in the colony.

Other more recent uses of the term 'grog' include:

> We grogged on till closing time; it was evident we all had one thing in common—a liking for the amber liquid.
>
> John Beede, *They Hosed Them Out* (1965)

> Hammo had been on the grog and he didn't give way to his right and this bloke smashed into him.
>
> Alexander Buzo's *Rooted* (1973)

All liquor is BOOZE so that a man can be ON THE BOOZE and BOOZED UP. He can also be FULL AS A GOOG (egg), or SHICKERED, STUNG, DRUNK AS CHLOE or simply PISSED TO THE EYEBALLS.

A stiff drink (of any kind) is sometimes referred to as a ROSINER (alternate spellings: ROZENER, ROSNER). The term comes from the old English expression TO ROSIN (to supply with liquor) and often refers to a pick-me-up. Tom Ronan in *Vision Splendid* (1954) used the term this way:

> Two nips that old Block had and the one I poured into Peter. They were rozeners I'll admit, but still the three I've had out of this second bottle haven't been exactly small.

Donald Stuart in 1973 used the expression in a slightly different context:

There's no harm in a bit of a rosiner after a hard day's travel, just once in a while.

Wines have also attracted nicknames, the most popular of which are PLONK (a term which still survives), BOMBO, RED NED and STEAM. From these are derived the terms ON THE PLONK, BOMBED OUT and he was all STEAMED UP.

Sid Baker notes that in the 1930s wine was also sometimes named CLEVER MARY after a household cleanser of that name because after drinking it a 'man goes home and cleans up the house'.

Methylated spirits, the drink of the down-and-outs, is simply METHO and the drinker of the stuff a METHO ARTIST.

PISS is a good old Anglo-Saxon slang word for urine, to wit the ancient rhyme.

> *He who once a good name gets,*
> *May piss a bed, and say he sweats.*

Australians, of course, use this word in the same sense as their English forbears, but they also use the word as a term for liquor in general. From there it was only one step to the further terms of GETTING ON THE PISS (to get drunk), to BE PISSED OUT OF HIS MIND (to be drunk) and PISS OFF, MATE (make yourself scarce).

A person who drinks to excess is said to be a PISSPOT. In 1974 Sydney Garbage Contractor Ron Walters was quoted as follows:

Eventually every house in the (North Sydney) area will have a bottle collection crate and we'll be collecting more than Mosman. As the mayor told me, they're much bigger pisspots over here.

In 1974 Sydney advertising agency executive John Singleton used the expression in a way that all true Australians would clearly understand.

The advertising industry lives a very cyclical sort of life. December is the month for getting pissed.

Credit must go to the *Bulletin* for turning up a story where these terms are given a slightly new twist. The story comes from the 1978 Commonwealth Heads of Government Regional Meeting in Sydney when the NSW Premier, Neville Wran, gave a reception for the Heads of State, including the Indian Prime Minister, Morarji Desai, who not long before the event had rather bemused the western world by admitting that each morning he drank a pint of his own urine.

Amongst the local guests at the reception was former Prime Minister Gough Whitlam and a prominent Jewish member of

Parliament, a very temperate drinker. The latter observed that he didn't want to stay too late at the reception, whereupon Gough Whitlam commented:

Oh, yes, that'd be right. A good temperate Jew like you would want to get away before all these Indians get on the piss.

The problem of reporting the actions of prominent personalities who become inebriated is one that has long exercised the minds of newspaper sub-editors. Most of them tend to pussy-foot around the matter by ignoring the incidents entirely, but sometimes the occasion or the personality is so public that the incident cannot be ignored. Then they are in real trouble trying to get around established guidelines.

One such occasion was the 1977 Melbourne Cup presentation ceremony by the then Governor General, the very controversial Sir John Kerr. It was quite obvious to all present, and to TV viewers watching the ceremony with great fascination, that the chief participant had partaken too well, and none too wisely. The unanimous verdict of a million or so Australians gathered in clubs and pubs around the country was quite clear and unequivocal: *He's pissed to the eyeballs.*

This also was the verdict of journalists present and sub-editors around the nation, but one and all felt that the verdict of their fellow countrymen could not be expressed *quite* that way in public print. The incident had to be referred to somehow, but in what form? They took refuge in the oldest sanctuary of the Fourth Estate—the euphemism. The next day readers around the continent were rather bemused to read that Sir John Kerr 'had been in a mood less restrained than usual', that he was 'flushed from his official duties', that he was 'flushed and obviously tired', that he somewhat 'discarded usual regal restraint' and that he was 'in high spirits'.

Of the major daily newspapers only the *Australian* subsequently allowed open reference to Sir John Kerr's condition, and that only in quoting a statement by Sir John's former friend and subsequent bitter critic, Labor Senator James McClelland:

. . . But the beneficiaries of Kerr's favors did not expect the titular Head of State to fall over in the mud when opening a country fair or to conduct himself like a drunken lout before half the population watching him on television present the Melbourne Cup.

In Australia teetotallers are known as 'cold water men' and this has always been an expression of contempt, viz Sir John Robertson (1816–1891), five times Premier of New South Wales:

None of the men who in this country have left footprints behind them have been cold water men.

Not that there were many of the cold water breed around in the hot, thirsty Australian climate if we are to take the word of one of Robertson's contemporaries, Sir George Reid when he opened the Kalgoorlie pipe line:

Never have I seen so much enthusiasm for water—and so little of it drunk.

Robertson incidentally went out of his way to prove that he wasn't a cold-water man. The *Encyclopaedia of Ridiculous Facts* reports that he drank a pint of rum every morning for thirty-five years.

Chapter Thirty-nine

BEER, GLORIOUS BEER

Beer makes you feel as you
ought to feel without beer.

Henry Lawson

Beer has always played such an important role in the
Australian way of life, that I have thought it advisable to devote
a separate chapter to the beverage.

The blame (or credit) for introducing beer to Australia would
seem to rest on the shoulders of a free settler named John
Boston, who in 1794 produced the colony's first brew with a malt
made of maize and flavoured with the leaves and stalks of the
cape gooseberry.

This, of course, was not a true beer as it lacked the essential
ingredient of hops. A convict named James Squires stepped into
the breach here by growing the colony's first crop of hops. Later
when he was freed, he set up a brewery at Kissing Point on the
Parramatta River, where he brewed the first quality beer in the
colony.

Squires died in 1822 but his fame lived on. In *Two Years in
New South Wales*, P Cunningham (1828) wrote:

About seven miles up (the Parramatta River), to the right, is
Squires's tavern, with its boat-wharf, and adjoining cleared enclosures
and ample orchards. Its enterprising proprietor, now no more, was the
first colonial brewer, and long too the only one who prepared a colonial
solatium for our drouthy population. Squires's beer therefore was

as well known and as celebrated in this as Meux and Co.s in your hemisphere. An epitaph on one of its votaries in Parramatta churchyard (which the jocose compounder of the beverage took a pleasure in quoting), records its virtues in these two expressive lines:—

> *Ye who wish to lie here,*
> *Drink Squires's beer!*

For about a century and a half beer came either in draught form in casks or in bottles, and the drinking men of the nation evidently found it difficult to think up a slang expression for such containers, though a publican was generally referred to as a BUNG—after the plug (or bung) which he removed from old-time casks.

When beer started to appear in steel kegs of nine or eighteen gallon capacity, the word KEG was quickly dispensed with and they were (and are) simply referred to as NINES or EIGHTEENS.

In the 1960s a smaller version of the traditional beer bottle found its way on to the market, and this was instantly named the STUBBIE. Because more of them were being consumed and discarded on the highways of the continent they also attracted the wrath of the temperance movement and the environmentalists. Bishop Shevill, Anglican Bishop of North Queensland, in 1970 solemnly proclaimed:

The stubbie is one of the most malevolent institutions of the decade.

Do not however, make the mistake of assuming that the word STUBBIE has the same meaning in all parts of the continent. Up in Darwin the perverse sense of humour of the Top End has led the locals to brand a monster bottle of draught beer (two and a quarter litres) as the DARWIN STUBBIE. Many a visitor from the south has been tricked into losing a wager that he can drink a stubbie in a minute.

The word STUBBIE can also be the cause of confusion in another direction, as it is the slang word used for football shorts with pockets.

Criticism of the STUBBIE tended to die down when beer started to be packed in cans for the first time, and these inevitably attracted what criticism was flying around about liquor containers. They also inevitably collected some new nicknames.

Cans of beer initially were referred to as TUBES, but vying with popularity was the nickname TINNY, particularly after the appearance in 1977 of a series of 'Life Be In It' TV advertisements which were initiated in Victoria but soon aired around the continent. In these a self-confessed do-nothing type named Norm mentioned that he would 'Cool the tinnies and warm the tube', which meant that he would put a few cans of beer in the refrigerator and switch on the TV.

In New South Wales a MIDDY of beer is a small glass (of 10 oz) whilst in Western Australia it shrinks in size down to a 7 oz measure. A similar thing happens with a SCHOONER which is a large-size drink in New South Wales (15 oz) but is a small drink in South Australia (9 oz).

John O'Grady in *It's Your Shout Mate* (1972) did his best to explain the crazy situation as follows:

A glass is a five ounces (in Western Australia), a middy is a seven ounces, an' a pot's ten. Got it? . . . (in Queensland) they call a pot a middy because its midway between nothing and a pint.

The confusion all this causes to the interstate (not to mention the overseas) traveller is well illustrated by this comment in an article in the *Sydney Morning Herald* in 1954:

'In Adelaide we call that a schooner' . . . I expressed sympathy at such extreme myopia. 'A schooner, my friends, is a large glass,' I told him.

David Ireland in *The Glass Canoe* (1976) has some sympathy for the character who has to reduce his or her drinking intake, viz:

Poor Liz . . . She didn't have the same old bounce, and she went down from schooners to middies.

The old terms of LADY'S WAIST (Sydney) and PIXIE (Melbourne) for small glasses appear to have disappeared from the scene, although the South Australian term BUTCHER for a 6 oz glass survives.

A few years ago the *Sydney Morning Herald* Column 8 recorded how, in some circumstances, a bottle of beer could be called LAUNDRY. It could only happen in Queensland, of course, and the columnist explained the situation as follows:

By chance a colleague booked into a north Queensland motel before learning that its dining-room was not licensed. 'Think nothing of it', said the waitress. 'If you want a bottle of beer with your steak just say, Steak and Laundry. It doesn't show on the records.'

I somehow think this transposition of terms would be difficult to get across to a foreigner with only limited command of English.

Beer drinkers are fanatically devoted to brands in Australia as they are in other parts of the world. The TOOTHS or

TOOHEY drinkers of New South Wales, won't have a bar of Queensland's BULIMBA or Victorian FOSTERS or COURAGE, not to mention Tasmania's CASCADE, South Australian COOPERS or the SWAN brand of Western Australia.

All these brands are clearly identified in the mind of the Australian drinker even if he doesn't consume them, except when travelling interstate or when his own favourite brew isn't on tap. He sees nothing incongruous in the fact that numerous tests have quite clearly shown that when blindfolded the average drinker cannot tell one brand from another.

He still tends to become confused when confronted with a brand he doesn't recognise. Maybe that's what caused such a problem in 1977 when a supposedly new brand of beer began to circulate surreptitiously underground in Brisbane and other capital cities. The new brew was named BJELKE BITTER and the label proclaimed it was Queensland's *Premier* Beer for *discriminating* drinkers and produced under Appointment to Her Majesty the Queen (of Queensland, of course). The joke was soon out however. It wasn't a new brew at all—simply a new label produced by students of Queensland University and applied over the labels of other more legitimate brands.

The target of this piece of beery satire—Queensland's Premier Joh Bjelke-Petersen—a 'cold-water man' himself, like Queen Victoria, was said to be 'not amused' when the hoax was drawn to his notice.

Beer can at times inspire brand loyalties of a surprising kind even in school-yard rhymes. In the 1970s Peters' Icecream ran a series of television commercials promoting their product as the 'Health Food of the Nation'. In Melbourne this resulted in the following parody popping up in the playgrounds:

> *Carlton Bitter, Carlton Bitter,*
> *Carlton Bitter, can or glass,*
> *It's the health food of a nation,*
> *Stick the icecream up your arse.*

Drinkers who consume large quantities of beer frequently develop BEER GUTS. According to David McNicoll, writing in the *Bulletin* in 1977, these men are 'beeraholics'—as distinct from alcoholics. McNicoll went on to explain the matter this way:

Some years ago a prominent doctor told me that a very large percentage of the population of Australia were 'beeraholics'.

Their systems were impregnated, saturated by their steady intake of beer. Their tolerance to the drinking of vast quantities was such that they seldom showed any ill-effects—except beer guts.

But, unknowingly, they had become dependent on that daily intake —in other words, 'beeraholics'.

Australians have long been aware that large-scale consumption of alcohol can affect their sex lives by making them (temporarily) impotent. They have not let this knowledge interfere with their drinking habits however, and, in true Australian tradition, have even coined a nickname for this unhappy male condition. It is known as BREWER'S DROOP.

Chapter Forty

DRINKING RITUALS

The Greeks always buried their dead with a coin in their mouths to pay the ferryman across the Styx. So why aren't Australians buried with a can of Foster's, even more poignant when you recall that most great Australians have been drunks?

T J McKenna, 1977

Australian drinking is steeped in ritual, most of it built around the SHOUT and the ROUND in a SESSION (all Australian expressions), and woe betide the visitor who fails to observe the social niceties in these traditions.

When one person buys another a drink in Australia it is a SHOUT, and there is an obligation on the recipient to SHOUT back, whether or not he wants another drink. The easiest way to get a bad reputation amongst the drinking fraternity is to fail to SHOUT when your turn comes around. The term itself is interesting, having been derived from the early colonial expression of STANDING SHOT or paying someone else's bill, and it has a long history in the drinking haunts of the nation. Raffaello Carboni in *The Eureka Stockade* (1855) commented:

You shouted nobblers round for all hands—that's all right; it's no more than fair and square now for the boys to shout for you.

Thatcher's Colonial Minstrel (1864) noted:

At ten o'clock we'd then toss up to see who was to shout. (An example of the combination of a ritual with the Australian love of gambling.)

Not all drinkers were in favour of the practice however, as a sour note was struck by A J Boyd in *Old Colonials* (1882):

This 'shouting', as 'treating' is termed in the colonies, is the curse of the Northern goldfields. If you buy a horse you must shout, the vendor must shout, and the bystanders who have been shouted to must shout in their turn.

Although the term is used predominantly in the drinking arena, it is not exclusive to it as a SHOUT can also apply to a gift or treats. For example, Henry Lawson's *The Stranger's Friend* (1899):

For he'd shout the stranger a suit of clothers, and he'd pay for the stranger's board.

Kylie Tennant in *Foveaux* (1939):

Any time Tommy tried to shout the family to the picture show there was a unanimous firm refusal.

When two or more people settle down to a period of steady drinking it is a SESSION, and the individual who merely wants to quench his thirst with a quick drink or two and then be off must always be on his guard against getting trapped into a SESSION which will go on for hours. Thus Lawson Glassop in *Lucky Palmer* (1949):

I'll join you in a beer later, but I don't want to get into a session.

What happens if you don't heed this warning is best expressed by D'Arcy Niland in *The Shiralee* (1955):

I don't want to make a session of it. I had a helluva night.

A session is sometimes referred to as a SCHOOL, though this expression is more usually reserved for a group of gamblers (i.e. of Two-up).

When a session starts the members are in a ROUND (probably derived from the original ROUND ROBIN) with each member in turn being obliged to SHOUT. The member who dodges his obligation is known contemptuously as a FOX. The person whose turn it is to SHOUT is said to be IN THE CHAIR and the obligation is on him to order, pay for and often to transport the drinks physically from the bar to the location of the session.

Sidney Baker puts it this way:

To be in the chair is to be the person who pays for the next round of drinks (the pertinent question is often Who's in the chair?).

A person who has intentions of quitting a SESSION early, or who wants to big-note himself will often volunteer to SHOUT early in the piece, knowing that the SESSION is likely to expand in numbers as the hours go by. Thus Geoff Morley in *Jockey Rides and Honest Race* (1972):

Just to show you what sort of fellow I am, I'll go first in the chair.

In an article on drinking in the *National Times* in January 1978 Elisabeth Wynhausen, after an extensive Sydney pub crawl, reported on the phenomenon of the ROUND and the SHOUT as follows:

In tribal societies in which gift giving is economically important, there may be exchanges of identical (or useless) gifts which serve to stress or maintain the relationship between the donors. In Australia, the ritual of the round, known to virtually all adult members of the society has some parallel functions. It symbolises entree to a group (and, for that matter, makes pointed an exclusion). It binds a group together. It can serve as a display of wealth or generosity. It publicly demonstrates a drinker's capacity.

You can drink from here to San Francisco and you always find there's one fox in the school and he foxes all the bloody time.

The shout involves contractual obligations which are generally taken seriously. It is shocking form for a drinker to drop out of a round before his turn to buy. In some pubs, especially in the country the offence of jumping the shout will be widely publicised and long remembered. The drinker who forgets his turn will probably be resoundingly abused. Someone who has to leave after the first drink is expected to offer to stand the round . . .

The Cowboy was a bit vague about it, but it seemed to him that when they first came into the pub, drinkers would re-order a middy in about five minutes. It is a common sight in any pub to see a drinker holding a brimming glass being handed another one. There is usually fair pressure to keep up the pace. Getting drunk is no breach of form. Drinking too little often is.

In August 1978 the Federal Government brought down what was described as a 'horror budget' with greatly increased excise charges which in turn considerably increased the retail price of beer and spirits. A week after the event Max Jessop reported in the *Australian* that the Budget had destroyed a great Australian tradition—the SHOUT. He said his investigations showed that friends still mixed in the bars of the nation, but they tended to drink more slowly and to buy their own. He quoted Mr Ron Nielsen, the licensee of one of Queensland's largest hotels, the North Star at Ipswich as follows:

It was a sad day when John Howard (the Treasurer) killed a legend of camaraderie that once helped Australia to be a great nation . . . Instead of the hail-fellow-well-met and the what-are-you-having, people, since the Budget, are sneaking in, shuffling alongside their mates and furtively asking for 'one on my own', or 'one on the side, please'. I fear for a community that can't afford to shout. My bank balance is suffering and somehow friendship isn't the same any more.

In the same issue, the *Australian* ran an editorial commenting on the story. The editorial writer was more optimistic than the paper's reporter and noted that the tradition of the SHOUT had survived many Budget-bashings in the past. The editorial writer considered the report on the SHOUT premature and added this linguistic note:

... It is to be hoped so, if only for the sake of the language. It will be much less colourful without: 'He wouldn't shout in a shark attack' and 'If those two blokes were alone in a bar together they'd die of thirst'.

In 1978 Mr David Herbert, the Superintendent of the NSW Traffic Accident Research Bureau, blamed the high road toll on the system of SHOUTING in clubs and pubs. He put his views as follows:

People feel they must keep up with every round. They have to learn to be strong when others try to force drinks on them. We're trying to break the 'shout' system.

His campaign to have the SHOUT banned fell on totally deaf ears so far as the legion of drinkers was concerned.

Whilst the SCHOOLS of drinkers with their ROUNDS and SHOUTS are an established tradition in pubs and clubs throughout Australia, there are always the solitary types who drink alone—or who 'drink with the flies'. They are known as Jimmy Woodsers, after some character, real or mythical named Jimmy Woods, who established this un-Australian practice. Needless to say the Jimmy Woodsers of the community are looked upon with considerable disfavour by the more social drinkers.

Chapter Forty-one

THE SPORTING LIFE

In a land where sport is sacred,
Where the laborer is God,
You must pander to the people,
Make a hero of a clod.

> Henry Lawson,
> in **A Son of Southern Writers**

Visitors to this country are unanimous on one point: that Australians appear to be obsessed with sport. The English fast bowler John Snow probably summed up the views of most outsiders when he wrote:

> In my opinion Melburnians are like piranha fish when it comes to sport. They will devour anything that will satisfy their appetite for competition . . . you can almost feel the jaws of the Melbourne mob snapping at you.

Snow was talking specifically about Melbourne, which perhaps has more volatile sporting crowds than are to be found in other Australian cities, but it is only a matter of degree. Anyone who has found himself on the receiving end of the hostility of the crowd on *The Hill* of the Sydney Cricket Ground would hesitate to award top honours for abusiveness to Melbourne.

Keith Dunstan in his amusing book *Sports* (1973) claimed that sport was the ultimate Australian super-religion, the one thing every Australian believes in passionately!

Sport is wholesome. It can do no wrong. It builds stronger Australian men and women and, best of all, it spreads the fame of Australia overseas. It helps unify Australia as a nation . . . not to be keen on sport is, therefore, unclean, unmanly, even homosexual, and definitely contrary to the ethics and super-religion of the nation.

To ridicule sport in Australia is to invite retribution in some form. Dunstan went on to relate how in 1967, becoming somewhat tired of the vast amounts of media attention being given to Australian Rules Football, he started an Anti-Football League as a fun thing. He expected some reaction from football fans but was startled by the hostility of the letters which poured in accusing him of being everything from a poofter to a Communist! One typical missive read:

If you and other fairies like you don't like Australian Rules football, then why don't you go and live in Sydney, go and live anywhere, and leave the place to decent people who like it.

Given the climate and the general outdoor life followed by most Australians, the inhabitants of the Lucky Country probably do play more sport than do the people of other nations. But what distinguishes them from the rest of the world is the intensive *interest*—as distinct from actual participation—in almost all forms of sporting activities. The man-in-the-street in England may be wedded to one sport (usually soccer), and may take only a cursory interest in other sporting activities. However the average Australian will follow with intense passion events on the race tracks of the nation, at least one football code, and cricket and have more than a passing interest in perhaps half a dozen other sports. The bars of the clubs and pubs of the nation literally buzz with sport talk and the newspapers—well aware of the interests of their readers—strive mightily to deplete the world's forests by providing an unprecedented (by international standards) coverage of sporting activities. Even the Australian Broadcasting Commission has allowed itself to be trapped into the sportsmania of the nation by providing a national sporting coverage that astounds visitors from abroad.

With such a preoccupation with sport, it is little wonder that the sporting world has been such a prolific contributor to the Australian-English language. Many of the new words and phrases on the nation's sporting fields, of course, have remained within the confines of the sports concerned, but many others have found their way out into the general language of the nation.

The word SPORT itself is even a slang term of some standing

in Australia, G'DAY SPORT being a national greeting from Perth to Cairns, whilst the term 'He's a good sport' is recognisable anywhere as referring to someone who is hundred per cent true blue Aussie. In Australia, sport is often a violent affair, and this is reflected in the fact that the term SPORT can also be used in an aggressive form: 'Where do you think you're going, eh SPORT?'

Apart from horse-racing (which is covered in a separate chapter), football is the biggest spectator sport in Australia, attracting far greater crowds than any of the other traditional games.

Australian football fans have four codes they can follow—the imported Rugby League, Rugby Union and Soccer codes or the indigenous Australian Rules, a high-kicking game which its detractors (and they are legion) describe as AERIAL PING PONG.

Australian Rules originated in Melbourne, where it is classed as a religion, and has strong followings in Tasmania, South Australia and Western Australia. Despite many strenuous promotional efforts it has made no progress in New South Wales and Queensland where the two imported Rugby codes reign supreme. Soccer is a johnny-come-lately on the scene having blossomed only in the post-war years as a result of the influx of huge numbers of English and European migrants— all dedicated soccer fans back in their homelands.

Whichever code they follow, the fans take their football very seriously in the Antipodes, and mayhem on and off the field is by no means uncommon for all codes. Perhaps this is because Australians are weaned on contact sports—including some of its worst aspects—at a very early age.

In 1973 a Sydney Roman Catholic School, Holy Cross Primary School, Woollahra, withdrew its under-six-year-old team from the Junior Rugby League competition because parents were 'bribing' their offspring. The school principal, Sister Mary Julian, explained:

A dollar for a tackle or a try, and more after the game is common. It is a sick atmosphere and not one to be encouraged.

In the same year another Sydney schoolboy footballer, 8-year-old Martin Fletcher was 'banned for life' by the Junior Rugby League following a tripping incident in a game.

One Australian slang invention common to all football codes is TO RABBIT meaning to (illegally) trip an opposing player.

Australian sporting crowds are not alone in assigning nicknames to their football teams. Fans everywhere do it, but in

Australia the names seem more inventive than their overseas counterparts. On the Sydney Rugby League scene for instance there are such long-established teams as the SEA EAGLES (sometimes just EAGLES), the RABBITOHS, the SHARKS, the EELS, the ROOSTERS, the MAGPIES, the TIGERS and the SAINTS. In Melbourne's Australian rules territory there are to be found such names as BULLDOGS, DEMONS, MAGPIES, SAINTS, TIGERS and SWANS, just to mention a few.

Such names, and scores of others, mostly with a distinctive Australian flavour, can be found in all capital cities and the country districts around the nation.

A widely used Australian rallying cry UP THERE, CAZALY had its origin in Australian Rules football, dating to the peak years of a noted VFL champion Roy Cazaly (1893–1963), a South Melbourne player whose specialty was high marking.

Footy, and the Clubs that Make It (Melbourne 1954) gives the background to the term:

> Melbourne rang with it for years. Every youngster punting his first football to a mate delighted to yell it. The Diggers of World War II took it into battle with them in the Middle East. And how did it originate? Harry Fleiter, another great South Melbourne player of the time, was responsible. 'Cazzer' had become the mainstay of a great South Melbourne ruck with Fleiter and Mark Tandy. When Roy was to go up for the ball Fleiter would shout 'Up there, Cazaly'. The crowds soon caught on, and they would echo the call.

The expression passed out of the football grounds as a general action cry and was extensively used, particularly by Victorian soldiers, during World War II. Ray Lawler introduced it into his *Summer of the Seventeenth Doll* (1957) when he had his heroine send a telegram:

> Up there Cazaly, lots of love—Nance.

The expression gained a new lease of life in 1979 when a song called 'Up there Cazaly' became a national hit tune.

Australian Rules has also given an amusing new phrase to the world in the form of BUM TO MUM—this being another way of saying 'no sex with the wife'. Melbourne coaches have long used the injunction BUMS TO MUMS on Friday nights before a big game, all fearing that a little bit of sex might sap the energy of the players on the morrow. As Ian Moffit expressed it in *The U-Jack Society* (1972):

> Australian Rules in Victoria, is, of course, a religion which divides man and wife.

It seems that the term was one known only to insiders in the mysterious world of football in Melbourne until 1973 when someone slipped under the guard of a sub-editor of the *Australian*, and the expression appeared for the first time in public print. Sydney Rugby League coaches, who had long been used to giving their charges similar instructions on Friday nights preceding big games, but in different words, then picked up the phrase. BUMS TO MUMS now seems a standard order around the nation on Friday nights in winter. It is not known what the wives of the nation's footballers think of the expression as no one has yet done a survey on the subject.

In the early 1970s a very strange change came over the football (soccer) grounds of England as players started to hug and even kiss one another after each goal was scored. Probably due to the influence of television this madness swept around the globe, and soon scenes of manly love play were being witnessed on playing fields everywhere. Even the hallowed turf of the cricket field is now witness to strange sights on the fall of a wicket.

Psychologists were not slow to comment on this phenomenon, and quite a few solemnly proclaimed that it was all just a public manifestation of what they had suspected all along—namely that the big manly footballers of the world were really just a bunch of suppressed homosexuals—nothing but a pack of poofters in fact.

The shock waves of these pronouncements are still reverberating. Coaches, managers and officials were appalled by the accusations and exhorted their players to restore their manly image. In most cases their pleas fell on deaf ears, and the television screens are still filled with shots of activities on football grounds that would result in charges of indecent behaviour if enacted on the streets of any Australian city.

In 1973 an anonymous writer in *Pelican*, the University of Western Australia student magazine, reprinted what he claimed was part of a newspaper report of an Australian Rules game between Victoria and Western Australia. In earlier years the report would have excited no comment whatever, but in the light of the charges of the psychologists, the report became a series of very funny double entendres, indicating what a minefield the English language is for a sports writer who does not keep up with evolutionary changes in colloquial speech. The report is reprinted below to illustrate the linguistic traps that now face all sports writers:

Once again WA lost many opportunities through their hesitancy in shooting for the goal, and overindulgence in fore-play around the flanks and their rather inept ballhandling.

Victoria found this pressure very light and consequently piled on the score. For WA the reverse applied and it was the tight pressure which forced them to put their shots into the behinds. Victoria had many players holding their own whereas only very few WA players were able to withstand such a tense situation. Fitzpatrick was having a bad day and was pulled off by the coach in the third quarter, allowing Alexander to come on and have a go at the Vic's 'big guns' which had been firing well up until that stage. In the rucking duels he was able to match them inch for inch and proved to be one of the few bright spots for WA. Another was Green, who played brilliantly over the back flanks for four quarters and must have been well satisfied when he came off at the end of the game.

Polocross, which has been described variously as 'the poor man's Polo' and as 'Rugby League played on horseback' is the only other recognised indigenous sport, and that does not appear to have developed any distinctive language as yet.

Cricket was once considered a sedate, gentlemanly sport. However all that changed in the 1930s with the introduction by English fast bowler Harold Larwood of a new technique of aiming at the batsman's body, rather than the stumps in an attempt to intimidate him. The Australians promptly labelled this *Bodyline*, and its introduction almost caused a severing of diplomatic relations between the *Old Country* and its former colony down under. From that date cricket became a bloodsport rather than a pastime, with crowds being roused to a fever pitch of anticipation (of bodily mayhem) when particularly fast bowlers were operating.

This probably reached an all-time high (or low, depending on your point of view) in the England-Australia cricket tests in 1976 when Dennis Lillee and Jeff Thomson were bowling over the hated Poms like ninepins. The result was that Australian sporting crowds found themselves a new battlecry of LILL-EE, LILL-EE which reverberated around the sports grounds much as the battlecry of UP THERE, CAZALY had done in a previous generation.

In the *Bulletin* in 1977, Keith Dunstan described the cricket scene of the previous year as follows:

In 30 years of cricket reporting I can't remember anything like the Lillee phenomenon. The adoration is complete. I was fascinated to observe the crowd even when he came in to bat. They cheered him just for being at the wicket. They were thrilled when he actually made contact with the ball. But Lillee making a run, that was bliss, that was heaven, and the cheers and the thunderous applause was the equivalent of a goal on grand final day.

Then there's this 'Lill-ee, Lill-ee, Lill-ee' thing. It goes on non-stop, all the time he is bowling. But as he starts his run it becomes louder and louder like an approaching locomotive. Under those concrete stands the noise is so loud it actually hurts the ear drums. When he first started to bowl to Amiss, honestly it was awe-inspiring and quite terrifying. There were those who shouted 'kill, kill' and I don't really think it was done in the gladatorial sense; it was just a boozy yob thing for most of them, but it didn't come over that way.

When no wicket had fallen for a few minutes they had another tactic 'bounce, bounce, bounce' and 'come arn Lillee get the pommy bastards'.

Cricket has also spawned a few interesting nicknames. The most famous of course was THE DON for the great Sir Donald Bradman. A well known Queensland opening batsman renowned for his stodgy, cramped play quickly earned the ironic national nickname of SLASHER MACKAY, whilst fast bowler Jeff Thomson is always referred to simply as THOMO. One of the most interesting nicknames however came into being as a result of a problem of the operators of cricket ground scoreboards. When the two Chappell brothers, Ian and Greg, were playing some way had to be devised for distinguishing the two on the scoreboards, so the scorers hit on the idea of tacking each player's initial on the end of the surname. As a result Ian Chappell appeared on scoreboards around Australia as CHAPPELLI and Greg Chappell as CHAPPELLG. Australian crowds instantly seized the opportunity to apply a new nickname to a cricket hero and from then on Ian became known as CHAPPELLI. When he published his biography in 1978 Ian Chappell appropriately called the book *Chappelli*. The nickname is mainly confined to Australia and this led a well-known English cricket writer, who was not aware of its origin, into a curious error. When Chappell's book appeared the writer acidly commented on the title 'as if he were some mafia leader' and added: 'If the Sicilian cap fits, let them wear it.'

Apart from nicknames, cricket has not contributed much to the Australian language, though the term IT'S NOT CRICKET is widely used to mean something that is not fair. To be ON A GOOD WICKET means to have an easy job or a life of luxury, and this term is equated with similar slang expressions of THE LIFE OF RILEY and HE'S ON CLOVER. On the other hand, to be on a STICKY WICKET is to be in trouble of some kind, whilst to be on a VERY STICKY WICKET is to be UP SHIT CREEK WITHOUT A PADDLE. Whilst the original cricketing terms might have English origins, they are certainly used colloquially in Australia in many ways different from their usage in England.

Cricket umpires (UMPS) and football referees (REFS) have one thing in common: they are subjected to a lot of abuse from angry fans. In Australia they are frequently accused of being AS BLIND AS BATS, and very often their eyesight is compared to that of a mythical BLIND FREDDIE ('Even Blind Freddie coulda seen he was leg before'). It is also alleged that most umpires and referees WOULDN'T HAVE A CLUE about the rules of the game, and anyway most of them WOULDN'T KNOW WHETHER THEY WERE ARTHUR OR MARTHA.

If the fast bowlers of cricket seem to have prompted Australian sporting crowds to go wild with their cries, there is another type of bowler who seems to be at the very opposite end of the sporting scale. Lawn bowls attracts more participants than any other single game played in Australia, but it is not a game which can arouse killer passions in the participants, and the onlookers stay calm. David Dale summed it up very well when he wrote in an article in the *National Times* (1974):

> ... bowlers behave with extreme gentility on the green. Men who utter the foulest expletives elsewhere suddenly use expressions like 'Oh, bad luck', 'that doesn't help' or 'great bowl, Ken' when their feet touch the grass.

Bowlers have their own jargon of technical terms with GREENS, MATS, SKIPS, LEADS, HEADS, KITTY, BIAS, ENDS, RINKS etc. which tend to be a mystery to the non-bowler, but so far as I know they haven't produced any notable slang terms worth incorporating into the general vocabulary of the nation, though I do have a friend who comes close to qualifying for this honour. Every bowl has an inbuilt bias which means it curves as it runs, either to left or right depending on which side (bias) it is bowled. If a player allows too much green for the bias it will stay 'out' and is said to be WIDE. If he does not allow enough green for the bias it swings in too far and is said to be NARROW or SKINNY. My friend takes this expression a step further. After delivering a particular narrow delivery he is apt to exclaim with disgust: 'Skinny as a flamin' Mogriguy wether'. (Mogriguy being an area in the district noted for its poor country. Sheep there are never in very good condition.)

Although the major spectator sports have been the chief contributors to sporting slang, some notable examples of Australian humour and inventiveness have turned up in some of the more exotic sports.

During the Big Game Fishing season each year considerable numbers of wealthy fishermen, with Americans predominating, descend on Cairns in north Queensland to pit their skills against the marlin. As if by magic, Cairns at the same time is invaded by numbers of extremely attractive young southern ladies whose bikini-clad bodies form a very decorative background on the decks (and below decks) of the fishing fleet. With superb irony, and with perfectly straight faces, the inhabitants of Cairns refer to these young ladies, one and all, as MARINE BIOLOGISTS, no doubt to the considerable distress of any genuine, particularly female, Marine Biologists who happen to be in the area on legitimate business at the time.

Chapter Forty-two

THE SPORT OF KINGS

Oh! Betting and Beer are the basis
Of the only respectable life.
Much better to go to the races
Than moulder at home with the wife.

Sir John Medley
in **An Australian Alphabet,** 1953

In the Old World of Europe horse racing may be the 'Sport of Kings', but in Australia it is the plaything of the proletariat, and has been since the first race meeting was staged in Sydney's Hyde Park in October 1810. From that humble beginning, racing flourished to become somewhat of an obsession with millions of Australians.

When Mr David Kay, Secretary of the New Zealand Thoroughbred Breeders' Association learned of the death of the top sire Oncidium he brokenheartedly proclaimed:

I almost felt my wife died.

Although uttered by a New Zealander, the sentiment was one that would be echoed by most Australian racegoers.

Australia is probably the only country in the world where a person could make reference simply to THE CUP being perfectly certain that any listener, young or old in any part of the country would know instantly that he was referring to a specific event—the Melbourne Cup—staged on the first Tuesday of each November. Australia is also probably the only country in the world where such a single sporting event can bring the entire industry and commerce of a nation to a halt for five minutes while the result of the Cup is being broadcast or televised.

The reason why horse-racing occupies such a dominant role in Australian life is two-fold: Australia has a climate which permits all-the-year-round racing in all capital cities and most country centres, thus maintaining a continuity of interest not enjoyed by seasonal sports, and it provides the means whereby countless Australians can express one of their deepest urges: to gamble.

Given the great interest in the NAGS, as the racegoer affectionately refers to horses, it is not surprising to find that the argot of the race track has penetrated into the general language of the nation to a very considerable degree.

Race followers have many colourful terms for the horses they back with such hope each week. A DEAD CERT or a SURE COP is a horse that is bound to win, but usually doesn't. A ROUGHIE is a horse at very long odds in the betting, a PEA or a GOER is a horse that is being ridden to win whilst one that is not trying is DEAD.

The race track also has spawned many expressions which have gained general circulation:

TO GO FOR THE DOCTOR (originally when a jockey went for the whip, but now a common expression meaning to take action of any kind).

HE WAS OFF LIKE A BRIDE'S NIGHTIE (A quick starter).

HE COULDN'T WIN IF HE STARTED THE NIGHT BEFORE (Now a general term for a born loser).

HE WAS SO SLOW HIS JOCKEY NEEDED A HURRICANE LAMP (to see him finish in the dark).

HE RAN LIKE A HAIRY GOAT (originally applied to racehorses but now a general description of any poor performer).

Racing commentators and writers also have always used colourful language when describing events of the turf. For instance during a Channel 9 broadcast from Sydney on 15 January 1978, sports commentator Ken Callender was so carried away by the speed of a field of horses that he expressed the opinion that:

. . . one would think the jockeys had been promised a blonde for the first into the straight.

Some other expressions culled from newspaper columns:

He's home and hosed (i.e. can't be beaten).

. . . with a furlong to go, a glass eye would have seen she could win it.

... he has travelled more miles than a blackfellow's dog.

... he ran about in the straight like mercury on a marble slab.

Blandstream looked like doing the trick for punters when he poked his bib in at the Leger, but King Lear, with Teddy Bottle in the pigskin, uncorked a terrific run on the inside to roll home the best part of a length to the good.

One of the chief cat-whippers in Melbourne today must be Scobie Breasley.

... had salt rubbed into his wound when the Lewis cuddy Valour curled the mo in the Bond Handicap.

... He came poking through on the rails (i.e. comes through the field on the inside).

Other expressions often used by sports writers include: 'To run up a lane' (to finish out of a place); 'To get beaten by an eyelash' (narrowly beaten); 'To burn up the track' (go fast); 'It's as dead as mutton' (not a trier); 'To stand at the peg' (to be left at the post); 'To enter the calculations' (to join the leaders at the turn); 'To salute the judge' (to be the winner); 'To be rubbed out' (when a jockey, owner or trainer is disqualified).

Jockeys are HOOPS whilst in charge of the general confusion and mayhem on all race tracks, and the Stipendiary Stewards known simply as STIPES. It is interesting to note that the same abbreviation is *not* applied to Stipendiary Magistrates.

If you have racing then you must have betting. At least in Australia. You might get away with a racecourse minus betting in Russia, but no full-blooded OCKER racegoer would tolerate such blasphemy, and if you have betting you must either have an impersonal totalisator system or bookmakers, known as BOOKIES or BAGMEN. The Sydney *Daily Telegraph* in 1941 gave this amusing definition of the various types of bookmakers then operating:

There are MEDICAL Bookmakers, EGG Bookmakers and NOTHING UNDER Bookmakers.

You've all heard the answers when you go up to price a horse.

The MEDICAL bookmaker says, 'You'll get better'.

The EGG man says, 'I've laid that'.

The NOTHING UNDER bookmaker is the one who won't accept a bet of less than ten shillings.

The newspaper made no mention of the most important of all bookmakers—the Starting Price Bookie—known to generations of small punters simply as the SP. Illegal, legislated against and hounded by the police, the SP BOOKIE must be one of Australia's most enduring species of animal life as their establishments, known as SP JOINTS, continue to thrive all over Australia.

Australia also gave to the world the word TOTE as an abbreviation of totalizator, the mechanical betting marvel, which is only fair because it was an Australian, the late Sir George Julius, who invented the machine. And from the betting ring have sprung such slang terms as URGERS, TIPSTERS, TIP-SLINGER, CRUSH BETTING, ALL-UP, QUINELLA, TRIFECTA, as well as some colourful expressions.

To BET ON THE NOD is to bet on credit, to BET ON THE COAT is to lodge a dummy bet with a bookmaker to induce genuine investors to bet on that horse, TO BE WITHOUT A MINTIE after a race is to be without money.

The term LONDON TO A BRICK, meaning a statement of betting odds (a brick being ten pounds) wasn't invented by Ken Howard, a popular broadcasting race caller, but he certainly popularised it by constant usage. When a close finish was being fought out in the straight, Howard would get very excited and proclaim that So-and-So seemed LONDON TO A BRICK to win. Once, when asked where he had picked up the expression he replied:

I don't know, but I probably picked it up in the billiards halls when I was younger. I used to meet a lot of Damon Runyon characters, listen to their talk and pick up some of their expressions.

Some people—or horses—seem born losers. That certainly seems to be the case of a well-bred colt foaled in 1921. His then proud owner gave him the name of DRONGO, probably after a well known bird *Chibia bracteata* whose common name was the SPANGLED DRONGO, or sometimes simply DRONGO. W O Legge in *Australasian Association for the Advancement of Science* (Brisbane 1895) wrote:

There being but one member of the interesting Asiatic genus DRONGO in Australia, it was thought best to characterise it simply as the DRONGO without any qualifying term.

It wasn't that DRONGO was a poor galloper, but luck never was with him on the race track. In 37 starts he failed to manage a win, though he was second in the VRC Derby and VRC St Leger, third in the AJC St Leger and fifth in the 1924 Sydney Cup. After that his unlucky owner gave up and retired him in 1925.

Even in retirement he was unlucky because racegoers began to attach the tag DRONGO to all consistently unlucky horses. Then the word passed out into the community to be applied as a derisive term for anyone who is stupid, clumsy or worthless.

Thus Ruth Park in *Poor Man's Orange* (1949):

> It wasn't his fault he was a drongo . . . he didn't want to have pimples, or a thin neck, or that hair all snowflaked with dandruff.

The word had such wide community acceptance by 1975 that even the *Sydney Morning Herald* allowed it into its august columns:

> There's no doubt that Australia fields a very poor political team, that our orating drongoes pose a more serious threat to democracy than the falling dominoes of Asia.

In Tom Ronan's *The Pearling Master* (1958) there is a vivid description of how the name can pursue some individual unlucky enough *not* to be winner in the stakes of life:

> His continued run of second placings, both in and out of the classroom, brought from a senior of some standing the comment that . . . 'Weyland was another Drongo' . . . They all knew about Drongo: the colt had been a popular fancy for the previous Derby at Flemington. After a careful preparation . . . he had run second. Throughout Oliver's first year at school the horse continued running seconds. He dropped out of the quality races and competed in moderate class handicaps, but he never managed to have his number hoisted first by the judge . . . Drongo, first synonymous with a capacity for always being narrowly beaten, gradually changed to be an epithet flung at anything or anybody too cow-hearted to try to win.

The Concise English Dictionary defines a DRONGO as a simpleton, but its Australian meaning goes far beyond that pallid term. In 1977 the *Australian* columnist Buzz Kennedy wrote an amusing item of what he thought was the definition of a true Australian DRONGO. Here it is:

> A drongo is a simpleton but a complicated one: he is a simpleton who might be expected to come the raw prawn; the sort who not only falls over his feet but does so at Government House; who asks his future mother-in-law to pass-the-magic-word salt the first time the girl asks him home, who, when having nothing to do, sits in a corner counting his nose and getting the wrong answer. In an emergency he runs heroically in the wrong direction. If he were Superman he would get locked in the telephone box. He never wins. So he is a drongo.

The word is still widely used despite the efforts of Sydney poet Len Fox (in 1958) in writing a poem 'Drongo wasn't such a drongo' which sought to show that people shouldn't despise the also-rans of this world:

> *Drongo wasn't such a drongo*
> *But of course the legend grew*

And legends are stronger than truth
So everyone believes now
That Drongo was an old camel
Who always ran last.

But some of us remember a colt
Running second in a Derby;
He didn't look so clumsy
Just for that second ...

Sure he never won a race,
Neither did I, mate;
Most of us never win races
And so they call us drongoes.

The original DRONGO achieved some sort of posthumous fame on 15 February 1977 when a 1600 m Drongo Handicap was included in the Epsom Programme at Flemington (Victoria). Even this however, was a bit of a back-handed swipe at the old fellow since the race was only for apprentice jockeys and horses without a win to their name in the previous twelve months— DRONGOES in embryo as it were. Still someone had to win the event, thus taking him out of the DRONGO class.

Chapter Forty-three

THE COUNTER CULTURE

When you're driving hard and fast down the wall, with the soup curling behind yer, or doing this backside turn on a big one about to tube, it's just this feeling. Yer know, it leaves yer feeling stoked.

A Surfie quoted by
Hugh Atkinson in **Quadrant**

In the post-war years there has been a tremendous proliferation throughout the world of cults—religions and secular—of all types as the youth of the world turned away from the traditional values of their fathers in search of new values of their own. The fact that in the great majority of cases the search has been in vain, has not had any impact on successive waves of adherents to the Counter Culture in its many forms. And many of the resulting clashes between the old and the new in western societies have arisen because the cults have developed their own languages which are meaningless to traditionalists, therefore making communication between the groups extremely difficult.

At a meeting of the Australian Institute of Mining and Metallurgy in Brisbane in 1976 Dr John Covey, a senior advisor in Mining and Metallurgy from Canada, spoke for all of us when he read out the following poem:

Remember when hippie
meant big in the hips,
And a trip involved travel in
cars, planes and ships?

> *When pot was a vessel for*
> *cooking things in,*
> *And hooked was what*
> *grandmother's rug may have been?*
> *When fix was a verb that*
> *meant mend or repair*
> *And be-in meant merely*
> *existing somewhere?*
> *And bread came from bakeries*
> *—and not from the mint?*
> *When roll meant a bun, and*
> *rock was a stone,*
> *And hang-up was something*
> *you did with the phone?*
> *It's groovy man, groovy, but*
> *English it's not,*
> *Methinks that our language*
> *Is going to pot.*

Every society comprises a myriad of 'Interest Groups', that is to say groupings, some large, some small, of people with common interests. Some of these groupings, such as people with a common religious faith, can be in great numbers, whilst others are so specialised that they may comprise only a handful of enthusiasts. Most people belong to a number of different interest groups, some with overlapping, or at times even conflicting, objectives. The totality of these interest groups is a giant mosaic with each piece, no matter how tiny, contributing something to the overall fabric of the society. And the fabric, I might add, is one of a constantly changing pattern, since the influence of the various interest groups waxes and wanes as ideas and opinions of the individual members change.

On the surface there may seem little difference between a cult (defined as a 'system of religious worship; devotion to a person or thing') and an interest group. Both comprise a number of persons banded together to further a common interest, but there the resemblance ends. An interest group is very much part of a society, and accepted by the majority of the members of that society as such. A cult, on the other hand, attracts only minority support from the members of the society to which it attaches itself, and is generally felt by most members as having aims and ideals contrary to the overall values of the society. It is felt, whether rightly or wrongly, to be an incubus on that society, and a thing to be rooted out and destroyed where possible. Of course, there have been many examples in history—and

Christianity is perhaps the most obvious—where the majority of people in a community have been wrong about the motives or threat of a cult. What may start out as being a cult that is thoroughly reviled in its infancy may in time become a valued part of society—an accepted interest group.

When tobacco smoking was first introduced into western society, its adherents were subjected to considerable odium and ridicule. They persisted until a majority of adults in most western countries were smokers and the habit became socially acceptable. Now the wheel has swung full circle, and in recent years the anti-smoking brigade have been out in force in their efforts to stamp out the evil of nicotine. As a result smokers again are very much on the defensive, and eventually may be forced back into despised cult status.

Sometimes the transition of a movement from a reviled cult status to that of an accepted interest group can be quite swift as a result of changes in the law or of community attitudes. This was the case with the CB Radio which developed (complete with a new language) almost overnight in the United States in the early 1970s. Originally used almost exclusively by truckies, the CB cult rapidly spread to the motoring community in general, and then out into the non-mobile back yards of the nation.

Officialdom tried desperately to stop it spreading to Australia. But their bans and restrictions were the action of King Canute, and the illegal tide of CB simply swept over them, forcing official recognition of the cult. By early 1978 CB radio was legal (though expensively so) in Australia and causing havoc in quiet neighbourhoods by jamming TV receptions, and introducing to the airwaves a whole new language imported direct from America. Overnight the public had to cope with such new terms as:

ACE (an important CB operator)
ASHPHALT PILOT (truck driver)
BATTERY ACID (trucker's coffee)
BIG DADDY (Telecom)
CAMERA (police radar)
CUSO (a CB conversation)
EMU (policeman)
EYEBALL (face to face confrontation)
MOTION LOTION (petrol)
PEDAL TO THE METAL (speeding)
RACHET JAWS (over-talkative CBer. Also known as a WIND-JAMMER)
XYL (wife, the initials stand for EX-YOUNG-LADY)

In 1978 the ABC sent a *This Day Tonight* reporter to interview a young CB radio enthusiast who had just acquired a set. The youngster triumphantly informed the somewhat bemused reporter that:

> . . . last night me and me mate had a CUSO (talk) and this morning we had an EYEBALL (meeting).

Some of the problems facing CB radio operators who are not 'with it' language wise were explained by an anonymous correspondent writing in *Forum* of March 1978.

> If you don't bone up on the correct lingo you may arrange an eyeball with a 'dress for sale' and find yourself face-to-face with a hooker instead of a frock. Or you might miss the most fantastic looking woman of your life because you mistakenly assume that all that talk on the channel about a 'beaver' refers to a small furry animal with big teeth. Or you might never get to eyeball a sexy-sounding young lady because you impolitely refer to her as a beaver instead of a 'YL'. Or, if you're a woman whose car has wornout upholstery, you might find yourself in an unexpected lesbian encounter simply by asking where you can find a new 'seatcover'.

One distinctive feature of cults is that they quickly cross national boundaries to become part of the 'global village'. As a result the languages of the cults and the Counter Culture are generally international, making it difficult to determine the country of origin of many of the 'in' words and phrases of their followers. Even the world of the surfie extends well beyond the beaches of Australia's east coast to such far-off places as Hawaii and southern California.

The cult of the surfie—a post-war phenomenon—has presented Australians with a dilemma. On the one hand the average OCKER enjoys the lotus-eating life of sand and surf himself—at least on weekends and during holidays—but he is also deeply committed to the Protestant work ethic. The idea of young men turning their backs on honest toil to spend their days loafing in the sun seems to him as something sinful. From this comes the paradox that within the world of the beach brigade the appellation of SURFIE is an honourable badge, whilst to the average adult (male) Australian the word has almost become a term of abuse, often being used in conjunction with such pejorative expressions as HIPPIE, DROPOUT, LAYABOUT, WORKSHY and DOLE BLUDGER.

There is some little suspicion that many of these aspersions are cast as a result of envy rather than moral conviction. Whatever the motive however, the scorn which is directed by the average

Australian at surfies is not helped by the fact that they speak a language which he finds totally incomprehensible.

A Sydney surfie quoted by Jonathan Aitken gives some idea of the communication problem involved with this cult:

> Well, I was out there riding the Dee Why swell when along comes this beaut set of tubes, so I front up and get m'plank hard on the green shoulder. Then away we shoot and before you can say Ned Kelly I'm sliding the curl, and then I'm riding the nose, hanging five, then hanging ten, and just when I'm real stoked along comes a bloody egg who clobbers my tab and it's a real dead loss wipe out, hit by a dumper so bad that I chundered real terrible, and had to hit the sack until one of the femlins woke me.

In *Good Australian English* (1972) Professor John Gunn noted that the language of the surfie was based on social distinctions and he commented:

> Surfing is a good example of a special group, not at all restrictive, but still implying some cutting off of its devotees from the rest of society. The 'with it' feeling of the true surfer appears to be like a drug which makes him at one with his world—he is away from others and is blissfully content. Somehow one can't help feeling a little jealous, and I deliberately refrain from criticising groups which appear so special, almost isolationist, demanding freedom from the curbs of their society yet insisting on the full service and benefits it has to offer.

Professor Gunn also noted that many surfie words and terms were quite technical (i.e. referred to types of waves or surfing conditions) and amongst them he recorded: CUSHION, CUSTOM, DECK, FLAT, FLEX, HANDBOARD, HIP, HULL, PINTAIL, POD, POPOUT, RAIL, ROCKER, TWIN FIN, BOWL, BREAK, CLOSE OUT, CURL, DEAD SPOT, THE FALLS, FLAT, GOBBLY, HEAVY, INSIDE BREAK, LEFTS, LINE UP, LIP, PEAK, PIPELINE, POCKET, PUMP, RIP, SET, SLOPPY, STACK UP, STEAMING, TIGHT, TRACK LINE, TUBE, BACK HAND, COFFIN, CUT BACK, DING, DROP OUT, DUD, GOOFY FOOT, GREMMIE, HANG FIVE, HODAD, HOG A WAVE, HOT DOG, JUICE, KAMIKAZE, LAY UP, NOSE RIDE, PEARLING, POP OUT, PUSH WATER, SIDESLIP, SKEG, SPIN OUT, SPINNER, SOUP and WIPEOUT.

Australian youth are as much addicted to fast cars (HOT RODS) as their counterparts overseas, and have adopted the universal language of the cult with some Antipodean variations. Just how confusing this language can be to a square oldie can be gauged from the following snippet put together in the 1960s by a writer in the now long defunct Oz magazine:

SATURDEE . . . On Saturdee morning I get up early and go over to Doug's. Then Doug and me go over to Mick's place. Mick has a HOT G. Really Hot! Can it PERFORM: Spliced sliced head . . . twin-fanged carbies, chrome grease nipples, triple flue perforated enigmatic exhausts, octagonal Vostok pleated cams . . . THE WORKS . . . TOO MUCH . . . givers her at least an extra 3 mph in top . . . We work on the G all the morning, then after lunch we fang up to the northern beaches . . . sometimes we go in convoy with some other G's and drag through the forest. Sometimes we just cruise around and wave at the other G's . . . then at night we drive up to the Cross and mock the pleb rodsers and whistle at the birds . . . We'd just done this GEAR wheelie round the traffic lights . . . we yelled out to these three birds . . . and y'know wot! We got caught in the traffic and they came over and tried to get into the G . . . talk about embarrassing . . . we just managed to get away . . . besides there's only ROOM for 3 in a G . . . besides who needs birds when your best mate's got a hot G with chromed grease nipples . . .

The world of music is a labyrinth of sub-cults which is far too complicated for any but the young activist to penetrate. But no parent of a modern teenager can hope to bridge the generation gap unless he or she is prepared to come to terms with a language which spawns such words and expressions as BEAT, BLOW THE MIND, BOMB, BUMMER, BUZZ, CAT, CATTING, CRACK THE CHARTS, COAL, COOL, DOWNER, FEEL, FREAKY, FLIPPED, FUNKY, GAS, GIG, HIP, HYPE, LICK, MOVER, RAP, RAVE UP, RIFF, SCENE, SPADE, SPLIT, UPPER, UPTIGHT and VIBES.

So far as I can ascertain, all these words are imports and to date the youthful with-it music lovers of Australia have not displayed anything like the linguistic inventiveness of the forefathers by developing a distinctive Antipodean language for their rock and pop activities. But it is early days yet.

Perhaps the most tragic segment of the Counter Culture of the twentieth century is the drug scene. The adherents on a world-wide basis must now be counted in the tens of millions. With such extensive participation, the emergence of a whole new language devoted to the scene was inevitable. And the world-wide spread of the drug scene also means that the new language is a universal one. If any of the words or phrases now being used by addicts around the globe had their origin in Australia, this has not been recorded—at least so far as I'm aware—and they have long since merged into the global scene.

Even the names of the various drugs in general use have a surprising (but universal) variety. The United States Narcotics Bureau has compiled a list of slang terms for most commonly used drugs and these terms are likely to be used just as much in Sydney as in Boston or Bangkok. A short summary of the list is enlightening:

AMPHETAMINES: Pep pills, bennies, wake-ups, eye-openers, lid-poppers, co-pilots, truck drivers, peaches, roses, hearts, cart-wheels, whites, browns, footballs, greenies, oranges, dexies, sweets, beans, uppers.

BARBITURATES: Yellows, nimby, nimbles, reds, pinks, red devils, seggy, pink ladies, blues, blue devils, blue heavens, double trouble, phennies, barbs.

COCAINE: The leaf, snow, C, Cecil, coke, dynamite, flake, speedball (when mixed with heroin), girli, happy dust, joy powder, gin, carrie, cholly, paradise.

HEROIN: Snow, stuff, H, junk, big Harry, boy, horse, white stuff, hairy, joy powder, salt, dope, smack, shit, skag, thing.

MARIHUANA: Smoke, straw, pod, bush, weed, grass, pot, tea, hash, hemp, griffo, loco weed, hay, herb, Mary Jane, joint sticks, reefers, roach.

MORPHINE: M, dreamer, white stuff, hard stuff, morpho, unkie, monkey, cube, morf, tab, emsel, hocus, morphie, melter.

METHADONE: Dolophine, Dollies, dolls, amidone.

The drug scene is loaded with ordinary English words or phrases which have special cult meanings: CAP, COLD TURKEY, CONNECTION, FREAK OUT, MAINLINE, PEDDLER, PUSHER, TRIP, DIRTY, SNIFFER, SPIKE, TICKET etc.

In *Good Australian English* (1972) Professor J S Gunn provided translations for some of these terms:

> . . . there is a surprising quasi-synonymy in the jargon of many sub-groups in our society, but with drugs it is particularly noticeable. For example, with limited research, I found that the effect of a drug can be A BANG, BLAST, BOOT, BUZZ, JOLT, KICK, to inject is to BANG, CHARGE UP, FIX, JOB, POP, SHOOT, being under the influence is CHARGED, COASTING, FLOATING, HIGH, HOPPED UP, LIT UP, LOADED, ON THE NOD, SMASHED, STONED, TURNED ON, WASTED, the injecting outfit is GEAR, JOINT, OUTFIT, WORKS, and to purchase drugs is to BUZZ, CONNECT, COP, BIT, MAKE IT, or SCORE.

Professor Gunn then went on to make this comment:

> One thing very clear in all of this is that what is added by Australian idiom to this unfortunate facet of our times is negligible. Like the drugs themselves, the terms come from overseas, but one must acknowledge that the colour of the naming loses nothing in comparison with any other slang. It was in the synonymy that I thought there might be an Australian variation and some sign of individuality, but this does not appear to be so.

Another very substantial segment of the Counter Culture has developed around homosexuals—both male and female. Homo-sexuals have been around on this planet for a long, long time, but, except for some periods of history when they were tolerated, mainly due to similar activities in high places, they were underground—out of sight and out of mind. We all knew they were there but didn't take much notice of them—except, that is, for the more obvious types who couldn't or wouldn't disguise their inclinations. Because they seemed so few, the average Australian was reasonably tolerant towards them. 'Poor buggers,' he was want to pontificate. 'They can't help it, can they?' This, of course, didn't stop him hurling epithets of QUEER or QUEAN or POOF at them when the need arose.

That all changed in the early 1970s when the permissive society had advanced to a stage where the homosexuals of Australia decided that at long last it was safe to emerge from the woodwork, to stand up and be counted and demand an end to discrimination. 'Coming out' they called it, and the numbers that emerged in this way provided quite a shock for the STRAIGHT community. It was a traumatic time for the Australian male who for the first time felt threatened in a way never previously experienced. His reaction was instantaneous and aggressive, perhaps understandable given the circumstances. For the first time POOFTER was used as a hard, aggressive epithet and POOFTER BASHING became an accepted after-dark Australian (male) pastime, particularly amongst members of the police force of several states, notably South Australia.

Even the little old ladies got into the act. The ABC 'Lateline' programme in July 1975 reported on one incident as follows:

Last week two elderly women were standing outside the Sydney ABC radio studios. After they had been there for some time an ABC employee ventured down to ask if he could help. 'Oh no,' said one of the ladies, 'my friend is here from the country; I'm just showing her where the poofters hang out.'

Now POOF or POOFTER isn't of Australian origin, but it is used so extensively here that many Australians feel quite possessive about it. An interesting thing has occurred in the evolution of the word—it is no longer applied exclusively to homosexuals but has become a general term of abuse to be directed at anyone who displeases the utterer.

After a visit to Australia in 1977 the British author Dr Richard Gordon thought that we had a problem on this front. He subsequently wrote:

And you have the poofter problem. There seem so many poofs in Sydney as might cause serious concern about overcrowding to the housing authorities of Sodom. It is a statistical and biological impossibility for all these poofters to be homosexuals. They are refugees from the other Australian tyrannical myth, the ocker.

Any young Australian man with a normal fondness for dressiness, an interest in the arts, a liking for a varied diet, a penchant for European travel, a preference for comfort, even a weakness for after-shave, measures himself against the ocker and instantly assumes himself queer. Once he thinks he is queer, he acts queer.

When homosexuals 'came out' in the early 1970s they brought into the open a whole new cult language which previously had existed underground. Whilst this may have added some dimension to the language, it also put the kiss of death on some perfectly respectable STRAIGHT words such as CAMP or GAY.

In *Cop It Sweet*, Jim Ramsay categorically states that the word QUEAN originated in Australia, but this is not correct as it is a very old English slang term for a prostitute. It may well be that Australians were the first to use it as a derogatory term for an effeminate type of male homosexual, but if so, it now has world-wide usage. Its most celebrated public use in Australia occurred in 1940 in the noted clash between Noel Coward and Lennie Lower at a big Sydney reception for the visiting celebrity. Lower, who shared the usual Australian male aversion for homosexuals, was a very reluctant guest at the reception, having been dragooned into attending by his employer Frank Packer.

In due course Noel Coward was introduced to Lower and, in a rather condescending manner, the great man exclaimed 'Ah, the King of the Australian humorists, one presumes!'

To which Lennie Lower, who had by then imbibed more liquor than was wise, retorted acidly: 'Ah, the great QUEAN of the English stage, one presumes!'

Pandemonium.

A very furious Frank Packer rushed up and demanded apologies and, when these weren't forthcoming, sacked Lower on the spot. Which was why Lennie Lower spent the remaining years of his working life until his death in 1947, at *Smith's Weekly*, whose management had always strongly espoused the myth of the big, bronzed Aussie male, and who were not at all concerned at the possibility of one of their writers offending visiting Pommie Poofs.

Chapter Forty-four

JARGON AND GOBBLEDYGOOK

The vacuum created by a failure to communicate will quickly be filled with rumour, misrepresentation, drivel and poison.

Law Propounded by
Professor Northcote Parkinson in 1978

One of the great problems of the world today is that people have almost lost the art of communicating with one another. And the chief cause of this sad state of affairs is the enormous proliferation of JARGON and GOBBLEDYGOOK which befouls the languages of the nations at almost every level where it matters.

Webster's definition of these two words is interesting. JARGON is defined as 'the technical, esoteric, or secret vocabulary of a science, art, trade, sect, profession, or other special group', whilst GOBBLEDYGOOK is defined as 'pretentious, redundant, and obscure speech or writing; jargon'.

A more down-to-earth definition of GOBBLEDYGOOK was given by Dennis Andersen in *The Book of Slang* (1975) as 'nonsense or confused writing or speaking'.

Andersen did not give a source for the word but I suspect that the inspiration for it was the *gobble gobble* sound that a turkey makes and which Lindsay in *Mind in the Lower Animals* referred to as follows:

The turkey-cock is another unfortunate bird, whose strut and GOBBLE have led it to be considered an emblem of . . . Bumbledom.

An alternate American term for GOBBLEDYGOOK is BAFFLEGAB but this is not in general use in Australia.

Back in 1916 Sir Arthur Quiller-Couch summed up official JARGON neatly when he wrote:

Caution is its father; the instinct to save everything and especially trouble; its mother, Indolence. It looks precise but it is not. It is, in these times, safe: a thousand men have said it before and not one to your knowledge has been prosecuted for it . . . it uses circumlocution rather than short, straight speech . . . and habitually chooses woolly abstract nouns rather than concrete ones.

In an article 'Menace of Jargon' in the *Sydney Morning Herald* in 1952 Eric Partridge described the enemies of the English language as JARGON, SLANG, DIALECT, FOREIGN WORDS and AMERICANISMS, though he admitted that the English language had long been enriched by recruits from these tainted sources. In explaining the apparent contradiction, he pointed out that war between good and evil takes place no less constantly in language than in the spiritual, moral and political spheres.

Partridge went on to single out JARGON as a special source of contamination of language, however, and commented that it was 'one of the most prolific of impurity'.

The chief culprit in creating and fostering both JARGON and GOBBLEDYGOOK however, is the bureaucracy of all nations. Civil servants now comprise about a quarter of the work force in all the developed nations, and their influence is enormous since it is through them that constant streams of information must be channelled from the lawmakers to the populace.

Unfortunately, the bureaucracy is entirely destructive since it continually befouls and muddies the linguistic waters of its host country, like some monstrous medieval creature continually threshing about in a pond. If there is one word that sums up completely the end results of all the frantic endeavours of the bureaucracy it is *obfuscate* which the dictionary neatly defines as to 'darken, obscure, stupify, bewilder'. That is exactly what the bureaucracy does every minute of its relatively short working day.

Some critics have accused the bureaucracy of doing this deliberately as part of some war or vendetta on society. I do not believe this to be so. I think that obfuscation which follows automatically from almost any act of a civil servant is largely unintentional. Most of them mean well, but are not able to escape from the predetermined grooves along which they must all move or crawl from the date of joining to twilight years of superannuation.

Their life is bound up entirely in rules which constantly

proliferate. Even the rules are couched in forms which outsiders cannot understand, and are hedged with 'ifs' and 'buts' and escape clauses, to strengthen the security of the civil servants concerned. This is not some diabolic plot against society, but simply an understandable defence mechanism on the part of a whole group of unhappy, unadventurous souls. We should not be too harsh on them, though it is difficult to think kindly of them when some of their more brazen attempts to obfuscate simple English cause us personal problems.

Sometimes, by sheer accident, some rule or regulation in the bureaucracy will be a model of simplicity capable of being understood by even the lowest intelligence. If this should happen, we can be sure that some horrified civil servant will soon appear to spread darkness where only light previously shone, by rewriting the rule in an incomprehensible form. This was particularly well illustrated when the Federal Budget was introduced in August 1978, altering, amongst other things, the system by which lump sum payments for accrued long service leave were to be taxed. Before that date the formula was excruciatingly simple: such monies were taxed at five per cent of the total payment.

That was far too easy for the bureaucratic mind, and the Treasury decided that forthwith, the income deriving from long service leave at the end of a taxpayer's employment should include an amount ascertained by the following formula:

$$\frac{A}{B}\left(\frac{C(B+D)}{E}\right)-F$$

The Treasury then provided an 'explanation' of the formula. The 'explanation' for F was particularly enlightening:

F is: In case where the number of whole days of long service leave that accrued in respect of the eligible service period and were used by the taxpayer after 15 August, 1978 exceeds the number (in this paragraph referred to as the 'relevant number') that bears to the number of whole days of long service leave that accrued in respect of the eligible service period (including days of long service leave that were used by the taxpayer before the retirement date) the same proportion as the number of whole days in the eligible service period that occurred after 15 August, 1978 bears to the number of whole days in the eligible service period—the relevant number; . . . in any other case—the number of whole days of long service leave that accrued in respect of the eligible service period and were used by the taxpayer after 15 August, 1978.

This is a typical example of bureaucratic jargon, whereby perfectly good English words are arranged in such a way as to make the meaning incomprehensible to anyone but another civil servant highly trained in the art of GOBBLEDYGOOK.

The language of the civil servant is crammed with mixed metaphors and tautological twists, dressed up with such bureaucratic favourites as ALBEIT, AT THIS POINT OF TIME, AT THIS JUNCTURE, IN RESPECT OF, IN THE CASE OF and ON THE QUESTION OF THE USE OF.

The bureaucrat also dreads having to call a spade a spade, let alone use the Australian method of describing it as a BLOODY SHOVEL. Because of this, he is inordinately fond of euphemisms, particularly in dredging up acceptable names for unpleasant tasks, such as: CUSTODIAL OFFICERS for prison warders and RODENT EXTERMINATORS for rat catchers. The best example I have encountered in recent years is that provided by the NSW Health Commission which insists on describing school tuckshops as SCHOOL FOOD SERVICE UNITS.

Surprisingly some of the worst offenders in the crime of obfuscation are professional communicators. Columnist 'Benelong' in the *Sunday Telegraph* (1978) provided a priceless example from the United States as follows:

> An American communications expert this week explained why some people can't communicate. 'They're digital people using their rational analytical channel,' he said. He meant they were rigid, uptight souls.

A prize example of murder of the English language from an unexpected source was provided by Dr Rupert Goodman, Reader of Education at the University of Queensland when he wrote in a letter to the Canberra *Times* of 8 February 1978:

> Sir, I am at present writing a book on the controversial social studies program MACOS, which is at present being trialled in a number of Australian primary schools. In Queensland, after several years of trialling, the course has been scrapped by State Cabinet.

Commenting on this piece of linguistic desecration by someone who should have known better, John Pringle in the *Sydney Morning Herald* expressed the opinion that:

> Dr Goodman should be immediately trialled, condemned, hanged and quartered, for treason to the English language.

Max Harris also has some harsh words to say about educationists who massacre English. Writing in the *Australian* (1978) he made these comments:

> The language of wine-buffery may be idiotic, but it isn't as slimy as the euphemistic jargon of educationists (who should, for the love of Gough/Mal set an example). These days there's no such thing as a child who comes up with lousy results. No school report declares that Gaelene could do better. These days Gaelene is mandatorily 'an under-

achiever'. The modern teacher provides 'unitary treatment of students' (gives individual attention). And when I'm made Commissar of Soviet South Australia I'm going to make the use of 'peer group' punishable by crucifixion. I'll not be so hard on those with motivational maladjustments who have to deal with child-centred procedural dysfunctions. Crook teachers will simply have both legs broken.

Academics also display considerable skill in the creation of jargon, a fact which prompted Donald Horne to comment (in 1977):

> They (academics) spend years writing a thesis in ridiculous jabber and jargon and when they want to make it into a book, they have to spend as many years unravelling it so people can understand what they are saying.

Even the Army has got into the linguistic act by creating a barrack-room jargon that is incomprehensible to civilians. A recruiting advertisement for the Australian Army in 1977 boasted of the achievement this way:

> Our guys do things most people have never seen. Want a job that gives you a blast? . . . Join the team. Then when your girl asks what you're into and you get heavy about high explosive or survey maps or airportable bridges, she won't understand a word. But she'll be impressed . . .

The curse of JARGON and GOBBLEDYGOOK will, of course, never be eliminated by the bureaucrats who created the problem in the first place, and any attempt to even marginally reduce the tide of official gibberish is doomed to failure. In 1978, the US Federal Administration decided that the language of American bureaucrats was too obscure and needed to be simplified so that the man in the street could understand government forms. So a committee was set up to bring about this worthy reform. And what were the guidelines given to this committee? we may ask. The committee, believe it or not, was charged with the duty of 'laymanising officialese'.

Closely allied to the civil service is the law in its many forms. In fact the two work in tandem to regulate what the rest of us should do or not do each day. The civil servant follows his tortuous path by means of rules; the legal man pursues the same end with a set of rules called laws which have considerably more teeth than those wielded by the bureaucrat. But the ends are the same: to force the populace into doing or not doing, and sometimes saying or not saying, what the rulemakers and the lawmakers deem right and proper.

The legal documents and statute books of the nation are a morass of JARGON and legal gibberish. From this, the legal men themselves derive considerable revenue as a result of the many appearances which they have to make in court to argue the interpretation of the words of their fellow professionals. It is clear that they have a considerable vested interest in maintaining a high level of incomprehensibility within the profession, which is why they have resisted for so long any effort to have legal documents expressed in plain English. For, as the *Sydney Morning Herald* said in a leading article on 4 February 1967:

> The law never moves more slowly than when it is involved in putting its own house in order.

The law is not particularly innovative in respect to language, as it prefers to obfuscate by hiding its activities in a smokescreen of centuries-old legal JARGON. However, on occasion it can commit cold-blooded murder of the English language with the best of the bureaucrats. In 1977 one of its practitioners was caught red-handed, and put in the dock, so to speak for such a crime. This was when Mr I B Maughan, the Chief Executive Officer of the Law Society of NSW wrote a letter to the editor of the *Financial Review* which referred to:

> . . . anonymitised copies of the files from which all identifying references have been deleted.

Perhaps the legal profession can be forgiven this particular lapse in the light of the fact that the law, in earlier times, attracted to itself several quite distinctive slang expressions which have added to the richness of the language. Solicitors and barristers in Australia invariably are referred to as LEGAL EAGLES (sometimes simply as EAGLES), whilst there are quite a few other interesting expressions relating to their calling.

A legal summons is a BLUE (or BLUEY) and the origins of this is not hard to fathom since summonses are printed on blue paper, but it is not so easy to determine the origin of BLISTER, an alternate term for a summons. TO BLISTER is also used as a slang expression for overcharging for goods.

A mortgage often is referred to as a POULTICE, probably because it is something which, when applied, is difficult to lift off the object (i.e. house or farm). Farmers in particular have always been very pessimistic about the prospect of 'lifting the poultice' and getting out of the clutches of the banks.

K S Prichard in *Kiss on the Lips* (1932) used the expression this way:

> Mick Mallone . . . sayin' if the bank wanted his farm, poultice or no poultice, it'd have to go out and take it from him, and he'd waitin' for 'm with his gun loaded.

Although the bureaucrats and the lawyers are the main culprits in the proliferation of JARGON, they certainly have no monopoly on it. It is to be found at all levels of the business world.

In 1978 for example, the Mobil Oil Company produced an expensive poster which was displayed throughout its plants and offices, 'explaining' the petrol discount system, and which read, in part:

> . . . the existence of discounts today is largely the result of a uniform reference price being superimposed for price justification purposes on a non-uniform market.

As a piece of communication, that must surely have ranked as the failure of the decade.

Trade and commerce, whether carried out on land, sea or in the air, is splintered into thousands of different segments—often at war with one another—just as is the case with their mutual enemy the bureaucracy.

Each of these groups—the trades or professions—has developed its own private JARGON of 'in' language or 'shop talk', but this is so highly specialised or technical that it rarely has any impact on the language of the community. An exception is the advertising industry which has a record, not entirely enviable, of inventing new words to sell some of the products of its masters—the manufacturers and entrepreneurs of the nation. These word inventions are professional creations which sometimes find their way into the colloquial mainstream, but all too often their artificiality ensures that they will disappear without trace after the advertising campaign in which they were introduced ceases to appear in print or on TV.

The commercial world also has a habit of dredging up atrocious new words such as FRUITOLOGIST (for one who sells fruit), EATERY (for restaurant), GARBOLOGIST (for a garbage collector), RECLAMATION ENGINEER (for junk dealer), FIDUCIARY GRANTOR (for pawnbroker) and TONSORIAL ARTIST (for barber).

The business world also contributes to the development of the language in other ways. Manufacturers of products which are so successful that they become household words run the risk of their brand names becoming generic words and part of the common language. This can be disastrous for sales since the names can no longer be associated with a single product, but apply to a range of like-products, some of which are manufactured by rival firms. Over the years, words which originated as trade names for specific products but which have become generic include: aspirin, brassiere, cola, linoleum, yoyo, shredded wheat, cornflakes and trampoline. Owners of the trademarks of Cellophane, Xerox and Formica are amongst the many companies fighting an expensive (but probably losing) battle to keep their names from the generic pit.

Whole dictionaries have been compiled on the jargon of some of society's most influential groups. One such effort is *The Doomsday Dictionary* (1965) compiled by Donald M Kaplan and Armand Schwerner on the new wordage of the atomic age. It is a very frightening publication indeed. Another even larger, but rather more amusing, book is William Safire's *The New Language of Politics*, a dictionary of political JARGON (almost entirely American) running to almost 800 pages. American politicians and bureaucrats, it would seem are a wordy lot.

Outbursts against Jargon and Gobbledygook seem to fall on deaf ears even when uttered by someone in authority. In 1977 the *Medical Journal* reported one such outburst by Dr R St. J M Butler, an Australian Medical Association Councillor at a medical seminar:

We are lolling in an absolutely unbelievable morass of Gobbledygook. I have heard the English language bastardised and prostituted and raped today in a manner I never thought I would see. I have been lectured by many experts in my time, but if this goes on much longer I would rather go to sleep.

There is no record of the good doctor's words having had the slightest effect on the following speakers at the seminar.

This chapter has dealt only with a few selected groups of word manglers. At every level of society however, there are other busy little groups working away at the English language and developing their own little brands of JARGON and GOBBLEDYGOOK to confuse those not familiar with today's 'in' words and phrases. Their individual contributions feed into the mainstream of JARGON being produced in a really big way by the masters of the art—the bureaucracy, the legal profession and the business world—threatening a flood so great that it will sweep away entirely the English language as we know it. It is a depressing thought.

Chapter Forty-five

UNPARLIAMENTARY LANGUAGE

Before coming to Australia it was explained to me that political preferment was awarded to people who have shown the highest degree of tactlessness and mediocrity over the longest period of time.

British author Clement Freud, 1970.

Visitors to the public galleries of any of the State or Federal Parliaments will quickly discover that the standard of debate—with rare exceptions—is of a deplorably low level. If they are present during some of the more animated exchanges between members of opposing parties, they will also note that politicians do not set any example to their constituents in the matter of name-calling, but tend to trade insults with all the enthusiasm and taste of Mediterranean fishwives. Almost totally lacking is sophisticated wit of the type used in 1970 by Don Dunstan, then South Australian Opposition Leader, during a debate on the Dartmouth Dam site. He said of a member of the other side of the House that on this issue he had taken more stands than were described in the 'Kama Sutra' and 'some of them even more difficult'.

Sir Paul Hasluck, for many years a Liberal member (and Minister) in the Federal Parliament, and later Governor General of Australia, in 1970 expressed some disillusionment with his rowdier parliamentary colleagues when he commented:

In my more extensive acquaintanceship with politicians, I have wondered why a man who uses words only for political purposes—including the yelling of interjections such as 'Sit down, mug'—is considered to have shown talents more worthy of respect than the writing of a sonnet.

For some reason State Parliaments have always had a greater reputation for verbal brawls than Federal Parliament—but then they have been in business much longer so members have had more collective practice in name-calling.

Probably the depths in parliamentary language were reached in the New South Wales Legislative Assembly in the early years of the present century. In this period the State was rocked with land and other scandals which enabled political rabble-rousers to indulge in muck-raking to an unprecedented degree. Leading the field in this respect was that quite extraordinary character John Norton, founder of the scandal sheet *Truth*, long-time member of State Parliament and a man who made numerous appearances in Sydney Courts—usually as a defendant.

The style of debate in the Legislative Assembly of the period is perhaps best illustrated by the following extracts from Parliamentary speeches by Norton in full flight:

... that black-hearted, bawdy, blackguard and barbarous brutal benedict, Baldy Black, who has befooled, befouled and betrayed women, should be banned and blackballed from brotherhood until he behaves himself better.

I always did regard you as a press-puffed nincompoop and a parson-boosted humbug, while your past connubial conduct makes you the concupiscent compeer of some of the pornographic pulpiteers who have taken you under their pious parsonical protection ... you're a beautiful bludger from a brothel to brag about dignity and decency.

He was ... like a bladder out of a sewer, and burst and made a nasty smell.

Admittedly Parliamentary debates have produced some amusing 'one liners' which have contributed something to the Australian idiom, such as:

... the Victorian Country Party is now furiously trying to pick the maggots off its bum.

He is like the Condamine Bell. He has a great tongue and a head full of nothingness.

... he (Henry Bolte) couldn't handle the petty cash at a hot dog stand at the local Sunday school picnic.

The Labor Party's rural policy is as full of kid as a pregnant goat.

... his speech contained as many falsehoods as a suet pudding contains currants.

You can be a rooster one day and a feather duster the next.

Politicians are like bananas: They come in green, turn yellow and there's not a straight one in the bunch.

You can't shut him up. He'd talk under wet cement.

Charlie (Jones) had a thorn up his bum and you couldn't stop him bucking.

He has a penchant for opening his mouth and letting the wind blow his tongue about.

He (Malcolm Fraser) is an insensitive totalitarian toff.

The only sport the Member for Light indulges in is playing with himself.

During a debate on security in the Senate in 1978, Liberal Senator Sir Magnus Cormack interrupted Labor Senator George Georges with the comment:

That is the greatest heap of bulldust since Marx first enunciated his Mein Kampf or whatever it was.

Which would surely have made both Karl Marx and Adolf Hitler roll over in the bulldust of their respective graves.

All parliaments operate under codes of conduct under which their members must operate both in terms of general behaviour and in speech. These codes differ from parliament to parliament, and from time to time. Thus an expression which may be completely acceptable in Federal Parliament today may be ruled 'Unparliamentary' in a State Parliament, or may have been so ruled by some former Federal Speaker of the House.

Because language is such a volatile thing, no current list of 'unparliamentary' expressions is kept by present-day officers of the House of Representatives, but a list of an earlier age does survive. This was compiled in 1952 at the direction of the then Speaker, the Honourable A G ('Archie') Cameron, a great stickler for correct Parliamentary language and procedures. The list covers terms and expressions which were ruled 'unparliamentary' in the period of the Tenth Federal Parliament (1926–1928) and they are reproduced here, together with the principles governing them, as they not only represent a fascinating glimpse into the language of the nation's politicians, but also provide an insight into the slang in currency (even in Parliament) in the late 1920s.

Principles

If a Member uses an expression which is regarded by another Member as personally offensive it must be withdrawn, but exception cannot be taken to expressions used in a general sense which are not distinctly unparliamentary.

The Chair will not order withdrawal of statements merely because of error or misrepresentation.

A Bill passed by the House cannot be referred to as 'iniquitous'.

A Member cannot evade the rules by saying that he would say so-and-so if it were parliamentary.

It is disorderly to imply that a subsidy has been paid to a Member or that a Minister is an echo of his officers.

It is disorderly to impute to Members improper notives but it is not imputing improper motives to say that a motion was supported merely to get kudos out of it.

Words and expressions

Abasing (himself), Abortion (of a Bill), Abuse their privileges, Adept at libel and slander, Alleged leader (speaking of the Prime Minister in relation to another Minister), Anarchists consort with, Arranged the thing very well (re favouring a Member), Ashamed of himself—ought to be, Asinine attitude, Ass (long-haired emotional), Assassin, Assassination (political), Asses, Atrocity performing any.

Back-scratching proceedings, Bag (a Member is in a Minister's bag), Be a man for once, Beauties, Believe—do not believe a word that the Minister says etc, Betraying the people, Bias—blinded by etc, Bidder—section of House—up for the highest bidder, Blackguard, Blackguardly utterance, Black-labour man, Blackmail, Blatherskited etc, Blood-drinker, Bloodthirsty conduct, Bounder, Bluffer champion political, Body snatcher (miserable), Bogus attitude, Bogus commission, Bribe a member etc, Bribery, Brother Smut, Brutal majority, Brutal statement, Brutal tactics, Brutality to keep Members etc. Brute, Brute (insulting), Buffoonery of a Member, Bulldoze, Bully, Bunkum, Burglars, Burke legislation, Buy political support.

Cad, Cant and hypocrisy etc, Capable of anything, Canting humbug, Chair a Member in the ear if he were outside, Chinese-like remarks, Circus (better fitted for), Claptrap, Claquirs petty, Clean hands (saying a Member has not), Cloven hoof (showing), Clownish tricks, Cocktailism, Coffin (helped a man into his coffin), Conduct unseemly, Conniving at (at an election), Conspiracy, Conspiracy against the manhood etc of Australia, Contempt beneath, Contemptible, Contemptible and dirty insinuation etc, Contemptible remark, Contemptible method, Contemptible tricks tactics etc, Corrupt gang of burglars, Corruption (imputing), Coward, Cowardice, Cowardly, Cowardly attacks etc, Cowardly action dirty, Cowardly dirty hound, Cowardly thing etc, Cowardly to say so, Crawling (Jingo etc), Creature, Crime (political), Criminal class friends of the, Creaking (speech), Cur.

Damnable lies, Damnable nonsense, Damned, Damned impu-

dence, Damned little to do, Damned nonsense, Damned thing.
Damned well ashamed of yourself (ought to be), Dare not to give
his opinions (saying a Member), Dastardly attempt, Dastardly
trick, Death of Mr Speaker (blaming Member for hastening),
Deceived the electors etc, Deceiving the House, Decent
electioneering (used offensively), Deception, Deception accusing Government of attempt at (before standing Orders adopted),
Debt of dishonor, Degraded the House, Delay business etc,
Deliberate mis-statement etc, Deliberately talking out a question, Despicable (trick), Diabolical act, Diabolical position
(placing House in), Dingoes, Dirtiest thing done in the House,
Dirty, Dirty charges (making), Dirty insinuation, Dirty mind,
Dirty Ministry etc (in bad taste but not certainly unparliamentary), Dirty political job, Dirty (statement), Dirty work,
Discourteous reply, Discredit to His Honor, Discreditable Bill
foisted upon the country without discussion, Discreditable
proceedings, Disgrace to a Member etc, Disgrace to the
Government, Disgrace upon the House, Disgraceful (use of the
'gag') etc, Disgustingly seryile, Dishonest, Dishonorable and
dishonest, Distort absolutely a Member's meaning, Do as they
are told (Members have to), Do not believe a word the Minister
says, Doctoring Hansard proof, Dog sitting like a dumb etc,
Dogs (sitting like a row of chained), Doing as they are told by
Ministers, Drivel, Drunken interjections, Dumb Dogs, Dumb
driven cattle, Dumb representation, Duped, Dupes, Duplicity.

Fabrication, Faked Hansard etc, False Coon, False pretences
and deceit, False statements, False to his oath, Falsehood etc,
Falsity of the imputations, Farce, Felony compound a, Hypocritical farce, Fenian language, Ferocious, Figures—wrong—
deliberately quoting, Filch from the Exchequer, Flounder, Fool
(Member or other person), Fools, Fooling, Forgery, Figures
faked, Form of House availed of to procure a postponement,
Foul insinuations and filthy slanders, Fraud, Fraud and
corruption (Opening door to), Fraudulent practice, Fungus
party.

Gag and smother up, Gaggers, Gagging, Gang one of the old,
Garrotters, Gas bags, German party, German vote (returned on
etc), Gerrymandering, Member is a good authority on goat
(playing the), Government subservient of shopwalkers,
Grinning jackanapes, Grins like an ape at his own lack of
intelligence, Groggy, Butter tactics.

Heathens, Hell (what the hell), Hell of a mess, Hirching,
Hogwash, Hold his tongue, Holding up business, Humbug,
Humbug and sham, Humbugged the electors etc or the House,
Humiliating spectacle in Parliament (a State), Hunt a Member

until he is politically dead (a Member saying he would), Hypocrisy, Hypocrites (political), Hypocrites and shams, Hypocritical amendment, Hypocritical pretence.

Idiotic question, Ignoramus, Imbecile, Imbecility etc, Immoral, Immorality, Impertinence gross etc, Impossible for him to represent anything fairly, Imposter, Improper influence, Impudence of three and intelligence of half a man, Impudent remarks, Inaccurate—and he knows it etc, Inaccurate (grossly), Insane, Incorrect—and he knows it etc, Not made a correct statement this morning, Infamous statement, Infamously (treating), Informer, Insect, Insincerity, Insinuations cruel—mean—unmanly, Insinuations of improper motives (See references to Members), Insinuations of untruth, Insult and gab (applied to Mr Gabb), Insulting argument, Insulting, as he always is, Interrupting business (purpose of), Intriguing.

Jackals (calling Members), Jackass, chattering, Jabbering nincompoops, Jesuitical, Jesuitical casuistry, Job gross alluding to a visit by Senators, Job—putup job, Judas.

Kaiser friend, Knaves and idiots, Knows nothing about the matter.

Lackeys (Government's), Lap-dog of a Minister, Larrikin—sanctified political etc, Laughing at the case of starving men, Liar, Lie etc, Lie—apology insisted on, Lie bloody, Log-rolling, Little minded, Low, Lunatic asylum (committing to), Lunatic—half a, Lying insinuations etc.

Mad statements, Malevolent charges, Malice actuated by, Maliciously, Malignity and spleen, Masters gratifying a Member's, Member—referring to as Bartonizing or 'Georgie', Mean advantage, Mean contemptible trick, Mean contemptible or untruthful, Member's old age pension, Mendacious, Miserable low-down way, Misleading deliberately, Misleading wilfully, Misled Members etc, Misrepresentations, Misstatement deliberate, Mockery (of a Bill), Mongrel political etc, Mountebank, Murdering gang of thieves.

Nasty way he says it, Neglecting his duty, Nobbled, Nonsense, No sincerity, Not discussing the merits of the Bill, Not sincere, Not honest (in his expression), Not honorable, Not in accordance with facts, and well he knows it, Not made a correct statement in the whole of his speech, Not man enough, Not sober, Not true see in this list Untrue, Not want to play fair, Not worthy of notice, Notorious (make himself), Nuisance (calling Member a).

Obstructed business, Obstruction, Offensive statements, Outrage (said of a speech).

Paid to make interjections, Parrot-chattering like a, Party

hack, Personal animus, Pitiable things, who cannot give a vote according to their wishes, Pimp or pimple, Playing it low down, Playing to the gallery, Plotted, Poison the minds of the people, Porcupine (bally), Pretence and sham etc., Pretence of Bills, Pretend to represent etc., Prevarication, Principles—a Member who would swallow his, Pro-Boer, Prostitute their positions, Pup an insignificant, Puppet, Purposely deferred a matter, Push (the Opposition party), Put him out, Putting up a Member to prevent a decision.

Question beginning at the risk of receiving another discourteous reply, Quorum re want of—sent men out of the Chamber.

Rat, Rats (dirty), Ratted, Ratting (if unworthy motive imputed), Rebel, reflecting on Members, Reflecting on Mr Speaker—See Speaker, Mr, Renegade, Renegade wretches, Reprobate, Revengeful conduct, Rigged-up question, Ring employed by a, Rob the farmers etc, Rob the public, Robbery describing proposed tax as and see, Robbery, Roughish acts, Rot, Rowdy ex-Speaker, Rubbish, Rude.

Sacrifice principle for payment, Sacrifice this country (would), Same old game, Sausage skin (political) filled with wind and water and painted like a Chinese God, Savagery unbridled, Scab, Scandal (public), Scandalous statement etc, Scandals arguments would support, Scarecrow, Scoundrel, Scramble for pay, Screw the necks of Members threatening to, Sells his soul and principles, Servile or Slavish majority, Sewer rat, Sewerage politics, Sham placard (motion), Shame the only thing he has the shame to do, Shame and scandal, Shame (Bills), Shirker, Shortening the life of the late Speaker blaming Member for, Shuffle (pleader for), Shuffling in an indecent manner, Shut his mouth, Shut-up! This is a piece of impertinence, Side-wind attempt to bring about by a side wind what cannot be done directly, Skeleton, Skulking, Skunks, Slanderer, Slewed mind, Slimy reptile, Slippery eel, Slipping (from principles), Sneak, Sneering and superfine, Sneering and grinning nasty replies of a Minister, Snipe, Snob, Snobbish trick, Sobered by that time, Sold the Ministry etc, Sold their State for eight months of office, Square Members to, Squib (political), stabbed in the back, Standing up for foreign company, Stole, Stolen by a Member, Stone wall, Stonewalling applied to a Member individually, Straight—nothing straight about you, Stupid, Stupid party, Subterfuges, Supercilious and elongated, Suspicious minds, Suspicious of his bona fides, Sweeping the gutter (when the honorable Member was), Swindle (apology insisted on), Swindling the electors.

Take one Member's word in preference to another's, Taking

in constituents (making speech so as to), Talking out a motion etc, Tammany gang, Tap-room only fit for, Thieves forty— comparing Members with, Threatening to obstruct a Bill or making any other threat, Thug, Time-wasting tactics, Toad in a Cesspit (has a mind like a), Tongue in cheek, Tool of the Caucus etc, Tool of the Government, Trading on his reputation as a Colonel, Traitor, Treachery, Treats as a farce, Trick, Trickery, Trickery and Treachery, Trickster, Tripe (referring to a Member's speech etc), Truth cannot be spoken in this House etc, Truth saying you cannot tell the truth, Truth deliberately keeping back the, Truth must not be spoken in this House, Try to be truthful, Turned dog, Twaddle, Twisters and torturers, Tyrants (potty).

Underhand, Unfair statements (grossly), Ungentlemanly conduct, Unreasoning animal, Unruly gentleman, Unscrupulous, Unscrupulous (politically), Unscrupulous and contemptible, Untrue sometimes with the addition and he knows it, Untruth, Unworthy character, Unworthy uses accusing of putting to, Usurping the Treasury benches.

Venom, Veracity absolutely no consideration for, Vicious, degrading despicable conduct, Vile, Vile slander, Villainous treatment, Vindictive amendment, Vindictiveness and revenge (Bill conceived in spirit of), Violating the Act, Vote against their own judgement, Voting against their own speeches, Vulgar expressions.

Wasting time, Waste time etc, Waste time deliberately, Wasting time shamefully, Wasting time wickedly, Wickedness, Winey friend, Wipe our Labor votes, Wrong—and he knows it.

SUPPLEMENTARY GLOSSARY

ACT: To put on airs ('He's bungin' on an act').

AUNTIE: The Australian Broadcasting Commission.

BANDIT (ONE ARMED): A poker machine.

BANKER: A flooded river.

BARNEY: An argument.

BATHERS: Swimming costume.

BEAUT (or BEWDY): Good, great.

BELT UP: Belligerent expression meaning 'Shut up'.

BIBLE BASHER: Anyone considered too sanctimonious.

BILLY: A can in which water is boiled over a campfire to make tea.

BINGE: A drinking session.

BITE: To borrow money (to 'put the bite on'. Alternatively to 'put the nips into' or 'put the acid on').

BITSER: Mongrel dog. (Also known as A HEINZ, i.e. 57 varieties.)

BITUMEN BLONDE: Aboriginal woman.

BLACK MARIA: Police van.

BLACK VELVET: Aboriginal girl.

BLIND: Drunk ('He was blind as a bat, he was').

BLIND FREDDY: A person who is not one to be deceived (i.e. 'Blind Freddy could see the joker was lying').

BLOKE: A male person.

BLOW-HARD: A garrulous person.

BLOW-IN: An unexpected visitor or newcomer to an area.

BLUE: A fight or an error. ('We put on a good blue' or 'That was a bad blue you made'.)

BOBBY DAZZLER: Admiring·expression for someone who is special or an expert at something. ('He's a bloody Bobby Dazzler, he is'.)

BOMB: An old car.

BOMBO: Cheap wine.

BONKERS: Of unsound mind.

BONZER: Good, excellent.

BOOZER: A heavy drinker. Also name for a Hotel.

BOSS: Employer.

BOTTLER: A first-class person ('He's a bloody bottler, he is').

BREAKERS: Surfing waves.

BROWN BOMBER: Parking policeman in NSW.

BRUMBY: A wild horse.

BUCKLEY'S (CHANCE): No chance at all or one chance in a million.

BULL: Abbreviation for bullshit. A derogatory expression. BULLDUST is used in a similar form.

BULLET: To be sacked.

BULL'S WOOL: A tall tale.

BUNNY: A victim ('He's a proper Bunny').

BUNYIP: Mythological creature said to live in waterholes.

BURL: To make an attempt, to have a go (to give it a Burl).

CACKLEBERRIES: Eggs.

CARPETED: To be reprimanded or 'asked to explain'.

CENTRE: The central area of Australia usually focused on Alice Springs.

CHEW AND SPEW: A cheap cafe.

CHIACK: To taunt or to tease.

CHIP IN: To pay one's share.

CHIPS: Fine-cut kindling wood. Also term for potato crisps or French fried potatoes.

CHOOK: A fowl. Also slang expression for a woman.

CHOOM: Nickname for Englishman.

CHOP: A share of the loot or to get the sack. Also a wood-chopping contest.

CHOPPERS: Teeth. A helicopter is also a CHOPPER.

CHUCK: To throw. To CHUCK IN is to contribute funds for something, usually a party.

CLOBBER: To strike a person. Also clothing.

CLOCK: To punch.

CLOUT: To hit. Also used as a term for influence (i.e. 'He has a lot of clout').

CLUCKY: A woman with desires to become pregnant.

CLUED UP: Very knowledgeable. (Also 'He is very CLUEY that one'.)

COAL CITY: Newcastle, NSW.

COAT HANGER: Sydney Harbour Bridge.

CONK: Nose, but to CONK OUT means to be exhausted. Mechanical things can also CONK OUT.

COOT: Man of inferior quality. Usually prefaced by adjective such as SILLY COOT.

COSSIE: Swimming costume.

COUNTER JUMPER: A shop assistant.

COW: An unpleasant happening ('It was a fair cow').

CRAWLER: A person who curries favour with another (usually the boss).

CROAK: To die.

CROOK: To be ill.

CROOKED ON: To be hostile towards.

CRUST: Money.

DAG: A droll person ('He's a proper dag, that one').

DAGGY: Dirty.

DAMAGES: The cost ('What's the damages, sport?').

DEAD SET: Absolutely sure.

DEKKO: To look.

DILL: A simpleton.

DILLYBAG: Small carry bag.

DINGALING: A stupid person.

DINGBAT: One who is slightly mad.

DINGO: A native dog. Derogatory expression directed to a coward or sneak.

DINKIE DIE: The truth.

DINKUM: True, Honest. Also FAIR DINKUM meaning one hundred per cent correct.

DINKUM OIL: Inside information.

DIRTY: To use unfair tactics ('He did the dirty on me').

DIVVY: A share of the proceeds.

DO: A party or function.

DOB IN: To betray. A DOBBER is a betrayer.

DOG BOX: Passenger Carriage on a country railway train.

DOG'S BREAKFAST: A state of great confusion.

DOG'S DISEASE: Influenza.

DOLE: Unemployed benefits. One who takes these benefits when he could get work is a DOLE BLUDGER.

DONE: To be overcharged or cheated. ('I was done like a dinner'.)

DONG: To hit.

DRUM: Sound advice ('To give him the drum').

DUD: Something that doesn't work. '(It was a dud, so help me'.)

DUNNY: Toilet.

DUDS: Trousers.

EARBASH: To talk too much. A constant talker is an EARBASHER.

EASY: Agreeable. ('I'm easy, mate'.)

ENDLESS BELT: A prostitute.

ENZEDDER: A person from New Zealand.

EXTRA GROUSE: Very good.

FAIR ENOUGH: An expression of approval.

FAIR GO: To be reasonable.

FANG: To borrow ('I'll put the fangs into him').

FIZZGIG: A police informer.

FIZZLE: To fade away.

FLAKE: To pass out, go to sleep, i.e. to FLAKE OUT.

FLOATER: Pie covered in peas and gravy.

FRIGGED: Tired, worn out.

GALAH: A fool, an idiot.

GAME (as Ned Kelly): Courageous.

GANDER: A look, a peak ('get a Gander of that willya').

GARGLE: A drink.

GHAN: Nickname of a train that runs from Adelaide (SA) to Alice Springs (NT).

GIN: Aboriginal woman.

GIZZARD: Stomach. ('Get that down your gizzard matey'.)

GO: To try ('I'll give it a go').

GOOD NICK: To be in excellent health.

GOOD OIL: The correct information.

GOOD SORT: An attractive woman.

GOOG: Egg.

GRANNY: Nickname for *Sydney Morning Herald*.

GROTTY: Dirty, unattractive.

GROUSE: Good.

GULF: Country in the Gulf of Carpentaria.

GULLY: A small valley.

GUMTREE, UP A: To be lost, bushed.

GUTZER: A fall. ('He came a proper gutzer'.)

GYP: To swindle.

HAD IT: Finished. ('The poor old bastard's had it'.)

HARD CASE: A tough person, a survivor, one who is admired.

HEAD 'EM: To toss the coins in two-up.

HERBS: Motoring expression for power. To 'give her the herbs' is to go flat out or rev. the motor.

HIDE: Impudence or cheek. ('He's got the hide of Jacky'.)

HIT THE SACK: Go to bed.

HOLD: To be flush with funds. ('I'm holding OK, mate'.)

HOLD YOUR HORSES: Expression meaning 'Not so fast'.

HOLE IN ONE: To have sex at first meeting with a woman.

HOLY JOE: A puritan, a Wowser.

HOLY-DOOLY: An exclamation of surprise.

HOME: The term for Great Britain, used even by second and third generation Australians.

HOORAY: Goodbye.

HOP INTO: To make short work of a task.

HUMDINGER: Excellent.

HUMPY: A small shack.

HUNGRY: To be mean or selfish.

ICEBERG: One who swims in wintry conditions. There is an Iceberg Club at Bondi Beach, Sydney, for the all-winter swimming brigade.

ICKY: A tricky situation.

IDENTITY: A well known local character.

INCOHERENT: Blind drunk.

IN SMOKE: To hide out.

IN THE BAG: As good as done.

JACKASS: Kookaburra.

JACK OF: To be fed up, tired of.

JACK UP: To refuse to proceed.

JACKY: Nickname for almost any male Aborigine.

JAILBAIT: Girls who are under the legal age for sex.

JAKE, SHE'S: Expression meaning 'everything is fine'. ('She's Jake, mate, she's apples'.)

JAM: Affected accent.

JELLY: Gelignite.

JOB: To punch.

JOEY: A baby kangaroo. Sometimes used for the young generally.

JONAH: A bringer of bad luck. ('He's a regular Jonah'.)

JUNGLE JUICE: Illegally brewed alcoholic drink. Originated in New Guinea in World War II.

KICK: To put in (i.e. contribute money for a party or present).

KICK THE BUCKET: To die.

KIP: To sleep. Also term for instrument used to toss pennies in two-up.

KITCHEN TEA: A gathering for a bride-to-be, each guest bringing a present.

KIWI: New Zealander.

KNACKERED: Tired.

KNACKERS: Testicles.

KNEE TREMBLER: Sexual intercourse standing up.

KNOCK: To criticise.

KNUCKLE: To hit with the fist. To be struck is to receive a 'knuckle sandwich'.

KYBOSH: To put a stop to some activity is to 'put the Kybosh on it'.

LAIR: A male who dresses flamboyantly or behaves in a boorish manner. ('He's a two bob lair, that's all he is'.)

LARRIKIN: Street tough or hoodlum.

LETTUCE: Money.

LINE UP: To make an approach.

LOAF: To do nothing ('He's just loafing about these days').

LOG: A person lacking in brains.

LONG SHOT: Outsider in a race.

LOUSY: Mean.

LUCKY COUNTRY, THE: Name for Australia coined by author Donald Horne.

LURK: A racket, a dodge or an illegal scheme.

MAKINGS: The materials (paper, tobacco) to roll your own cigarette.

MANGLE: Bicycle.

MANGY: Mean ('He's a mangy bastard').

MARKET, GO TO: To become angry.

MICK: A Roman Catholic.

MIX IT: To have a fight.

MOB: A large number of people or things.

MOLLY DOCKERS: Left-handed people.

MOONLIGHT FLIT: To depart at night from premises without paying the rent.

MOONLIGHTING: To have a second job, usually under an assumed name to avoid paying taxation.

MORAL: A sure thing, a certainty.

MUG: A gullible fool. A fool who thinks he is being smart is a 'Mug Alec'.

NARK: A spoilsport.

NECESSARY, THE: Money.

NEVER NEVER: Hire purchase.

NEW CHUM: Newly arrived immigrant.

NICE LINE: A good-looking girl.

NIP: To borrow money or to beg (i.e. 'To put the nips in'). Nickname for Japanese during World War II.

NIPPER: A male child.

NIT: A fool. But to 'keep nit' means to keep a lookout.

NO HOPER: A useless person.

OIL: Information ('I've got the good oil on it').

OLD COUNTRY: Great Britain. Another term is OLD DART.

OLD MAN: An adult male kangaroo.

ON AT: To continually nag. ('She's always on at me. One of these days I'll do me block and knock her head off.')

ONKUS: All wrong.

OODLES: Plenty of.

OUT TO GRASS: Retired.

OUT TO IT: To be dead drunk.

OVERLANDER: Stockman who herds stock over long distances.

OVER THE FENCE: Too much, unreasonable, unfair.

PACK, TO GO TO THE: To collapse, or to go downhill.

PADDOCK: Any fenced area, irrespective of size.

PARALYTIC: To be dead drunk.

PARK THE CARCASS: Sit down.

PASSION PIT: Drive-in movie.

PEA: A certainty. A racetrack term.

PEANUT: An idiot.

PENGUIN: A nun.

PERFORM: To lose one's temper or to carry on.

PERISH, DO A: To suffer from thirst or cold.

PERK: A special privilege or an 'extra'—there are plenty of LURKS and PERKS for an opportunist in Australia.

PERVE: To watch openly with admiration a young woman. ('Hey, Harry, get a perve at those sheilas'.)

PICNIC: A good time. But a NICE PICNIC can mean something unpleasant. ('That's a nice old picnic you've got us into, now'.)

PIECE OF CAKE: Anything achieved with ease.

PIE-EATER: A derogatory term for person of no importance.

PIGS: Derisory expression. Sometimes PIG'S ARSE.

PLONK: Cheap wine.

POKIES: Poker machines.

PONGO: An Englishman.

POSSIE: Position or place. ('Not a bad possie, eh mate?')

PRANG: An accident.

PROVERBIAL: Something elusive ('He's in for the proverbial').

PULL: Meaning a person has a lot of influence. ('Great guy, Harry is. He's gotta lotta pull around this place.')

PULL UP STAKES: To depart.

PUNT: To bet on something.

PURPLE PATCH: A run of good luck.

PUSH: A gang of larrikins, louts.

QUACK: A doctor.

QUANDONG: A woman who denies sexual favours after being wined and dined.

QUART POT: Tin pot for boiling water or cooking.

QUID: One pound (two dollars), but 'Not the full quid' means a person who is mentally defective.

RABBIT, TO: To tackle around the ankles in a football game.

RAFFERTY RULES: The absence of rules. To run things in a slipshod or irregular manner (i.e. by Rafferty Rules).

RATBAG: A person who acts foolishly.

RAZOO: A non-existent brass coin. ('He hasn't a razoo' or 'He hasn't a brass razoo'.)

READY: Cash ('I've got the ready').

RED CENTRE (or RED HEART): Central Australia.

RIGHTO: All right.

RIGHT OIL: Correct information.

RING: Centre of operations in a two-up school.

RIPPER: Term of approval ('She's a real ripper, mate'). Alternate term is RIPSNORTER.

ROCKHOPPER: Angler who fishes from rocks on coast.

ROCKING-HORSE MANURE: A term for any non-existent commodity. ('It's as scarce as rocking-horse manure'.) An alternate is SCARCE AS HEN'S TEETH.

ROOTED: Worn out or confounded. ('I'm really rooted, mate' or 'That rooted him, the bugger didn't know whether he was comin' or goin''.)

RORT: A dodge or scheme. Also a term for a wild party. ('It was a rort, I can tellya'.)

ROTTEN: To be drunk.

ROUGHIE: An outsider (racing term).

ROUSEABOUT: A handy man on a property.

RUBBEDY: Hotel.

RUNS: An attack of diarrhoea.

SACK: Bed. Also to be dismissed from a job. ('I reckon I'll hit the sack now' or 'He got the sack last Friday, poor bastard'.)

SADDLE UP: To prepare for work.

SANDY BLIGHT: Eye complaint prevalent in inland areas. A form of ophthalmia.

SCALE: To ride on public transport without paying the fare.

SET: All ready to go, or all ready to win. Sometimes SET LIKE A JELLY.

SHAG: To have sex, but SHAG ON A ROCK is an alternate expression meaning 'left high and dry'. ('He was like a shag on a rock when we finished with him'.)

SHAKY ISLES: New Zealand.

SHARKBAIT: A swimmer who ventures too far out to sea.

SHIRTY: To be extremely annoyed about something or with someone.

SHOOT THROUGH: To depart in a hurry.

SICKIE: Taking a day off work, whether sick or not. ('I gotta do some shopping with the missus tomorrow. I think I'll take a sickie.')

SKITE: To boast or description of a boaster.

SLY GROG: Illegal alcohol.

SMACKERS: Pounds or dollars (not used in singular form).

SMART ALEC: A flash person.

SMOKO: Short (!) break from work for morning or afternoon tea.

SOUTHERLY BUSTER: A southerly gale.

SOUVENIR: To steal.

SPARROWFART: The crack of dawn.

SPINE BASHER: A perpetual loafer, a parasite.

STEAMED UP: To be angry.

STICKY: Humid weather.

STONKERED: Drunk.

STREWTH: Exclamation of surprise.

SUNBEAM: A plate not used after completion of meal and which can be put away without being washed.

SWEAT ON: To wait apprehensively for something to happen. But NO SWEAT is an alternative term for 'She'll be right'.

SWEET: Right. ('She'll be sweet, mate, I'll see to it meself'.)

SWY: Two-up game.

TALK TURKEY: Plain talking.

TANKED: Drunk.

TARPAULIN MUSTER: To make a collection to aid some victim of a disaster or to buy more liquor.

TEE UP: To make an arrangement.

TICK: Credit.

TINNY: A person who is unusually lucky. Also a can of beer.

TOGS: Swimming costume.

TOP END: Far northern section of Northern Territory—usually the area around Darwin.

TROPPO: One who acts as if mentally disturbed.

TROTS: Diarrhoea. However TROT is a run of luck (good or bad).

TRUMPS: A good fellow. ('He's trumps, is old Harry'.)

TRUNKS: Swimming shorts for males.

TURN IT UP: A warning to stop.

TURN OUT: A part or even, or to make an appearance is to TURN OUT.

TURPS: Alcohol in general.

TWICER: A double-crosser.

TWO-UP: A popular gambling game in which two pennies are tossed in the air and bets are made on whether they fall heads or tails. Also known as SWY.

TYKE: A dog. Also sometimes used as derogatory term for a Roman Catholic.

UNBELIEVABLE: A general expression of incredulity.

UNDERGROUND MUTTON: Rabbit.

UPHILL: Facing a difficult task.

URGER: A conman or trickster.

VAGGED: Gaoled for vagrancy, having no visible means of support.

WAKE-UP: An alert person ('I'm a WAKE-UP to you, matey, what do you think you're trying to pull?')

WALKABOUT: To travel aimlessly. To disappear for a period.

WALLOPED: Beaten in a fight.

WARB: A dirty or untidy person. WARBY is a term applying to such a person.

WET: A simpleton (i.e. 'Wet behind the ears'). THE WET, on the other hand, is a term for the rainy season in Northern Australia, whilst to WET THE BABY'S HEAD is a drink to celebrate a birth.

WHACK: A ration or share of something (usually food).

WHACKED: Intoxicated or very tired.

WHACKO: An expression of approval. Sometimes WHACKO THE DIDDLEO.

WHINGE: To complain. A WHINGER is a constant complainer whilst a WHINGE ARTIST is one who has developed complaining to a fine art.

WHITE ANT: To sabotage.

WILLY WILLY: Small dust storm which races across the countryside with circular wind action like a corkscrew. Also called WHIRLWIND.

WING DING: A party.

WOOD: Advantage. ('He's got the wood on me'.)

WORKS: Everything, the lot. ('Give it the works, mate'.)

YAKKA: Hard work. Also term for talk. ('He yakkers a lot'.)

YOU BEAUT: Expression of approval.

YOUR TOUCH: Expression meaning 'It is your turn to pay' (for the drinks).

ZACK: Sixpence (five cents).

INDEX

ACKNOWLEDGEMENTS

For permission to reproduce copyright material the author and publisher wish to thank the following:
Sidney J Baker, *New Zealand Slang* (Currawong Press P/L) p. 17–18; Sidney J Baker, *The Drum* (Currawong Press P/L) p. 57, 62, 63, 77, 155, 194, 195; Sidney J Baker, *The Australian Language* (Currawong Press P/L) p. 39; C Hartley-Grattan, *Introducing Australia* (Angus & Robertson Publishers P/L) p. 16, 37–8, 98; Alistair Morrison, *Let Stalk Strine* and *Nose Tone Unturned* (Paul Hamlyn P/L) p. 25, 26; Eric Partridge, *Slang Today and Yesterday* (Routledge & Kegan Paul Limited, London) p. 76; Brian Penton, *The Landtakers* (Angus & Robertson Publishers P/L) p. 42; Elisabeth Wynhausen, the *National Times*, January 1978. The extracts from *Pronunciation of English in Australia* by Professor A G Mitchell are reprinted by permission of Angus & Robertson Publishers (p. 16, 37–8, 98). Thomas Wood, *Cobbers*, reprinted by permission of Oxford University Press, Oxford (p. 33).